ONE LIFE
ONE CHANCE

ONE LIFE
ONE CHANCE

A STORY OF ADRENALINE AND ADVENTURE
IN THE MOST UNFORGIVING PLACES ON EARTH

LUKE RICHMOND

IMPACT PRESS

First published in 2018 by Impact Press
an imprint of Ventura Press
PO Box 780, Edgecliff NSW 2027 Australia
www.impactpress.com.au

10 9 8 7 6 5 4 3 2 1

National Library of Australia Cataloguing-in-Publication entry:
One life one chance: a story of adrenaline and adventure in the most unforgiving places on earth
/ Richmond, Luke.

ISBN: 978-1-925384-37-6 (paperback)
ISBN: 978-1-925384-38-3 (ebook)

Category: Memoir

Cover and internal design: Brugel Creative
Cover image: Luke Richmond

The paper in this book is FSC® certified. FSC® promotes environmentally responsible, socially beneficial and economically viable management of the world's forests.

PRAISE FOR

ONE LIFE ONE CHANCE

❝ The "dignity of risk" is a human right and the human race's greatest accomplishments have often been on the back of enormous risk to human life. Luke embraces risk as a necessary means to an end in this inspiring account of his incredible adventures. A true inspiration and a reminder to those who discourage the expression of risk in today's workplaces, schools and playgrounds that you will never get much back out of life without taking risk. ❞

KEN WARE, founder of NeuroPhysics Therapy

❝ An honest and inspiring story about a man living his life to its absolute maximum. ❞

'JAY', 10-year Australian SAS and Commando veteran

❝ Luke's story and life shows us all that with conviction and discipline the world and what it has to offer is on tap just waiting to be experienced. We just need to find the courage and strength to break out of our comfort zone to embrace life and begin living. ❞

COMMANDO STEVE, host of *The Biggest Loser Australia*

❝ Luke is proof of both the incredible strength of the human spirit and the need to push our personal boundaries. He is also intent on living up to what Helen Keller said better than anyone: "Life is either a daring adventure or nothing at all." ❞

TIM JARVIS AM, Australian Adventurer of the Year in 2013, Conservationist of the Year in 2016 (Australian Geographic Society)

❝ Luke's story brings home three things to me, we have one life...make it count, never be told you can't do something, and anticipation is worse than participation. ❞

DEAN STOTT, former British Special Boat Service (SBS) operator

❝ Luke's story is an honest one that many will be able to relate to. By laying bare his own dark times and documenting how he personally got back on track, Luke has produced a work that will resonate with anyone experiencing difficulties and who wants to find happiness and vibrancy. A life full of extremes, this is a rollercoaster of a book and well worth chucking in your backpack. ❞

ED STAFFORD, star of *Left for Dead* and the first person to walk the full length of the Amazon River

❝ Luke is an inspiration! His story is a great yarn in overcoming adversity and a true living example of "have a go, ya mug!" Uplifting, harrowing at times and incredible! ❞

JAMES CASTRISSION, Australian adventurer and author of *Crossing the Ditch* and *Extreme South*

❝ Luke's life has taken him from partying like Ronnie Wood, training like Schwarzenegger, to exploring like Sir Ranulph Fiennes...and the scariest thing is, to those that know him, the best is yet to come. ❞

MATHEW BENNETT, ocean rowing world record holder and CEO of Acorn Children's Homes

❝ If your life feels like a deep dark hole and it seems that there is no way out, this book is your ladder into the light. It's inspiring and empowering. ❞

PAT FARMER AM, multiple endurance running world record holder, National Geographic's Adventurer of the Year.

❝ Wow, carpe diem! This is an amazing story of a man from humble beginnings that won't let anything stand in the way of achieving his dreams. Don't know how to row, why not paddle the Atlantic? Don't know how to climb, why not tackle the famed Seven Summits? A great story about a regular guy taking on big challenges. ❞

MIKE HAMILL, premier high altitude guide and author of *Climbing the Seven Summits*

For Mandy and Clive, my gypsy parents
who taught me the way of the road

ABOUT THE AUTHOR

Luke Richmond is an Aussie adventurer who has conquered the odds during many internationally acclaimed expeditions. Growing up on various cattle stations across the Northern Territory, Luke joined the army at 17 years old, which gave him the discipline and world knowledge he needed, and lit a fire for adventure that he pursues to this day. Luke has climbed the highest mountain on six continents, completed a world record ocean row across the Atlantic, and was the first Australian male to trek 1800 kilometres across the Gobi Desert in Mongolia, dragging a cart that contained all his food and water. Luke's lifelong passion is to make adventure accessible to everyone, and to inspire others to feel the reward of conquering a physical and mental challenge. His life motto is OLOC which stands for 'one life one chance', a belief that has driven him into harder and longer challenges every single year.

CONTENTS

PROLOGUE

...

The barrel of his AK-47 assault rifle was pointed straight at my head; the tip was shaking and I wondered whether it was the Russian soldier's anger that was causing him to tremble or the freezing temperatures brought on by the blizzard raging outside the helicopter. Either way, I thought, this is it. This was the moment my life would get snatched away in the blink of an eye, and it was a silly misunderstanding that would cost me everything. I could see the inside of the barrel inches from my face; I noticed the rifling honed into the steel designed to rotate the bullet and make it more accurate. It was impossible for him to miss this shot, and as I looked at his trigger finger already moving into firing position I had that moment that others have written about, the flashback to times gone past, to family, friends and crazy adventures.

Dad saved me from drowning when I was a little kid, the brown fresh water of the river took me under its murky depths but I was brought back to the land of the living and given a second chance. I always thought my military service might have taken me; to die bravely while serving the greatest country on earth would have been a better way to go. The drugs couldn't get me – the addiction left me lying on the cold cobbled streets of London yet I still survived. Or the mountains I had climbed that had taken the lives of more experienced mountaineers than I, right in front of my eyes, but had allowed me to climb down their steep cliffs shaken but alive. I had escaped death many times before but now my luck seemed to have run out.

The last thing I heard was my climbing partner Valentine yell something in Russian; I could have easily shut my eyes and turned my head away but I chose to stand tall with my eyes wide open, to meet what was coming as I have with everything in life. I thought, please don't let this be it. How did a country kid from the Australian outback end up inside a crashed helicopter on top of the tallest mountain in Russia, facing the barrel of a gun? I noticed the howling wind outside, before the silence.

CHAPTER 1

OUTBACK AUSTRALIA

...

The head of a feral pig detaches from its body with one-and-a-quarter turns to the left or right before the vertebrae fracture and separation is achieved. This is of course after the throat is slit and the tough meat and sinew are cut down to the bone around the circumference of its powerful neck. The weight of the head always surprised me and a strong hold of the ear, turned carry handle, is needed to avoid dropping it and possibly damaging the prize. The large, protruding, razor-sharp white tusks of a feral boar are the trophy and once the head reaches our backyard the skin is removed and the jaw is cut off. The jaw is boiled to loosen the teeth and extraction of the full-length undamaged tusks can be achieved. A large portion of the tusk is hidden inside the jawbone and it's only at the final extraction point we get to see the finished product.

This was one of many life skills my dad taught me growing up and as primitive as some of them seem to me now, I wouldn't change a single thing about my childhood, where every day seemed like an adventure and behind every gum tree a lesson was learnt.

My sister and I were little kids in the back seat of a cream-coloured V8 Holden Kingswood wagon. There was no such thing as air conditioning so the hot, dry air blew through the open window, bringing with it a mixture of Eucalyptus trees, dust and highway exhaust.

Bruce, our black kelpie dog, and adopted family member, was panting with his tongue fully extended, and drooling over the back seat behind me. The drool would build up in large waterfalls on the vinyl seat forcing me into a sideways seated position to avoid the cascade. Mum and Dad were in the front seats and there was nothing but the bitumen highway and the shimmering red centre of the Australian outback through the windscreen ahead of us.

Our upbringing, although not normal, was adventurous, and as little kids we knew no other way, nor did we want to. We grew up on the road like gypsies, our parents moving from town to town searching for their little niche in a big open country. Australia is one of the most diverse places on earth. It covers an area the size of Europe and in its northern regions grow some of the thickest rainforest and jungle in the world; a place I would spend many weeks of training in the coming years. Inland from the picturesque coast is a dry, barren landscape stretching for thousands of kilometres, with the Simpson desert and its enormous red sand dunes taking centre stage.

Australia's red centre is part of the Northern Territory and is a definite favourite of my dad's. He loved the wide-open spaces, beautiful landscapes and that unforgettable smell of rain as the monsoon made its way across the red dirt. He said it made him feel free as soon as he left a town behind and made his way into the remote regions. He always referred to this part of the world as 'God's country'.

My parents are Mandy and Clive Richmond. Mum was born in Australia in the southern state of Victoria, to Patricia and Noel Willson. She is one of eight kids who loves her AFL (Australia football) and is good at anything she puts time and effort into. She is funny, loves to sing and dance and always cries whenever I leave on adventures, even to this day. When times are tough, or when I have been in a tricky situation, she has always been there with her resourceful mind, to get me out of trouble.

Dad was born in the small town of Durham in England to Jean and Harry Richmond, one of three boys and the middle child. When Dad turned five the Richmond clan boarded a boat bound for Australia. The immigration drive was in full swing and the £10 boat ride from England was the best way to relocate for a working class family. Dad only has one memory of the journey to Australia, making paper planes on board with my grandfather, throwing them off the back of the vessel and watching them gracefully glide into the churning sea below.

My dad is a smart man who comes from intelligent, traditional English stock, knowing no other way than to get a job done right the very first time. He worked with his mind and hands and could solve any structural or mechanical issue you put in front of him by the time he had finished rolling a smoke and had a cup of coffee. He is also a free-thinking rebel and chose to do whatever felt natural to him at the time, never being constrained by what was deemed normal or permissible. I inherited the same traits and it all began in these early years growing up with my free-spirited parents.

Mum and Dad met in Western Australia, where Dad had become the local motocross champion. They were married young and before the dust could settle from the occasion they were back on the road seeking adventure. Dad was working as a motor mechanic and he had designed a mounting frame that could attach his motorbike to the Holden, so that it could be taken everywhere with them. Mum had become a jack-of-all-trades, a person able to adapt to any scenario, locating a job within a day of arriving in a new town. They were always close to broke but they were happy and that's all that mattered.

Searching out some of the most remote cattle stations in the country, they would soon be calling them home. Some of the properties were so large it would take many hours, and sometimes days, of driving just to reach the boundaries. This land was wild, barren in parts but also majestically beautiful. The wildlife was plentiful, kangaroos in such abundance their numbers were too great to estimate. There were large goannas with razor-sharp teeth, birdlife ranging from tiny finches to kookaburras, emus and noisy cockatoos, large fish in any river or dam that could hold year-round water, and plenty of crocodiles to keep you on your toes.

I loved the bush as a boy, running off with a small calibre rifle under one arm and the fishing pole under the other. I can still hear my mum yelling 'be home for dinner' as I disappeared out of sight. I learnt the dangers of the bush and how to look after myself early on in life. Shooting venomous snakes on sight was nothing out of the ordinary. Other dangers such as heat stroke, poisonous spiders, wild cattle, horses, feral pigs and wild flowing rivers all had to be respected. As did infection. With no access to doctors or hospitals, a cut on a foot could turn septic, and the closest medical care was many hours' drive away down a rough dirt track.

The memory of a child is a wondrous thing. I could not tell you what year, month or even what day some of my memories come from or what else was happening around me at that time. I couldn't tell you how many head of cattle a property contained or how many people lived there, but a particular memory from one station has always been with me. The station was called Avon Downs and during our time there a plague of rats swept through the area in biblical proportions. They were the common house rats in unrelenting volume, which could decimate food stores in hours, and were driving the local residents crazy. Everyone hated the rats so no adult batted an eyelid when I went on operation extermination with the neighbours' little, but feisty, Jack Russell terrier.

The basic rat-killing expedition started with the location of a burrow. Once found, a garden hose had to be procured and shoved down the burrow as far as you could get it in. Then it was crank the water pressure on full steam and wait. I gave it about two to three minutes for the twisting system of tunnels to fill up with water and force the rats towards the surface. Once they showed their faces it was party time.

The rats would come flying out of their homes at full speed trying to escape the flood. The little dog instantly reacted, as if he had ingested a pint of adrenaline, quickly snatching them up and tearing them to shreds. I would stand by watching the festivities and when a lone rodent escaped towards me I'd do my best Don Bradman impression with the cricket bat to end their furry little life.

It seems barbaric now when I tell the story, and I'm sure if you were caught today slaying rodents with bats there is a high likelihood you would end up on the evening news. But back then when I was a boy and witnessing my father butcher a cow for the station's food, swatting a rat didn't even register on my radar.

Another pest in the bush are the wild pigs. Their numbers have swollen to millions and have provided hunters, who shoot them for money all year round, with jobs for decades. They are big, angry, and the males have massive tusks hanging out of the side of their bottom jaw. These tusks can slice like a razor and I have witnessed their effects on horses, dogs and people that have gotten too close to them.

On special occasions Dad would take me out on 'bore runs', which was one of his jobs, driving around the entire property to all of the man-made dams. He would fix all of the broken windmills and pumps that power the water bores and fill the troughs for the cattle. During these bore runs we would get the chance to do lots of shooting at one of the biggest pests the cattle station had, feral cats. The domestic cat had exploded in numbers in the bush, living off the vast array of birdlife Australia has to offer. They grew big and were tough enough to survive the harsh conditions of the desert country. They tended to be in large numbers around the man-made dams; my dad and I took it upon ourselves to clear out these pests for the sake of the birds and other native wildlife.

We always knew when there was a large cat population at a dam because there would not be a single bird anywhere. Upon inspection of the closest trees we would see the cats lying over the branches, not bothered by our presence. On one such occasion my dad and I eradicated forty-two of these pests at one small dam. I was only ten years old but in the bush you learnt to shoot, drive and take part in the work as soon as you were capable.

The entire community would take it upon themselves to rid the bush of feral animals, which to me meant two or three times a week going off on hunting trips with my parents after they had finished work for the day. We all loved the outback and hated to see the pests take over and destroy the native birds or the beautiful landscape. Mum was by far the best shot in the family. She could kill a pig from miles away with her steady hands guiding the bullet to its mark, while Dad and I would squint to even see what she was shooting at. Many times she would fire a round, tell me it dropped the target and send me out to fetch it. I wouldn't believe she had hit anything at all until I had walked the distance and stumbled upon the animal, now motionless. My parents taught me some of the first lessons of shooting, which I would put to good use in the Army many years later.

A vital service to the remote communities was the Royal Flying Doctor Service (RFDS). These guys were on call from Mount Isa for any emergency: they would have a doctor or paramedic in the air and on their way to a remote cattle station within minutes of being called. I am truly grateful for these heroic people more than any others because without their help, I would have lost my mum when I was a kid instead of having her by my side today.

It was in the very early hours, just after midnight, that my mother's appendix ruptured on Lorraine cattle station, many hours' drive from the closest emergency service. If we had to drive her to a hospital she would not have made it halfway, that was certain. The Royal Flying Doctors were called and after giving us some immediate things to do to help her they were in the air and en route to us.

The station had an airstrip that had been carved into the red dirt and even though it wasn't exactly Boeing 747 ready it was just enough for light aircraft, or so we hoped. Before the plane arrived we had to prepare the runway. At night kangaroos moved onto the strip to drain the remaining heat out of the earth, so we had to drive up and down many times to ensure that the landing area was kangaroo-free for their approach.

The next problem was lighting; we had to fill empty tins and coffee cans with a mixture of petrol and diesel and place these at intervals all the way around the landing area. We would then have every available vehicle on the station park around the airstrip with their headlights illuminating as far out as possible. Both of these combined would provide just enough light to give the pilot the best chance of landing safely.

The plane arrived and completed a fly-by to scare off any remaining kangaroos and to check the illumination of the area. We found out later that the pilot wasn't happy with the lighting and that he had a lot of trouble seeing the ground, yet in true Australian style he brought the plane in anyway and landed it perfectly on this patch of red dirt in the middle of nowhere.

Mum was loaded on board and given a healthy dose of morphine, so much so that all she recalls is feeling like she was having an amazing foot massage all the way to hospital. The plane was turned around and took off without incident into the darkness. The RFDS saved my mother's life that night and I will be forever grateful to the brave pilots who took a chance and got her out.

A good education is essential in life and even though my sister and I were in the middle of nowhere we still managed to get one. With all the kids spread throughout the most remote regions of outback Australia there is a schooling program called the school of distance education and it is all controlled via the radio.

Imagine a teacher sitting in a small radio-shack room, far away in the regional city of Mount Isa, which is on the border of the Northern Territory and Queensland. From there the teacher can broadcast across the desert for hundreds of kilometres, reaching any station with a radio and all of the kids who need a teacher. Your textbooks and work pads are sent out from the city at the start of the year. Every morning at a designated time we would turn on the radio and wait for class to begin.

The radio would crackle to life and the teacher in Mount Isa would start the class by asking across the wire, 'Who is here today?' We would all say our names one by one and the teacher would write down her roll call and then away we would go with a normal primary school curriculum.

I remember mine was always a female teacher and she would usually ask all of us to tell a story at the beginning of the class, like a show-and-tell type of scenario. I realise now that it was probably a great way just to get kids comfortable on the radio and I really enjoyed the stories the other kids would tell. From fishing and hunting to working with the cattle, we were all just country kids not knowing any other way of life and loving it.

Classes on the air would typically run for an hour, this was unless you were fortunate enough to have a radio signal dropout. Any technical failure, to a country kid itching to get outside, was like getting an early jail release. Otherwise, at the end of the class, one by one all the kids would say goodbye and bring to an end our session for the day.

School of distance education isn't the most in-depth form of learning but with a tireless mother like mine and her home school program running side by side with it, I was getting an education just as good, if not better than the public school system of the cities. What it also does is give otherwise cut-off kids a chance to get their basic reading, writing and mathematics skills locked in, and if you ask me, that's all we really need.

As soon as the radio was placed back on its hook I was out the door and heading off towards the cattle yards to help the cowboys with their work. As a kid I would never wear shoes, no matter where I went, but when I wanted to go and work with the men, Mum would hold me up long enough to make me put my boots on. I can still remember those few minutes it took to pull on those boots being torturous, because in my head boots were the craziest waste of time and any hold up was hell.

The cattle yards were where the processing of all the cattle took place and were rough, wild and dirty places to be. In Australia people who start working with cattle are known as jackaroos, for men, and jillaroos for women, and once fully qualified they become ringers. They are all tough people working through a range of jobs from cutting off the horns, ear tagging, vaccinating and branding each beast. The person in charge was known as a head stockman and was typically the toughest of them all.

I would stand on the top row of the fence and watch the men and women at work, always keen to lend a hand but mindful of how easily you could get kicked or crushed in the yard.

The indigenous people of Australia, the Aboriginal people, have a long-standing attachment to the land. They can survive off the land, eating bush tucker, flourishing where other people would perish, and the men from these tribes were part of station life. They were a quiet bunch of guys while tending to the work of the day and would get most animated when one of their favourite foods was offered up for lunch.

One of the jobs in the yards was the removal of the testicles from young weaners before they had a chance to breed. These cattle nuts were removed with a knife and thrown onto a hotplate to be cooked up for everyone to enjoy, and the ones that enjoyed them the most were the Aboriginals. A few of the older veteran workers had tried the oyster-like delicacies before but almost everyone agreed that it wasn't a taste they could enjoy daily. If you ever have a chance to give them a go make sure they are cooked all the way through. The only thing worse than a testicle for lunch is a raw one.

My sister Kim is a year older than me and when we were both nearing the end of our primary school education my parents understood what had to come next. Secondary learning was going to be needed, which the radio could not provide. So with our best interests in mind, my parents packed up the entire house once again and moved out of the desert to a coastal town on the east coast of Australia.

It was a 1700-kilometre journey before we arrived at the town of Forrest Beach in Far North Queensland. I was enrolled at Ingham State High School and I caught the bus to school and back every day. Coming from the bush, where it was just my sister and me, to walking into a school with 700 kids was a massive shock to the system. These were not country kids, we had no common ground, we listened to different music, and at first it was a major struggle for me to make friends.

I was carrying the baby fat of a kid and was bullied for being tubby for the next two years at Ingham High; wearing my cowboy hat to school for the first few months didn't really help with my social standing either. When that glorious hormone of maturity shot its way through my system, I grew in height, lost the excess weight and began to train every day.

As my social skills and athletic ability improved, a group of friends grew around me who are still with me to this day. After playing my first season of rugby league I became captain of the side, and as I developed this enthusiastic approach to compete in every sport available, I also became the sports captain for the school.

After a rough beginning at Ingham High I took it upon myself to beat up every bully who had ever taunted me in those early years. I'd like to say it was out of some desire for a noble deed but it wasn't. It was pure revenge and it felt great at the time to take my anger out on someone who made a country kid's life hell. I had earned myself a reputation as a nice guy who should not be messed with and I was content with that.

All in all my high school years and city life were exactly what I needed to open my eyes to the world. I started to dream of adventure and as graduation approached I began to think about what my next step would be. Even though I had earned the grades to apply for university it didn't interest me in the slightest, neither did following in my father's footsteps and becoming a tradesman.

I was seventeen, young, ambitious, seeking adventure and didn't have a clue what I wanted in life. What institution would take me?

CHAPTER 2
ARMY STRONG

...

My great-grandfather on my mum's side served with the Australian Light Horse Regiment in World War I, a horse-mounted infantry unit used extensively in Turkey and Egypt. My grandfather on my dad's side was involved in World War II as an aircraft technician maintaining and repairing British aircraft fighting in Europe. I have always respected the history of military service in my family and felt honoured to be part of the lineage of such brave and patriotic men.

In Queensland, high school begins at grade 8 and finishes at grade 12. Upon enrolment we were asked to fill out a questionnaire that was to be placed into a time capsule and opened upon graduation. 'Who is the prettiest girl in school?' was one of the questions on the list and there was 'What occupation are you going to choose?'. I was thirteen years old when I answered that question, bursting with youthful pride and dreams of grandeur, writing ARMY in big block letters.

The idea of joining the military marinated during my high school years and was always at the forefront of my thoughts. During school I was playing lots of rugby league, competing in cross-country running, fishing and camping most weekends. I was absorbed with trying to get a girlfriend and generally doing what teenage boys do. Upon graduation we opened the time capsules from five years earlier – two answers to the questions remained the same. The prettiest girl in school hadn't changed and neither had my feelings towards a career with the Army. I enlisted in the Australian Infantry at seventeen years of age. I was too young to enlist myself directly and needed to have my parents' permission and signature on the enrolment forms. Mum and Dad are both patriotic Australians, and even though it was hard on Mum to let me go so young, they gave me their permission and their full support.

Before the hangover of the graduation parties had cleared, I had taken two flights and was sitting on a bus full of new recruits heading towards the town of Wagga Wagga in rural New South Wales. Just outside of town lay the training camps for the entire Army. It didn't matter what unit you were enlisting in, whether it was Catering Corps or the Infantry, everyone was put together for the initial six weeks of basic training. I looked around at the silent faces sitting on the bus and wondered if everyone was as nervous as I was. They all seemed much older than me and no-one seemed to be showing it.

When the bus pulled up in fading daylight a uniformed man stepped on board. He was dressed in pressed green camouflage clothing and with his immaculate appearance and thousand-yard stare he was very intimidating. After a brief pause as he took a moment to lock eyes with all of us, he bellowed out our first set of orders. We were told to get off the bus, grab our bag with our left hand and carry it off the ground as we followed another intimidating staff member. We were ordered to walk in two straight lines towards an area called the muster hall. Carrying a bag that had been packed in the belief it would be pulled on wheels proved to be a real challenge but there was no way I'd let it touch the ground. I gritted my teeth through the burning pain in my left shoulder and stumbled onwards.

Some new recruits couldn't carry their bags off the ground for more than a few paces and every time their bag touched the ground a bombardment of verbal abuse from circling staff soon followed. A look of terror covered the faces of the timid civilians getting screamed at for no other reason than to drive home the fact that we now belonged to an institution and not to ourselves. That day I heard for the first time a sentence I would hear repeatedly in the coming weeks: 'You joined us, we didn't join you'. It never seemed to lose its impact.

Once we were together inside the muster hall a roll call was taken and we were sorted into our platoons. A platoon is typically made up of thirty soldiers however ours were slightly bigger, the staff knowing not all of us would still be there in six weeks' time. I looked around and noticed Greek, Chinese, Aboriginal, Lebanese and European faces, all filled with the same look of fear and apprehension. We were a group of young people from different cultural backgrounds thrown together, all wanting to serve our country. Once sorted into platoons we were marched over to the barracks and given sleeping arrangements for the next six weeks. The barracks were split into ten rooms each containing four recruits. At one end of the hall was a fire escape exit and at the other end was a shower/toilet block and the staff office. Late that first night we were told to get to sleep: without meeting my new roommates I jumped into the rock-hard single bed with sheets tucked in tighter than a tourniquet and lay quiet. Sleep didn't come easy and I could feel the other three guys in my room also lying awake. As the hours ticked by with my imagination running wild about what was going to happen the following day, I dozed off.

At 6 am, forgetting where I was, a spray of commands and insults from the staff shocked me into reality. I was a new recruit of 15 Platoon and we were ordered out into the hallway and told to stand against the walls, facing our teammates on the opposite side. 'Back straight, toes forward, chin up, eyes forward, don't look at me', the commands didn't stop. The abuse was endless and intense and I was ordered to go and grab the sheets off my bed and return with them draped over my left shoulder. Returning, clutching the sheets and standing there half naked the barrage continued. Streams of information were forced upon us: how we fold our socks, how we make our beds, how to shave, shower and how to stand.

Every little detail was covered as we were indoctrinated into the system. Running through my head was 'You joined us, we didn't join you'.

During basic training a platoon is allocated a team of seasoned corporals. They would train and mould us into something resembling soldiers in just six weeks. This is done in a very systematic and proven way. First they must break down a platoon physically and mentally, stripping away personal ego and bringing the team together. If they made it hard enough the only way we could survive was to work together as one unit. Once a team hits rock bottom they could begin to build us up as one, utilising new skills, strengths and mottos driven into our brains daily by the military machine. If the corporals have done their job effectively a smaller group will remain who have survived the baptism of fire and could be called soldiers.

There was so much information to take in at once that we made mistake after mistake and the staff were waiting to give us our punishments. Hundreds of push-ups and stress-position holds, corporals coming within an inch of my face and unloading verbal abuse. Spit would be flying into my eyes as they simply repeated the tasks over and over again until we got it right. At one stage we got dressed and undressed going through the morning routine at least twenty times. It would have been borderline hilarious if I wasn't pouring sweat and desperately trying to figure out what I was doing wrong.

After the first day of endless 'beasting' (punishments) we had a super-tight schedule to stick to. The morning routine consisted of being woken up by a corporal yelling or Metallica music blaring out over the barracks' speaker system. We would need to make our bed, shave, brush our teeth, get dressed, straighten up our locker and be out in the hallway ready to go in under twenty minutes.

One time we didn't make the twenty-minute limit, so we continued to repeat the morning routine for the next three hours until the corporals were certain we had it nailed. Every recruit got a rash after shaving a dozen times, and even though I didn't have a whisker on my chin at seventeen, I still had to shave with the other guys. One morning when a fellow recruit's bed wasn't made to the staff's exact specification, his mattress was hurled out of the third-storey window crashing into the garden below. Every day while we were formed up in the hallway we had to sing the national anthem as a team at the top of our lungs. The first verse everybody already knew but we also had to learn the second verse, rarely heard before. It always sounded terrible yet singing out loud in front of everyone played a vital role in breaking down self-esteem issues and getting your voice primed for repeating commands.

I was the youngest recruit there by a few years and I was handling the orders and rules fairly well. I had only just completed my schooling and was living at home where there were plenty of rules and restrictions already, so I adjusted easily. Some of the other guys reached their limits early on in the breaking-down phase and by the second week we had lost four recruits. One guy repeatedly ran at top speed into his steel locker in an attempt to kill himself and was medically discharged. Every time a recruit quit it made me a little bit more determined to keep going, something about their weakness made me stronger. I would never do anything to make someone quit and I'd help out everybody I could, but when they gave up and couldn't take any more I turned away and kept pushing myself onward.

The physical side of the training was what I was enjoying the most. I had prepared myself well in my final year at home with constant sport, strength training and an ever-increasing distance of running. Dad had bought me some weights to use in the shed, welded a pull-up bar to the roof and made a boxing bag out of an old mattress rolled up and taped together. Anytime we had a birthday party or gathering at home it would inevitably end in pull-up competitions and arm wrestling championships. In Army training our PT sessions (physical training) involved weights circuits, running intervals, pool sessions, pack marches and sometimes a smash session of everything thrown in together. We had to complete the 'beep test' of just running as one of our first fitness classes. It utilises shuttle runs between markers following a series of beeps, starting very slow and over time getting faster until you are sprinting between the markers. If you failed to make it to the marker before the next beep you were out and given your score. That first session I was the last man sprinting and took out the highest score.

To build up our endurance in order to carry weight on our backs, we started doing short pack marches of around 5 kilometres with only 10 kilograms in weight. Then the week after it would be 8 kilometres with 12 kilograms building up the distances and weight until we could march 20 kilometres carrying 25 kilograms. The trick I found the best when carrying a pack was to never take it off. Any time we would stop for a break the others would take their packs off and sit down, I would just sit straight down with the pack still on my back and lean against it. This ensured that the pack remained in a comfortable position when we set off again with very little time wasted in finding a comfortable position. I enjoyed the physical and mental battle of the marches, little did I know that this skill would serve me well on high mountain expeditions in coming years.

I had grown up hunting with Mum and Dad out on the cattle properties and enjoyed using various bolt-action rifles and shotguns. I was excited to finally get my hands on the F88 Austeyr, the Austrian made fully automatic assault rifle. This is the number one rifle used throughout the Australian Army, it replaced the SLR (self loading rifle) in 1989 which had been used since 1960. The Austeyr has a plastic stock and can unload a thirty round magazine of 5.56-millimetre ammunition in less than five seconds. It all sounded like Rambo to me and I could not wait to play with it.

The next weapon to be placed in my hands, and little did I know would remain there for a very long time, was the F89 machine gun. Its ammunition is belt fed and it can pump out a thousand rounds a minute of the same 5.56 millimetre ammunition. It's a lot heavier than the F88 rifle and we became inseparable buddies. It came with two spare barrels for changing over when one got too hot from firing, and a night scope that is the size of a loaf of bread and produces an amazing magnified green image, even on the darkest of nights. Cleaning kit for maintenance had to

be carried and one thousand rounds of belt ammunition
Finding room for everything in my already full pack was
added over twenty extra kilograms, which never bother
because I got to carry the big gun and have the most fun.

Night vision was something I had only ever seen in movies so the day that we were going to be issued our own set of night-vision equipment I was very excited. Called Ninox, it was a single monocular the size of a small can of Red Bull, which painted a light-green picture of the world even on the blackest of nights. It is mounted on a head harness with a chin strap or it can be pulled out of a pocket and used sporadically. The monocular is very powerful, so to avoid any retina damage from overuse it must be continually rotated from left eye to right eye throughout the night. The Ninox functions by detecting all ambient light from the moon and stars then amplifying it. The picture seen when looking through the eye piece was exactly the same picture I could see during daylight, except now in shades of green. The device is extremely sensitive to any forms of artificial light, even a lit cigarette at 100 metres is very easy to detect and looks like a car headlight through the monocular. One place the Ninox was useless however was in very thick jungle, like what we have in North Queensland at the Army Jungle Training Wing in Tully, where the canopy blocks out all the ambient light.

Becoming a soldier wasn't just about playing with all the toys, we also had to be able to perform formal duties including parades. I'm sure you have seen groups of soldiers all synchronised, completing turns, salutes and firing rifles. It looks very impressive and getting up to that standard was going to be the one part of military life I did not enjoy. Parade movements were called 'drill' but it wasn't limited to the parade ground, everywhere we travelled on the military base and every movement we made while in uniform consisted of learning two or three movements of drill. Every day for at least two hours we had to form up on the parade ground and get lessons on doing everything to perfect drill timing. Performing salutes, learning to slow march, quick march, presenting arms (saluting with the F88) and all the halts and turns. Everything was to be done to a count and with perfect timing by everyone. If one person was out of time they stood out like a sore thumb bringing a barrage of verbal abuse from the staff.

Drill lessons tended to send the corporals a particular type of insane; I think they hated the sessions just as much as I did. Standing out on the hot parade ground and trying to get soft-skinned new recruits to pick up the fairly difficult art of drilling would have been extremely frustrating for them. Corporal Pearson was one of my favourites because he stayed calm and did not lose his temper as much as the others. He did explode once when sweat was pouring from his face and we continually messed up his commands, but I didn't hold it against him. During my first few sessions of drill I had doubts that I would ever move like I was supposed to, however after hours and days of repeated practice it started to come together. Slowly we were starting to look like one solid unit.

The three physical training sessions per day were the most enjoyable for me and so were the three meal times. The only downside during meal times was our restriction to a twenty-minute window for the entire process. We would be marched to the mess (dining hall), halted at the front door and then dismissed. The dismissal would start the twenty-minute clock and it turned into a literal feeding frenzy from there. Racing inside I would grab the tray, plate and cutlery as fast as possible. Then, proceeding to the buffet, I would load my plate with as much food as it could hold. Sticking to the stews or spaghetti was the key, it created a solid base for food to build on and I didn't have to chew it as much, saving valuable time. Spaghetti base, crumbed steak on top, eggs, pie and bread on the edges. I would always try to place a piece of cake at the very top of my mountain of food making it the first to get eaten, ensuring I never missed out on dessert.

Once loaded I'd move to the closest table among the hundreds of recruits feeding like animals; dropped trays and smashed plates were a common occurrence. There was no conversation at the tables, all that could be heard was the scoffing sounds of starving soldiers. I could clear an entire plate of food in under two minutes, giving me ample time to stand at the water machine drinking as much fluid as my stomach could hold. It was then a race to drop the dishes into the allocated bins and be outside formed up with the rest of my platoon. All in under twenty minutes.

Shooting is a critical skill for an infantry soldier and we spent many days out at the firing range learning the finer skills of marksmanship. I had a head start on the other recruits because I had grown up hunting but there was still plenty to learn. Taking an accurate long-range shot was something we had to master, and like everything else in the military there was a procedure in place to make it happen.

Lying on the range in good body position, having gone through all adjustments and my sight locked on target, I would take in a deep, slow breath and focus on relaxing my body and slowing my heart rate. I would start to release my breath and at the same time take my finger to the trigger, very softly beginning to apply pressure. At the very end of exhaling, when I'm at my steadiest, the shot should almost be a surprise. I would feel the recoil and see a perfect hit on target.

After the first few weeks I had passed all of the rifle shoots at the firing range, the physical fitness tests and even passed the drill test. It then came time for all of us to undergo bayonet assault course training.

Every combat soldier must know how to fight effectively with the use of a bayonet (combat knife) attached to the end of an assault rifle. Throughout history countless battles have come down to the use of bayonets, and the soldiers that were more aggressive and effective in its use were victorious. This is where war becomes up close and personal, and it was one of the most intense days of my entire life. At around five-thirty in the morning the training staff walked into the quiet halls of the fifteen platoon barracks, crept into our rooms with machine guns and opened fire with blank rounds, not more than a few feet from our heads. Shocked from deep sleep, my heart was thumping out of my chest and I didn't know what the hell was happening. We were rushed down the hallway in the dark and every time the corporal asked 'What are you going to do?' we were made to scream 'Kill, kill, kill' at the top of our lungs.

At the end of the hallway was a pitch-black room where we were all made to sit together cross-legged on the floor. Once sitting down and still screaming 'Kill, kill, kill' a projector screen flickered to life in front of us. Images of war, killing and battlefield clips were flashed across the screen over and over again to a soundtrack of heavy metal music. *Braveheart, Saving Private Ryan, Apocalypse Now* scenes, and images of bombing raids, all shown to us in order to do one thing: make us emotional and aggressive. It worked.

As the rage inside me was building I could feel the tears fall from my eyes. I had a quick glance around at the rest of the platoon and everybody looked to be in the same condition. Even the guys I thought were too tough to show emotion were welling up. The film clips and music continued on for half an hour in that dark, cramped space. Then the commanding officer of 15 platoon stopped the video and began to read us a story about Australian soldiers fixing their bayonets during World War I at the battle of Gallipoli. The soldiers in that battle knew they were going to die but still they fixed their blades to the end of the rifles and charged in with their mates behind them, never to return. That story was the tipping point for us, we were ready to begin. We were led out of the building and down to the bayonet assault course, the sound of 'Kill, kill, kill' being screamed by thirty passionate men was deafening. Over and over we were told that today was all about aggression and it was hard not to be swept up in the emotion and violence of the day.

We were put into lines, told to fix bayonets and then for the following ninety minutes were taught the bayonet fighting movements. Once the corporals were satisfied we knew what we were doing it was time to hit the assault course for the first time. The course consisted of a massive pit of water (bear pit) at the beginning that was neck deep. The bear pit was first so that when you emerged on the other side you were soaked from head to toe, making the rest of the course all the more difficult. There were tunnels filled with water and barbed wire, walls to climb, wooden beams to balance and move along and endless mud to crawl through on your stomach. Red, green and blue smoke grenades were set off everywhere, burning your eyes and lungs. Above everything was the constant sound of gunfire from the machine guns that were positioned all the way along the course and manned by the corporals. Just as I was nearing the point of exhaustion a target would appear and it would be time to put our aggression and fighting skills to the test.

At the time I was going through basic training the September 11 terrorist attacks were fresh in everyone's minds. The training staff used this to their advantage and made the bayonet targets with faces of Osama bin Laden. This added to the emotion of the day, giving us an extra burst of aggression as we stabbed, hacked and smashed our lifeless enemy to the ground. It was a physically gruelling course and at the end of the first run through I was shattered, after the second I was vomiting and after the third I thought I might black out at any second.

We were sat down at the start of the course absolutely shattered and barely moving. The commander came across again and read us another story about the Rats of Tobruk. The story was of an Australian soldier taking out three gun pits single-handedly after watching his mate die and being shot three times himself. He won the Victoria Cross for his efforts, our highest military commendation. The story got us firing and when the commander asked, 'Who wants to do the course again?' all of us jumped up and screamed. We lined up at the pit ready to charge in when the commander called the stop. It was the end and that was our final test. If we hadn't jumped up and gotten ready to go in again we would have failed. It was a physically and mentally draining day and one I will never forget. That night the halls were silent and I slept like the dead.

At the end of our six weeks of training there was a march out parade that showcased to our friends and family the beautiful drill that we had been practising every day. I had performed well during my time at Wagga and I was lucky enough to win the physical training trophy for fittest soldier. This meant that I had to march out in front of the entire parade with the other four trophy winners, call the halt for the five of us at a certain position on the tarmac and salute the governor of New South Wales. In the days leading up to the parade I couldn't manage the halt on the right spot, no matter how much I practised it. The night before, during our final dressed rehearsal, I stuffed it up again. The staff were not very impressed with me and there was talk that they would get someone else to call the halt instead. The commander came to my rescue and said that I would be fine on the day. I was shitting myself. The moment came during the real deal with everyone's families watching and I called the halt: it was perfect and exactly where I had to be. I was a bit stunned that it all went so well that I nearly forgot to salute the governor so it was a little bit delayed. The entire march out parade went really well and I was keen to see my mum who had travelled 2300 kilometres to Wagga from Far North Queensland just to see me.

Mum was a little shocked at my physique as I had lost 8 kilograms over the six weeks and I was already a skinny kid when I arrived. At the buffet dinner, Mum got to see some of the skills I had learnt in the Army. She followed behind me as I loaded my tray from the buffet with a full plate of spaghetti, crumb steak on top, mash potato and bread on the sides. Then to finish off my meal a large slab of chocolate cake at the summit. All of this was promptly shovelled into my mouth in four minutes flat. I turned to see my mum staring at me with shock on her face. All of the manners I had been taught at home were erased in a matter of weeks and I'm sorry to say they were going to remain that way. Basic training was over and I now had to get prepared for my next ten-week training course at the Singleton school of Infantry. I thought I had survived a hard six weeks in Wagga Wagga but it was only the beginning.

Every soldier in the Army goes to Wagga Wagga for the initial basic training course. On completion those going into cavalry, artillery, catering and other corps get sent out to their own training courses which the Army names IET (Initial Employment Training). For me, who was wishing to become an Infantry soldier, I was sent off to Singleton Infantry School for ten weeks. On arrival I was fairly confident and believed I was ready for anything. The course didn't start straight away so I had two weeks of waiting around for all of the other soldiers to arrive. I was in the gym lifting weights and eating well again, trying to put back on some of the weight I had lost in Wagga. As the men arrived I noticed they were all fit, strong and some of them had infantry experience in the past, so once again I was the youngest and most inexperienced of everyone. This didn't bother me, I had done well in Basic Training and had the unbeatable confidence of youth on my side.

The staff corporals this time were all hard infantry men called 'grunts'. All of them had seen some action in their careers and they were now tasked to turn us into warriors. They wouldn't yell for the sake of it like our last staff but these guys could put the fear of God into us when they wanted to. Our first physical training session was the hardest since I had joined the Army and at the end of it they said that the session was an easy one to judge where we were with our fitness. One of the first things we were taught was the role of the infantry, and we had to know it and be able to recite it on request. The role of the infantry soldier is: 'To seek out and close with the enemy. To kill or capture him. To seize and hold ground, and to repel attack. By day or by night, regardless of season, weather or terrain.'

For the next few weeks we spent long hours inside the lecture room learning everything from the history of the Infantry and rules of engagement to navigation and bushcraft. These were tough times for me due to the staff always putting a two-hour lecture straight after we had done a gruelling physical training session and had eaten a big meal. I could never stay awake no matter how hard I tried, but I wasn't alone. The corporals went mental any time someone fell asleep and they guaranteed we would all be punished for it. Punishments occurred whenever we had a spare ten minutes and at the end of every day, no matter how long the day was. A dirty rifle warranted 100 push-ups, failure to adhere to timings was another 100, not finishing runs in a decent time 100 and on it went. Falling asleep earns 200 push-ups to every man and once begun they would not stop until we couldn't do another single rep.

Becoming an infantry soldier also meant learning a whole new range of weapons and devices. One of my favourites was the M18A1 Claymore mine containing 700 grams of C4 and steel ball bearings with a kill range of 200 metres. I was getting paid to shoot and blow stuff up, I was in heaven. A thirty-man platoon has three sections, each containing ten men. Inside a section there are two machine gunners, a corporal leading as section commander, and a lance corporal as his second in charge. Most tasks were completed as a section and my section became my little family over the two and a half months at Singleton.

The corporals had to mould us into infantry soldiers and one of the tools used to carve out a soldier was the biggest obstacle course known to man. It could be completed in thirty minutes with good teamwork and high levels of fitness. The course encompassed everything from concrete tunnels narrow enough to get stuck in, rope climbs up and across muddy pits, barbed wire fences, 14-foot-tall walls, cargo nets, monkey swings and endless bars to climb. It was tough and gruelling and if we didn't attack it with everything we had it would chew us up and spit us out.

The second tool used by the staff was the bayonet assault course 2.0. This course was absolutely ridiculous, twice as long as the one in Wagga, double the targets to stab and kill, deep pits, tunnels filled with water, barbed wire walls, fallen trees, trenches full of logs and a huge bear pit at the beginning. The first time we went through was our hardest physical test so far. It was midday, scorching hot, leaving two of the men treated for heat exhaustion. Even though my fitness was great, I was destroyed by the end and we were all sent in for a second time. We did not come close to the expected time for completion so once again we had punishments to do.

My time in Singleton was progressing at a rapid rate, with lots of time out in the bush learning how to survive on patrol and how to attack and destroy the enemy. Living in the bush came very easy to me after all those years camping with Mum and Dad in the outback and on the side of a highway. I also enjoyed learning 'bushcraft', which was how to move through forests, jungle or grasslands leaving no sign for the enemy. We were taught how to cook meals without making smoke and how to cover long distances in rough terrain, knowing exactly where you are at all times with nothing but a map. I enjoyed the training and passed every test. My fitness was at the highest level it had ever been and we could now pack-march for hours carrying 35-kilogram packs. Talk among the men started to turn towards our last two weeks and the final test we had to endure before we could call ourselves infantry soldiers. The staff called it 'hardcore'. It was the last hurdle to finish the course, earn our infantry badges and get shipped out to an infantry unit, ready for deployment overseas.

Hardcore began with trucks dropping us off out in the bush at 4:30 am on a cold winter morning. It had started to rain and the weather forecast predicted more rain and sub-zero temperatures for the following week. The bush was grassland over rocky terrain with clusters of trees scattered throughout. The grass was ankle to knee height, just high enough to cover up rocks, causing trip hazards whenever we dropped to the ground or took a kneeling position. The trees were in winter mode and would provide very little shade from the sun during the middle of the day, however the temperature would be freezing until the sun poked its head over the horizon each morning. Our platoon commander placed us out on the ground in a large circular perimeter called all-around defence. He gave the order to 'dig in' and we went to work with our small fold-out shovels.

Digging in has three stages, stage one is called a shell scrape which is a hole in the ground about 40 centimetres deep with measurements long enough and wide enough for my body to lay in. The shell scrape is used to get my body below ground level for concealment and for some protection from rifle fire and fragmentation devices. Stage two is a pit big enough for two men to stand upright in with our chests at ground height. It takes solid work to get down to stage two depth and the trick was to start the pit wider at the top because we have a tendency to taper the sides in when we dig. This pit is a formidable fighting position as only the very top of my head would be visible to the enemy. It offers protection from small arms fire, fragmentation devices and artillery fire, everything except a direct hit from above. Stage three is the Taj Mahal of fighting pits. It is a pit above head height in depth, with sleeping quarters built into the walls and overhead protection made from sheets of tin. The sleeping positions however are small, cramped and vulnerable to flooding from rain. The overhead protection if built correctly and to the right standard will provide protection from mortars and artillery.

The order was given to dig in up to stage three and it was at that point we realised we would be digging for a week. The first swing of my little shovel made my heart sink, sparks shot up from the earth at the point of impact and I pictured the staff laughing at the look on my face. With all of my effort I broke out a piece of ground the size of a small banana. The earth was compact dirt known as shard and felt only slightly less dense than rock. We dug constantly in two-man teams, rotating in twenty-minute intervals. When we rested we were still required to be in defensive mode and on the lookout for the enemy. We dug for three days straight with no sleep and on the third night I was beginning to have hallucinations, seeing people and animals in the bush around us.

After the initial three days of sleep deprivation we were allowed to get four or five hours of sleep per night for the rest of the week, while maintaining our digging cycle. Completing stage three pits while sleep deprived was the main objective for the platoon that first week. To make conditions worse it was raining constantly and every hour we had to stop digging and bail out the water pooling up in our pit. At night the temperature dropped to two degrees and the only way to keep warm was to swing the shovel. Any time I stopped digging and tried to sleep shivers would grip my body and keep me awake. We managed to get down to stage three in eight days. I was hungry, tired, had lost a ton of weight and was feeling terrible.

During the second week we started to go out on patrols to practise all of the infantry skills we had been taught. Patrolling in different formations, learning to read ground signs left by the enemy, attacking enemy positions and lying in ambush on roadways and tracks. We had to know how to operate all of our weapon systems while in stressful situations. We laid trip wires, anti-personnel Claymore mines and called in imaginary mortars and artillery. The entire time we were being watched by the staff and assessed. The days and weeks were one big practical exam.

It was the last few days of the course and we were all trying to anticipate what was going to happen next. During our last night we came under attack by fifty soldiers playing enemy and using blank ammunition. The staff wrapped detonation cord around nearby trees and set them off to simulate enemy mortar-fire on our position. Mortars are short, smooth bore tubes on tripods utilised for firing shells onto an enemy. We needed to maintain communication throughout the attack, call in our own mortars and utilise all of the weapon systems effectively. We were using blank ammunition and even though there is no actual round going through the barrel the machine gun became scorching hot. I had to change out the barrel halfway through the attack because it was glowing red. The mock battle had lasted for over an hour before an order came over the radio to withdraw from our position.

We grabbed all of our waterlogged gear and retreated back under covering fire to a designated position and straight into a 10-kilometre pack march away from the area. It was dark, my pack was heavier than usual due to everything being soaked and the trail followed a series of hills which were steep and had me pushing hard to keep the pace. As I came up and over the largest hill I saw the platoon trucks waiting to pick us up in the distance and I smiled knowing it was the end of tonight's march. Once we were all on board, the trucks drove us to another location where we disembarked and started congratulating ourselves for surviving two weeks of hell in the bush. The staff told us to eat and get some sleep because the following day hardcore was due to begin.

I was woken by the staff four hours later at four-thirty and felt like I had only just closed my eyes. We were told to eat something and be ready to move in twenty minutes. I ate three hard biscuits, drank some water and mingled with the other guys in my section noticing that for once it wasn't raining. The platoon was divided up into our sections and once everyone was ready we set off on another march. I was carrying a full sodden pack, webbing full of ammunition, the F89 machine gun with all attachments, and I was feeling drained after only a few kilometres. A small hill rose up in the distance and we were told to attack the imaginary enemy gun pit on the summit. We had done mock attacks before so this was nothing new to us. We broke into formation and proceeded to take the hill. It took thirty-five minutes of crawling on our bellies, running and manoeuvring to clear the hill and regroup on the top. I was soaked through with sweat and feeling defeated under my heavy pack when the staff gave the order to move out again.

A few kilometres later we came upon a supply of big crates and ammo boxes. The ammo boxes were made out of steel with metal handles and weighed about 15 kilograms each, the crates were made out of timber with rope handles and weighed around 40 kilograms each. Our task was to gather up all the boxes and crates between the section and bring them with us. As a section we had two men to a crate and one man per ammo box, with everybody having something to carry. About 2 kilometres down the road my shoulders and arms were burning with fatigue. Changing hands helped for the following 2 kilometres but after that nothing would ease the pain and I simply had to deal with it.

Six kilometres later we arrived at a firing range. This was a place we had been to before while we were learning to shoot all of our weapon systems. We placed the boxes and crates to one side and were told to get ready on the range for the targets to pop up. I was drenched with sweat, my hands were fatigued and my heart was racing from the effort of the day but I had to shoot straight. We all had to pass this shoot to carry on and finish hardcore. The shooting distances varied from 100 metres to 400 metres and we had to run between the different firing positions. Each interval caused my heart rate to spike, which affected my shooting. As the target came up I took a few seconds to calm myself, adjust onto target, and then began firing. I passed the shoot, however two guys from another section were not as lucky. They would need to repeat the entire two weeks again from day one with another platoon.

We walked off the firing range, picked up the crates and boxes and continued marching. It was only ten minutes later a guy from my section dropped to the ground saying he couldn't go on. The staff only ask once if you want to carry on, if you say no then you get left behind. They asked him and he said no; off we went again, one man down. The next 4 kilometres went by in a blur of pain before we came upon bodies lying in a field creating a mock first-aid scenario for us to attend to.

The pretend casualties had bullet holes, broken legs, amputations and shock, all needing our newly acquired first-aid skills. We knew that all of these scenarios were treated as real and judged as such. First we secured our position on the ground in all-around defence and then tended to each casualty in order of most critical first. It took forty-five minutes to bring the scenario under control and radio for evacuations of the critical cases. The next scenario was radioed back telling us that no air evacuation was possible and we needed to carry out a critical casualty. We had two hours to get the patient to the landing zone or he would be confirmed dead and we would fail the stage.

The crates and boxes were left nearby and this time we set off with a stretcher weighing 90 kilograms. An object of this size is best carried between four men with the horizontal poles resting in between their backpacks and necks. Carrying duty is shared evenly between all of the men so that no single soldier does more work than the others. Carrying a stretcher is hard in the best of conditions and we had to move down a winding old track, knee-deep with mud and obstacles on either side to navigate around. It wasn't long before this arduous task took its first real casualties. The pain was excruciating and continuous; the small rest we had while not carrying was only a few minutes, before we were back on and hurting again. Two guys couldn't take it and dropped out within the first 2 kilometres, they were asked once but they didn't get up.

My back felt like it was about to break, my neck burned and my legs pumped battery acid, I broke. With the stretcher pushing down on my neck I began to cry. First just a little sob then full tears, but I didn't stop. Something strange was happening as I broke, I realised that I could keep going, I just told myself to put one foot in front of the other and don't drop. As I was starting to pull myself together another guy dropped, he chose not to continue and it made me feel stronger. I know it's harsh to say but seeing that person fail spurred me onwards; I was gaining strength from their weakness and as long as I stayed focused on the next step I wasn't going to drop. After what felt like an eternity but was in reality just under two hours, we made the landing zone before the cut-off time where we dropped the stretcher and all fell in a heap for a well-earned drink break.

'Get ready to move,' came the call from the staff ten minutes later and our hearts sank. We had been going for almost six hours and my tank was well below empty. Up I rose and continued on the march trying to think what else they could throw at us today. I should have known what was coming. The obstacle course came into view and I nearly cried again, I heard 'fuck off' and 'no way' come from the boys behind me. We were told to line up at the start, given the cut-off time to complete the course and in we went.

After six hours of punishment and pain we attacked one of the hardest obstacle courses in the Army. At the tunnel section I got down on my knees to crawl through and was seized by the worst cramps I had ever had. I was dragged through by one of the guys and in turn I dragged someone else through who was in the same condition. Climbing over walls, swinging on ropes, up cargo nets, down wooden logs, it was a team effort to complete the course; we were all dehydrated and physically exhausted but we got it done. It was painful and there were no records broken but we all made it through without anyone dropping.

After a ten-minute drink break off we walked. If we all passed today we would earn ourselves the 'skippy badge'. This is the infantry badge given to every soldier who marches out of this training centre at the completion of the course. We walked passed a huge replica of the infantry badge at the entry to our base and my chest swelled with pride as tears came into my eyes. This is what all the pain is for, to earn a place as a soldier on the frontline for Australia. We should have seen the next challenge coming as we pulled up to the start of the bayonet assault course. Our corporal looked at us and said that if we gave it everything we had we would only do it one time through. He then turned to me and said, 'Richo, get these boys going.' I exploded and began shouting to the guys to give it everything as we charged into the bear pit.

There was no pain, no feeling at all. I was running on the last bit of adrenaline left in my body. I was charging up from the rear screaming encouragement at the guys all the way until we were all standing at the finish line soaked in swamp water with steam coming off our bodies. The corporal came over and I thought for sure we were going to go through one more time as he said, 'Well done men, you are now infantry soldiers', and a cheer went up from the remaining guys and he shook all of our hands. It was seven hours from start to finish. Hardcore broke everybody who had completed it in some way, but we never dropped, and it turned me into a man at seventeen years of age. I learnt a lot about myself in those seven hours and I also realised that when the mind is willing the body will go through hell.

We started with thirty-one men that day but only nineteen skippy badges were given out. I was lucky enough to win awards for best shot and the fittest soldier. I was now a member of the Australian Army and I had received a posting to the 1st Battalion Royal Australian Regiment in Townsville, and so did a few of my closest mates on the course. We were heading up to a part of the country I knew well, sunny North Queensland, and I was ready to start my career as a soldier.

CHAPTER 3
EAST TIMOR

...

My first goal had been achieved; I was posted to the 1st Battalion part of the Royal Australian Regiment (RAR) and the 3rd Brigade as a qualified infantry soldier for the Australian Army. It was now time to become the best infantry soldier I could be. Our battalion consisted of four rifle companies, each company containing 100 men split into three platoons and each platoon broken into three sections. I was part of A company, 3 platoon, 8 section. The 1 RAR is based in Townsville in Far North Queensland and only 100 kilometres from my family, who lived further north in Ingham. With a population of 130,000 it was more like a big country town than a city.

Battalion life was like a dream to me: for a seventeen-year-old I was getting paid great money just to stay in perfect shape. The accommodation was provided, food readily available, medical and dental care was free and I had twenty-four hour access to gyms. The typical day involved a morning run, a pool training session around midday and then hitting the gym for weight training in the afternoon.

Everything I had learnt in Singleton got refined and perfected with my new company. The ten men in my section became my new family and even though I was the new recruit and still had to earn the respect of the senior soldiers, my biggest strength being fitness made for a smooth transition. If you couldn't pull your weight due to lack of strength or fitness it was very hard to get accepted by the team. So long as I stayed fit and strong and could do my job, there was no more yelling and it was a great place to be.

A journey to the Jungle Training Wing (JTW) was my first big military exercise as a new soldier. Twice a year for specific jungle training the battalion loads into buses and drives north from Townsville to Tully. It was a 210-kilometre drive to one of the wettest locations in Australia, averaging 4000 millimetres of rain per year and containing some of the thickest jungle in the world. This combination makes for a perfect environment of misery. Military units from all over the world come to JTW to get put through the hardships of living and navigating in this remote and unforgiving terrain.

JTW is a group of small wooden buildings at the end of a road in the middle of nowhere. The humidity hit me in the face as I stepped off the bus and I immediately started to sweat. It enveloped me like a wet blanket, whether I was in the sun or shade it was always present. The next thing that hit my senses was the vibrant smell of the jungle, a tropical greenhouse with a backdrop of birds and cicadas all fighting for an audience. Then it started to rain and a heavy deluge of the tropical rainforest soaked me to my core in a single minute.

I entered the thick bush on my first patrol in this new environment, searching the jungle for enemy, and I was excited. That excitement turned quickly to frustration as I began to realise how hard walking through thick jungle with a heavy pack and machine gun could be. The ground was ankle-to-knee-deep mud from the constant rain. Branches and vines snagged the barrel of my gun and slapped me in the face at every turn. Any brush of vegetation against my body sent the water that was settled on the leaves cascading down my back, leaving me constantly soggy and chafing in the overwhelming humidity. Then there was the 'Wait A While' vine, named due to the fact that when it snags you with its razor sharp barbs it forces you to wait a while to pick it off. Trying to force through it to keep moving, leaves you with torn clothing, or worse, torn skin with a high risk of infection.

The biggest lesson I learnt on my first night in the jay (jungle) was that all of our night vision equipment was useless. There is no ambient light that can make its way through the thick jungle canopy that the Ninox needs to operate. Once the sun went down we were literally blind and unable to patrol. To move around at night we needed to construct string lines between everyone's sleeping positions. It was an eerie feeling following a string line in full blackout conditions with the sounds of the jungle all around me.

It rained all night long, which meant staying wet and sleeping in the mud. We were warned against using too much leaf litter for a mattress as the leaves contain ticks that can latch hold of you and over time make you very sick. Big rats were everywhere and if a pack was left on the ground and not suspended from a tree they would eat through the canvas to get to the food supplies. I woke up on my third night with a rat nibbling on my left ear; he didn't get much of it.

Then there was the war against the leeches. They were all over us during the day, presenting themselves on leaves until we walked by and they would grab hold. Every afternoon we would check each other's bodies in those hard-to-see locations and without fail there was sure to be a cluster of leeches having a feast. One morning I woke up and couldn't see out of my right eye, as a big fat leech had been feeding on the corner of it all night and was now blocking my vision. I had to get one of the men to burn the leech with the head of a match until it dropped off. The corner of my eye didn't stop bleeding for three hours, it was an average start to the day.

We would normally do two or three weeks of jungle patrolling, enough to get the full effect of living in this inhospitable environment. The jungle left my morale low from being constantly wet and chafed and my body was drained, not just from the leeches but from the physical effort it takes to cover any distance in this unforgiving terrain. I couldn't imagine how the soldiers handled months and years of it in Vietnam; it would have been a true hell on earth.

A big motivation for joining the Army was to travel and talk started to float between the men about a little place called East Timor. The eastern province of Timor was a newly formed small country with a tragic past, located a short, ninety-minute flight from Australia. Indonesia's brutal dictator President Suharto first invaded East Timor in 1975 with the full support of the United States and Australia under the false pretext of anti-colonialism. The invasion led to a quarter-century occupation and the slaughter of soldiers and innocent people including women and children with lives lost estimated between 100,000 and 180,000. Suharto continued to have the full support of the West during the occupation years, constantly being supplied the latest weaponry until a referendum in 1999 when the majority of East Timorese voted for independence. It was then that the UN finally stopped turning a blind eye and ordered peacekeeping missions to Timor to help the East gain their independence.

The Australian Army, as a part of the United Nations force, was asked to go in to stop the killings and bring an end to the occupation. To trained infantry soldiers this was music to our ears. When people asked me why I would want to go to a war zone I could only say that it is like a fireman who never got a chance to fight a fire. We had trained for a long time to do a job and now we wanted to go and do it. Orders came down from the Commander of the Army for 1 RAR to be ready to go to East Timor on short notice. I started to get excited; this would be my first international trip, hunting down militia in the jungles of East Timor.

I didn't know the Timorese history until many years after I had discharged from the Army. I didn't know about the politics of war and at eighteen years of age I simply believed that good people were dying and we had a chance to go and put a stop to it. To me that sounded honourable and was exactly what I had enlisted to be a part of. I had two years of military service under my belt when we were given the go ahead for our tour. Within three months of getting the green light and the endless preparation training, we were sitting on the concrete waiting area for our Qantas flight out of the country and into a war zone. I was swelling with pride at the thought of serving my country in action. The flight from Townsville to Dili, the capital of East Timor, was short, only three hours, and upon landing we knew we were in a different world all together.

There were Australian soldiers providing security for the airport in full battle gear, ready for anything. Stepping off the plane my senses were overwhelmed with the smell of rubbish fires mixed with the occasional scent of sewage and the stifling humidity. With no customs or officials to stamp passports or check bags we were loaded straight onto flat-bed trucks to begin our long drive out of the smoky city and up into the hills, where we would be doing most of our patrolling.

It was a rough five-hour journey by truck with changing scenery and native people everywhere. I had an anxious feeling looking out at the locals; I knew we were there to protect them but at that point I didn't know how to interact with them. I ended up giving awkward smiles and big waves. We followed a coastal road along the northern edge of the country until we came upon Forward Operating Base Batugade. This would be my home for the next six months.

The local East Timorese lived very basic lives. In the cities they had running water, electricity and were well educated, however, a couple of hours out into the hills and it was a step back in time. Villages were broken into many small huts with no running water or electricity and the people lived off what they grew themselves or could hunt in the jungle. Many locals that I came across in the bush chewed a substance called betel nut. It's a little red nut that once chewed releases a big hit of caffeine. It turns the lips and tongue red and a big side effect of chewing it for long periods of time is that the teeth eventually fall out. Some people chew it from a young age, so by the time they reach their late twenties their teeth are well on their way to rotting. It's very hard to pass judgement on the locals who chew betel nut or drink too much rice wine, they have survived twenty-five years of occupation and genocide, which is going to leave social scarring for generations.

We were tasked to stop the militia that had committed atrocities from doing so again, and to help the East Timorese develop and maintain their own government. We were doing this in several ways. First, conducting green hat patrols out in the jungle for periods of up to two weeks. These were patrols where we sought out any militia that might be operating along the border, and upon locating them, engaged them.

Conducting blue-hat patrols was a part of the hearts and minds operations; blue hat meaning our UN-issue blue hats, known all over the world, being worn at all times to show that we came in peace. This meant showing our smiling, clean-shaven faces in local villages and around schools to gain a rapport with the locals. We did this to encourage them to not see us as a threat and possibly give us some intelligence on the militia.

We also trained the local police and border guards so that one day they could effectively protect their own people and secure the border. This was a hard task to undertake because even though these people had seen atrocities with their own eyes, they were still not motivated enough to meet up with us for the training sessions. We would have to walk around the police compound and round up as many as we could see and get them over for the class. It got very frustrating after a while; we were there to help and protect them but they didn't care enough to learn to protect themselves. So that was our basic cycle, two weeks of green face patrols, two weeks blue-hat, training the locals and securing our base for another week, then it started all over again.

While out on green face patrols at night in the bush I always knew when we were getting close to a village. First I might hear some sounds of coughing from villagers or farm animals crying out. Then I would smell the village toilet, that sometimes was nothing but a designated area of open ground. There are not many things worse than stepping in human faeces. Humans have a certain aroma that's very unpleasant, and once that smell's all over your boots it remains with you for the entire night and only comes off with scrubbing and lots of soapy water. I spent many sleepless nights lying awake with the smell of betel-nut faeces wafting up from the soles of my boots.

Going out on smuggler (rat-catching) patrols at night while we were on border guard were some of my favourite patrols. The border between East and West was hard to secure as it was just open jungle. The jungle was thick and full of little rabbit-warren passages through the undergrowth. So at around 1 am we would slip into the jungle and hide near some of these passages and wait for the militia or smugglers to come along. Most of the time it was locals bringing across petrol, food or other trinkets from the West to sell for a tiny profit in the East. We would wait in total silent ambush until we heard the sound of footsteps coming slowly towards us through the leaf litter. We let them get in front of our position only a few metres away and would then spring up and take them down. We would never intentionally hurt them unless they were resisting, which was very rare; they were usually too scared to talk and would surrender immediately. Most times we would seize whatever it was they were shipping across the border and let them go with a warning. It was only if they had some illegal firearms that we would detain them and hand them over to police.

One great thing about the Batugade Base was that it was directly opposite the beach and it had a killer set of beach-breaking waves. We were allowed to go swimming once a day at 4 pm once our other duties were complete. The only requirement was that our weapons had to be laid out on the beach ready in case we needed to grab them quickly, and we had to have two men fully dressed and armed, standing on the beach as protection. The men standing on the beach had two jobs to do. They had to maintain security for us in case we came under attack and they needed to keep an eye out for sharks and crocodiles. It was easy to forget where we were while enjoying ourselves on that beach in the afternoons. The sunset was beautiful, its reflection shimmering off the water as it made its way towards the horizon, and lying there on the sand I could just as easily have been lying on a beach back home in Australia.

Our base was for infantry only, which meant there were no women at all. With a habitat like that there were going to be magazines containing the naked female form lying around from time to time. One day a female officer from a base in Dili was driving through our area and wanted a tour of Batugade Base. It was simply by chance that the female officer encountered a magazine of that description and she was outraged. This led to a series of complaints to headquarters that concluded in an order coming down the chain of command to burn all the porn on Batugade Base and to screen all mail for the new contraband. It was our turn to be outraged but we had to follow orders, the burning took two full days of round the clock destruction of literature inside two big metal drums. This caused a drought of glossy magazines on an unprecedented scale and something needed to be done. My dad, who was known for being able to fix any problem, came to the rescue. The mail was now getting screened for banned magazines so Dad started splicing a page from a porn magazine in between the pages of motorcycle magazines. It worked perfectly and before we knew it the supplies were restocked and sanity was restored to the young infantry battalion. Cheers Dad!

We visited schools during our blue-hat patrols as part of the hearts and minds operations, which were great fun. The kids loved us and they would swarm around the vehicles asking for lollies, pens or in most cases simply 'aqua mister'. I'd throw them some water if I had some to spare and it would be shared around and guzzled down in a matter of seconds. They always seemed happy and glad to see us, most likely not fully understanding the reasons for us being there in the first place. The kids were one of the biggest motivating factors for me in doing what we did; it was an opportunity to give the next generation a chance at a life free of occupation and misery.

Our tour was cruising along at a rapid pace, we were so busy patrolling and doing a variety of things for the first time that as the old saying goes 'time flies when you're having fun'. Once we crossed into the second half of our six-month tour we had our departure date locked in, which gave me something to aim towards.

I had my nineteenth birthday while I was in East Timor and it was different to most of my birthdays before or since. We were out on a green face patrol when we received reports that there were going to be some smugglers coming in at a local boat ramp, fully loaded with cargo. Cargo of what nature we weren't sure, but we thought we should check it out. We made our position close to the ramp yet back in the thick jungle out of the way of the locals, and positioned two men forward under a log at the edge of the clearing, with eyes on the boat ramp. I had my turn up front with eyes on our target at 11.30 pm. Midnight arrived and my birthday ticked over while it was drizzling rain, the mozzies feasted on me and I was lying under a log in the mud. The song 'I Was Only 19' by a band called Red Gum about the Vietnam War started playing in my head, and I managed a smile.

It was only about half an hour after midnight when we noticed a boat starting to make its way towards the shore. I used the radio to wake up the rest of the section and get them ready for action. Moving onto my knees I shouldered my machine gun and clicked my safety catch off. As soon as the boat touched the bank we were going to charge out and take them down. My heart rate was jacked and my adrenaline was pumping. The boat was three metres from touching the bank when shouts from a local villager hidden on the other side of the clearing warning the boat of our presence called out. The boat spun around and hit full power as it vanished into the darkness. We didn't move. There was no point trying to catch the local, he would be back in the village and gone in seconds. A little pissed off, I settled back down into the mud. Even though we didn't apprehend the smugglers it made for an exciting night and a very memorable nineteenth birthday.

Anytime we came back to the base after long patrols one of the first things on my mind was getting mail. We had no access to mobile phones or internet and very limited access to a temperamental satellite phone. This made receiving letters and parcels from home very exciting and important for morale. The best packages I ever received were from my nanna. She would fill a box with random stuff from books and newspaper clippings, to little trinkets she had bought at the markets. She would also cook massive Christmas cakes, wrap them in aluminium foil and send those over as well. They were absolutely delicious and a big hit with the rest of the men in my unit. I really enjoyed sending handwritten letters back to her; it was a skill I kept up for years, until she passed away.

In the military there is a scenario referred to as getting a 'Dear John letter' which is a female breaking off a relationship via post while her man is away. This was a weekly occurrence in our company as husbands lost wives and men lost girlfriends. Being away for such long periods of time with minimal contact, only the hardiest of relationships would survive. I had a girlfriend before leaving Australia, let's call her Karen for the sake of this book, and to my nineteen-year-old heart she was the one. I managed a phone call via the satellite phone to my best mate back home after I hadn't heard from Karen for a few weeks and he told me he had seen her with someone else. I had joined the ranks of the Dear John family without receiving the mail.

Becoming a Dear John was hard but I don't think it's as hard as what happened to a couple of guys from my unit. One guy returned home to find that his wife had put a beautiful in-ground pool in the backyard of their home. She didn't seem to realise it was a rental property. Another guy had the most brutal one of all, when he returned home to find an empty house with every single stick of furniture missing, with his wife deciding to leave forever. I think I got off lightly in the grand scheme of things, but with a nineteen-year-old heart I had plenty to think about while out in the jungle.

I had recently returned to base and was recovering from a long, green-faced patrol out in the thick bush and big mountains. My platoon was placed on QRF, which meant we were the Quick Reaction Force, in case something happened. It was only the day after we arrived back to base that something did happen. There was a report that the local police were in a firefight with the militia down near a river that ran parallel to the border. We grabbed our gear and loaded onto the trucks, with me and the machine gun taking the turret position at the top.

Racing along the road, every possible scenario of what we might encounter was going through my head. I was going over the rules of engagement in my mind, checking my ammo and preparing my nerves for what we might encounter. When we arrived at the area it was quiet and I started to worry that it might all be over before we had a chance to see some action. As we patrolled down to the border, scanning the bush for militia, I saw the police standing around in a group. I knew it was all over and I was disappointed. We secured the area and then waited for the information to get back to us about what had happened.

The story from the police was that they were patrolling along the border when a man threw a spear at them, injuring one of the police in the thigh. In retaliation they opened fire and killed the guy. Later investigations revealed that the man who was killed was a high-up militia figure who was guilty of taking part in the massacres two years before. The twist in the story was that the police officer who shot him had his entire family killed in the massacres by that very man. So eventually the truth came out: the police officer saw the man that killed his entire family and wasted him; he then covered it up, so he had one of the men from his patrol throw a spear at his leg. He was charged for the murder and the cover-up, but I'm fairly sure he is sleeping comfortably in jail for getting the revenge he wanted.

When the area was secured, our section commander said we could go check out the body if we wanted to. I jumped at the chance, as did the rest of the men. Seeing my first dead body didn't affect me at all really. He looked like he was just sleeping but I knew, judging by the bullet holes riddling his body, that he was dead. I think I was that desensitised by all the books I had read about wars and genocides that a dead body in real life had lost its effect somehow. The fact that he was a mass murderer and deserved to be dead helped me handle the whole situation. He was typical Timorese build, short, skinny, and a rough beard. I took some photos while our commander wasn't looking then went back to my position. The entire scenario was a bit of an anticlimax at the time, but years later I would appreciate not being the man who pulled the trigger.

Our tour was coming to a close and all of us were glad to be going home. It's all we could talk about in the last couple of weeks. What we were going to do and what we were going to buy with all of our money. The tax-free pay and the danger bonus had all added up to a tidy amount after six months and Timor had given me the opportunity to see a different culture and had fortified the love of travelling and adventure that I had grown up with.

We withdrew from East Timor in much the same way that we had arrived, on the back of trucks and with the jungle and mountainous scenery whipping by. We had to spend a few days back in Dili getting debriefed and packing all of our equipment into trunks for the trip home. The debrief and packing base had a small security force of Fijian military looking after it. They were a great bunch of friendly guys and I got to enjoy two nights of singing songs and drinking kava with them. Kava is a drink made from the root of a pepper plant and looks like dirty dish water. It turns your lips numb and gives you an overall feeling of relaxation. I had a big evening on the kava with them on my last night before I was due to leave, leaving me feeling quite rough the next morning when a big, friendly Fijian face came in to wake me up and said, 'You go home today.' I was over the moon hearing those words, a feeling of accomplishment and pride swept through my body.

Getting back to Australia was the last hurdle to jump over before the celebrations could begin. We weren't flying commercial aircraft back home on the return journey, we were going to catch C130 Hercules aircraft back to Townsville instead. Three planes departed Townsville bound for Timor, enough for all the men due to go home. One had to turn back with engine trouble and another one made it to Dili safely but couldn't leave again, citing mechanical issues. This left one working plane with an entire company of men all keen to get home to their families.

The single plane was loaded to its capacity with men but one unlucky platoon was left behind on the runway and would have to wait until the next day to fly back. There was nowhere to sit down – bodies and bags were everywhere – so the only thing I could do was try and find a comfortable spot to get some sleep. The old plane was deafening and cold. The only place I could find was literally on the back tailgate. It was loud, freezing, but funny enough, I could stretch out because it was such a terrible spot to sleep that no-one wanted it.

Upon landing I'm sure I had mild hypothermia and I felt terrible, but I was home on Australian soil again.

My successful tour of East Timor was a big achievement for me and I had honoured my family legacy by serving my country. The travel and adventure was like a shot of adrenaline and I wanted more of it. I was a young man and I had my whole life ahead of me, I had seen the outside world, I had glimpsed its far horizons and I wanted to see more. I wanted to explore and experience the vastness of our world and the mediocre life was of no interest to me. Adventure and adrenaline had me hooked and I wanted it all.

CHAPTER 4

LONDON AND THE DEMON DAYS

...

My military service term of four years as an infantry soldier was fast approaching its end, and with six months to go I had decided it was time to move on. I had achieved my goal of serving my country and now I wanted to achieve my other goals of travelling the world and having adventures.

The discharge process was long, very tedious and I thought at one point I would never get discharged. The convoluted administrative nightmare took six months of lost records, sign here, lodge that, scan this, but in the end I was finally out and on my way to Europe. I had booked the long-haul flight from Sydney to London, I had sold all of my possessions and had a couple thousand dollars in my bank account. It was 2005 and I was twenty-one. Freedom never felt so good.

London is a city with its own life force, it's a city of cities filled with people from all over the world. I realised quickly that Australians and New Zealanders were everywhere, all with the same mindset of working and travelling. Jobs were easy to come by in London, travel to anywhere in Europe was cheap, and in summer the festival season was something that should be enjoyed by everyone at least once in their lives.

I arrived into town on a winter's day wearing flip flops and a pair of board shorts. It was drizzling with sleet, and a grey sky enveloped the city. The underground train system was easy enough to figure out and I made my way to Angel station, right in the heart of London. I had a friend with a place to stay and by the time I arrived at his front door I was shivering uncontrollably. My mate laughed as he opened the door and let me in.

I was living in a share house with Australians, Scottish travellers and some locals. I didn't have a bedroom, most of the time I slept on the floor in the lounge room. I was known as a 'dosser', someone who just sleeps anywhere and pays the absolute minimum of £5 a night for the privilege. My diet consisted of the bare necessities and during the coldest months of winter I lived off tomato soups and bread – it was hot comfort food that cost 55 pence per serve. It suited all of my needs at the time, sustaining my life for the cheapest possible price.

I snagged a job as a labourer in Kings Cross train station, where we were doing the refurbishment of the old St Pancras hotel and train decks. It was an amazing old building and easy work swinging a sledgehammer. It took time for me to adapt to the cold temperatures and when it started to snow at work one dark miserable morning, in my head I thought we would get to go home now. I was wrong. We were told to have an extra cup of tea and crack on with the job; they really wanted me to earn my £7 an hour.

I was riding the tube to work one morning when I saw an advertisement for human medical trials that payed a whopping £1000 per week to take untested medicines. I called them immediately and booked in for my pre-screening at the testing clinic. My mindset at the time was I'm young, invincible and this is going to be some quick easy cash. Upon walking into the waiting room it became clear that I was not the only traveller who thought this was a great idea. The nurse took all my details, then nearly all of my blood, and told me to come back the following week to get the screening results and to find out if I was eligible for the trial. I arrived back the next week and was told I was disease free and therefore eligible. I would need to stay in hospital for two full weeks and was not allowed to leave during that time once I committed to the trial. I thought 'why not, let's do it!' and checked myself in the following day. The trial was to test a new drug being developed to help stop blockages of the arteries in the brain that can cause a stroke.

The ward where we had to sleep was like a flashback to the Army barracks, one big room with ten beds down one side and ten down the other with only curtains to give some privacy. It was sterile clean, smelt like a laboratory and there were multiple doctors and random people in lab coats shuffling around. One young girl in a lab coat ushered me to my bed and told me that the administering of the drugs would begin in a couple of hours, until then just relax. There was a small library and internet cafe at the end of the ward for us to use, however I had brought with me a selection of books to keep my mind occupied so I opened one of those, crawled onto my bed and settled in.

Alec, also a human guinea pig, walked over to my bed to say hello and he told me this would be his fifth trial. Alec used the trial money to travel; upon completion of a trial he would head off to the far corners of the globe and when his money ran out come back and line up for the next one. It wasn't a bad plan in my opinion, food and shelter while you're at the hospital and a cheque on the way out. The only downside was the Russian roulette I was playing while taking the untested drugs. Considering how cold I was at work swinging that sledgehammer, Alec's way of life was very appealing.

The trial was due to start and we were given our final briefing and told we must consume only the food and drink given to us so that all patients ate exactly the same. This made me hungry immediately. I looked around to see normal-sized people who would eat normal-sized meals. I was a big guy and typically didn't hold back on the serving size; I began thinking this could have been a mistake. The rules were we had to take all the drugs they gave us and let them steal our blood every couple of hours.

The first week of the trial I must have been given the placebo. While some of the other patients were doubled over with migraines I was kicking back reading my books and planning how I was going to spend my money. I was right to be worried about the food situation; when the first tray came out for dinner I thought I was going to starve to death. It was a tiny meal of meat and vegetables which disappeared in two minutes leaving my stomach grumbling. I asked for some more from a passing worker but he ignored me. I had come from a military mess hall with unlimited troughs of food to meals measured to the gram.

Time flew by that first week. It was frustrating getting woken up every two hours throughout the night for blood samples but after three days of getting used to the roster I would typically be fast asleep when they drew blood at night. I didn't know it at the time, but years later, while on expedition this type of sleeping pattern would be the norm. The second week started and that was when I earned my money. Almost immediately after receiving the dose of medication I began to get a headache. The headache evolved into a migraine, which is something I had never had before, and it was absolutely brutal. I was curled up on my mattress with a throbbing head with no chance of pain relief.

The nurses told me I wasn't allowed any other medication to relieve the pain as it would compromise the results of the trial, I simply had to deal with it. The last few days crawled along at a snail's pace. I was unable to sleep, read or move around as my head would start to pound. The pain began to ease by the middle of the last day and I was able to sit up and start having conversations with the other patients. Some of them had a similar story to my own with only one week of migraines, while a few of them had migraines for the entire time. It was late afternoon when the trial was completed and we were told to get dressed and pick up our cheques at the office on the way out.

I walked out of the hospital entrance £2000 richer into the icy fresh air that hit me in the face. Although it was cold it was great to be outside. I guessed I had lost a few kilograms from the starvation rations we had been given but I consoled myself by thinking I had helped advance our medical knowledge for the good of humanity; or I just helped another big pharmaceutical company make more profit. Either way, I had three things on my mind: food, beer and sleep, in that order.

Labourer's wage just wasn't cutting it, I was really starting to struggle for money. My poverty line status forced me to develop a technique to eat for free, which involved getting to the cafe just as all the other workers were about to leave. I'd sit down with them to have a quick chat and as soon as they got up and were out of sight I quickly grabbed the leftover plates and piled all the remaining food onto one without the cafe staff noticing. Then when the staff came along a moment later to clear the table they would see me still finishing up and think nothing of it.

After a few months of working with other tradesmen I was promoted to a semi-skilled role. This simply meant that I had good skills for metal work but wasn't a qualified tradesman. It was a great pay rise, to £11 an hour, and I was given a labourer to help me. Finally I was starting to earn enough to eat a little better, get a gym membership and save some money for adventures.

My labourer was from Poland and he was a really great guy. He told me his name was Jerry but I think that was just a name he used to be better accepted in London. He was a qualified accountant in Poland but couldn't get that sort of work so he was labouring. We were both on the same level with our skills so we could help each other out. Whenever I would come in on a Monday feeling rough from a Sunday drinking session he would cover for me as I crawled up into the air conditioning vents and had a sleep for a few hours. Whenever he needed to go and do something for his family, instead of sacrificing hours of pay, I'd cover him. We were a solid team.

Once I was in the groove of working longer hours, training and saving my money I quickly built up enough cash to have some trips away. I ventured to Scotland to climb its tallest peak, Ben Nevis, and to learn ice climbing, I climbed England's biggest peak, Scafell Pike, and I drove over to the cliffs of Wales for rock climbing. I spent two months in Africa exploring overland from Nairobi to Cape Town and had multiple weekend escapes to Europe. One summer I even saved enough for a trekking trip to the Himalayas in Nepal with two friends Hal and Shannon. It was during that trip I first laid eyes on Everest and some of the biggest mountains on earth. That trip set in stone my desire to try to climb them, but I had a lot to learn and needed a lot more money.

London has a drinking culture much like Australia, and I started to develop a Sunday session ritual of going to Church. Not the church typically thought of but a place renowned for a good time of drinking and partying on a Sunday. The Church was an old building in northern London that opened at midday and closed at 4 pm. Only four hours to drink as much as you could and sing along to some classic tunes. As we entered the front of the building we bought our drink tickets first, usually estimated by how much we had consumed last time. Moving straight to the bar, which only sold beer in a four-pack of cans in a plastic bag, we purchased our first one and moved along. Sawdust blanketed the floor for ease of cleaning up after all the spilt drinks and whatever other fluids get deposited there over the following few hours. Then after jostling for a position near the front stage we waited for the show to begin.

The afternoon spiralled into classic pub songs, sweaty dancing bodies and the constant flow of booze. A comedian performed a set followed by drinking games and on occasion a stripper who rotated from male to female on alternate weekends, to keep everyone equally entertained, would do a show. Four hours went by in a flash and before we had time to finish our last bag of beers the lights were coming on and we'd leave the Church filled with more sin than when we arrived. It was then time to find the second best Sunday watering hole and there was only one establishment on everyone's lips, The Walkabout.

The Walkabout was a chain of pubs marketed directly at Aussies and New Zealanders living abroad. Our favourite was a big venue in Shepherd's Bush that would be jam-packed with our kin by the time the Church emptied into it. A short, sobering tube ride disembarked at Shepherd's Bush and we entered the Walkabout charged up for more. It was straight to the bar to order the specialty concoction known as Snakebite, a jug made with half beer, half cider and red cordial.

The afternoon turned into evening as we sang, danced and dyed our clothes red with spilled snakebite. Knowing I had work the following day I always tried to pull the plug and make it home by midnight, which was achieved a majority of the time. No matter how hungover or rough I was feeling on Monday mornings, when Sunday came around again the following week, I could never say no to the pull of the almighty Church.

As much as having a good time was a priority, so was keeping fit, which I know sounds like a contradiction, but I did my best to make it work. After getting a pay rise I was able to afford a membership at a local Virgin gym and made sure I trained every weekday after work, no matter what. Fitness was important to me and I had achieved so much with my physical abilities in the Army I didn't want to let myself relax those standards.

My fitness served me and my good mate Kieren well when a concert called Live 8 came to London. It was a massive event organised to raise awareness and funds to fight poverty in Africa and it had a headline of artists that was like nothing seen before or since. The only issue was it sold out in minutes and the only tickets we could get were for an event with a massive screen showing the concert in the same park. We decided that would have to do, so we went along to watch the show on the big screen. It turned out to be a family affair with picnics set up on the grass and kids running around having a great time. It wasn't really our scene but we settled in and had a few beers. The show itself was epic and by the time the first few beers had kicked in Kieren and I looked at each other and said, 'We have to get into this concert.' We jumped up, threw our empty cans in the bin and started to walk off in the direction of the main event on the other side of the park.

We had underestimated how hard this was going to be, the paths were blocked off with security, the bridge over the lake we had to cross had a police officer with his dog posted on it and there were fences everywhere sealing off the show. We were in Hyde Park, and the Serpentine lake stood between us and the greatest show on earth – there was only one solution, a military style incursion through the lake. I grabbed Kieren and told him the plan: because the police were on the bridge we needed to slip into the water gently so we didn't cause ripples on the surface that could be spotted from above. Then we needed to take a deep breath and swim underneath the water all the way across about 100 metres to the far bank.

I went first, gently easing myself into the water and taking a deep breath before dropping below the surface. The lake was only 5-feet deep and it was disgusting murky water that smelt like ducks. At the time, I thought I'd definitely get an ear infection from this swim. I had to gently break the surface three times to take another breath before diving under again and finally making it to the muddy bank on the far side. I looked back, gave Kieren the wave and it was now his turn.

I don't think Kieren had done any training on stealth operations or had much experience swimming under the water for any long distance. He entered the lake and dove under, returning to the surface moments later gasping for air and splashing about. I looked up at the bridge to check on the police but they hadn't seen the commotion in the lake, they were preoccupied blocking the path. He kept swimming and doing his best, finally hauling himself out on the far side next to me. It was a miracle we hadn't been seen! We laughed and recovered for a few minutes and then it was time for phase two.

There was a fence to get through next but it wasn't an issue as the clamps holding it together were not secured tightly and we managed to undo one section and slide through. Then we noticed how loud the concert had become; we were getting close and a hundred metres further on we could see it, or rather we could see the final wall separating us from it. As we got to the final wall we realised it was massive, probably 4 metres high, made from steel and seamless on the outside with no way to get through. The only option was over the top.

I had done plenty of wall drills back in Singleton during the obstacle course so I had the process ready in my mind. I placed Kieren with his back against the wall and his hands clasped together on top of his knee. I moved back to get a run up and as I sprinted towards him I planted my foot into his hands and jumped up with all my strength. I managed to catch the top lip of the wall with one hand and then pull myself on top where I balanced myself for the catch that was coming.

Kieren backed up to get ready for his big run at the wall, I was purchased with a solid grip on the back side of the wall and my arm reaching down as far as I could on Kieren's side. We could hear some security guards coming around the perimeter and knew it was now or never. Kieren hit top speed and launched up the wall where we caught each other's hand and I pulled him on top with me. It was the luckiest catch of all time considering how wet and muddy we were and how many beers we had consumed. We laughed with relief as we turned to face into the concert from the top of the wall; we were in awe.

What we saw would stay with us forever. There were 150,000 people all massed together in front of a main stage singing and dancing along to some of the world's best artists. The music was deafening but it was absolutely exhilarating. We had breached the wall behind the food trucks so when we dropped down to the ground we were immediately hidden by the stalls. We assessed ourselves for a moment deciding to remove our soaked shirts and then calmly walked out from behind the cover of the trucks.

One of the vendors yelled out, 'Don't piss behind there lads.' He must have assumed we were using the back as a toilet. We yelled out 'Sorry mate', and that was it, we were in. We entered the enormous crowd of singing humanity and for the remainder of the night we danced and sang our way to the middle of the pack. We were sopping wet and smelt like ducks but we had pulled off one of the greatest festival break-ins of all time, and it is still to this day the greatest concert I have ever witnessed.

• • •

The Kings Cross job was expanding. We were going to refurbish the adjoining St Pancras Hotel, building a massive new train deck that could host a Eurostar rail connection and the entire underground tube system was to be reworked. It was a rare glorious summer day as I worked away on the train deck when a deep rumble shook the entire site. Cries of evacuate sounded out and the supervisor ordered us all off the site as quick as possible telling us there had been an explosion in the underground.

It was 7 July 2005 and the London suicide bombings had just occurred. We were all gathered outside of the construction site and we could see the emergency services running into the underground. We had no idea at that moment that what we were witnessing was part of a series of suicide attacks across London involving three underground trains on the central line close to Kings Cross and a double-decker public bus in Tavistock Square. What I had known and been reading about occurring in the Middle East was in front of my very eyes and it was chilling to know I could easily have been one of the people working or travelling on those trains that day.

London was in turmoil, sirens were echoing throughout the city, everyone was hungry for information on what had happened and the phones crashed shortly after we were evacuated from work. I managed to get a quick message out to my parents letting them know I was okay before the phones went down. In the following days we would learn that four suicide bombers using homemade devices killed 52 innocent people and caused hundreds of injuries. It also left London in a state of fear that I could sense everywhere. The public were in shock and the tension could be felt wherever I went, especially on public transport.

The bombings, to me, were a reflection of a new era of war we were entering into. Since I had discharged from the Army some western nations, including Australia, led by the United States, had invaded Iraq and Afghanistan under the pretext of weapons of mass destruction and capturing Osama bin Laden. In our wake we have left millions of civilians dead and entire cultures destroyed. I didn't know it at the time but what I had witnessed on 7/7 was a consequence of our invasions, occupations and foreign policies as well as the terrorists' extreme interpretations of Islam. It wouldn't be the last attack.

By the end of summer, as the fear eased London slowly settled back into its normal rhythm and the party scene paradise returned. It was becoming a slippery slope of intensifying chaos for me as I began to party more and experiment with drugs. I was in two minds about putting the following pages into this book, however, my past has moulded me into the man I am today. I have no regrets in life and this was part of my journey that I now call my Demon Days. It was a big turning point which would ultimately lead me to a life of adventure. Before I was consumed by that adventurous life however, I ventured to the Camden Markets on a Sunday afternoon to buy mushrooms.

Magic mushrooms were legal in London in 2005 and Camden local markets were the bearer of such goods. I had never eaten mushrooms before and there was a large selection to choose from. Many types from various parts of the world and all carrying with them a different intensity. On a scale of one to ten with ten being out of this world strong hallucinating power. I bought a bag of the number two. The lady who sold them to me said to eat them with some yoghurt for your first time, it would help to settle the stomach. With a bag full of magic mushrooms and some dairy goodness I boarded the train for home. Once I was back at the house our small group of friends all settled in for a beer and began to eat the fungus and yogurt like they were a Doritos and salsa combination. Within twenty minutes they were all consumed and we sat back to wait for the ride.

Not much happened for a while and I was sitting on the couch with my arm around my girlfriend chatting away happily. One minute I was having a conversation with a friend and when I looked back to my arm it was 3 metres long and stretched out like I was a member of the Fantastic Four. I thought to myself, here we go it's show time.

The afternoon turned into evening as everyone started to go off on their 'trip'. I was having a great time floating around the apartment watching the walls melt and my limbs get stretched and pulled in random directions. At one stage I had a mini panic attack and had to tell myself that it was just a ride and it would all be over in a few hours. I passed two of the girls standing in the hallway lined up at the toilet door, I asked 'What are you girls up to?' They said, 'We are just lining up for the nightclub, you should come in with us.' I replied that I was fine thanks and floated on past back to the lounge room.

The effects began to wear off after a few hours and turned us all into giggling school children for the last hour. It was a fun experience but I'm very glad that we had started with one of the weakest varieties. It takes a solid mindset to handle hallucinations; it's very easy to get caught in a spiralling panic attack if you're not ready for everything the mushrooms will make your mind explore.

Alcohol has always been the main staple of the party animal and ever since my first boozer parade in the Army, where we were forced to drink huge amounts every week as a rite of passage, I have struggled with moderation. I could never just have one beer, it always turned into an exuberant amount until my brain eventually switched off and I went into autopilot for the remainder of the night. This often led to passing out and waking up in random locations with no idea how I had gotten there.

I once woke up in what looked like an elevator shaft. It was a bare concrete, square shaped box about 3 metres wide and there was an indent in the wall the size of a door that I assumed could be the way out. I was immediately in a panic and started to bang on the indent screaming at the top of my lungs 'Help me, help me, I'm trapped.' This went on for a few hysterical minutes until a small window slid open in front of me at about eye level. A man on the other side looked through at me and said, 'You're in jail you dickhead, now settle down.' It was then I realised I wasn't trapped at all, I was in the drunk cell of the local police station. I found out later this was the bare cell you get placed in first until you settle down and then they move you to a cell with a bed and toilet.

I woke up on an underground train once after the trains had finished running and were parked up for the night. I had fallen asleep on the last train home from Shepherd's Bush and the train staff had missed me in their final sweep. There was spew on the floor in front of me that I assumed was mine. I stepped off onto the platform and made my way through the eerily quiet station. When I made it to the front entrance the security gate was locked so I had to climb up over the gate to get out of the station and into the dark street outside. From there it was a bitterly cold walk home.

I hadn't seen cocaine back in North Queensland. I'm sure it was there but it had never crossed my path. In London however it seemed to be the lifeblood of the party scene; it was everywhere. I couldn't go to a local pub without someone eventually offering me a line in a casual way as if offering to buy me a beer. Since I was constantly placing myself in this type of environment it wasn't long before I had tried cocaine and started to use it on a weekly basis.

Cocaine made me feel invincible and without a worry in the world. It started with a couple of small lines shared with friends on a Saturday night to kick off the party and fight back the drunken stupor brought on by all the alcohol. It then slowly progressed into me buying my own gram for a night out as I wanted a little more for myself and could spread it out to cover the entire evening. Before long I was well into the party scene and consuming 3–4 grams of coke over a weekend, also ecstasy if we were planning on attending a rave, speed on occasion, and it was all washed down with a constant flow of alcohol.

Adding drugs into a party scene, especially when they are cheap and in abundant supply, has a tendency to lead to drug abuse. What started as a single line on a Saturday night in London was turning into weekend benders starting on Friday and not wrapping up until early Monday morning. Drugs carried me through the days, not needing sleep or food, and the alcohol was always there to lubricate the process. I knew I had hit rock bottom after one particular bender that lasted almost five days.

I had a weekend free of work so after finishing early on a Friday I first went and purchased enough coke to carry me through another wild few days. At this stage I was consuming half-gram lines at a time and needed to plan ahead, as there was nothing worse than running out of coke and desperately searching for more when you wanted to carry on. I had arranged to catch up with different groups of friends at different clubs and parties over the next few days. With this frame of mind my weekend quickly descended into chaos. I moved from party to party, club to club and house to house. Pausing to drink a glass of water on occasion and always trying to conserve supplies of the main ingredient during daylight hours. As was my style, I entered a blackout stage late Sunday evening and went off on another adventure by myself.

I came out of the haze as a blast of cold water hit me in the face. I was freezing and soaking wet, looking down I was naked and standing in a shower without walls and my body was covered in what looked to be my own shit. Looking around I could see three police officers standing behind me holding a fire hose with the look of disgust on their faces. I had been arrested for drunk and disorderly behaviour and drug possession while wandering the streets early Monday morning. I had soiled myself and the police were in the process of washing me down as my mind snapped harshly back to reality.

After the hose down I was placed in a cell, given some water and told to sleep it off. It was impossible to sleep due to the chemicals pumping through my veins and after five paranoid hours I was released with a warning. I was told the drug amount in my possession was very small and as this was my first offence as long as I contacted the drug and alcohol hotline they gave me there would be no charges. I was very lucky to get off so lightly; if they had picked me up a few days before there is no doubt I would have been in jail.

I arrived back to an empty house as all of my roommates were at work. I had one gram of cocaine in my room that I quickly procured, and sat down in the lounge room. I took a line and sat back to analyse my situation. I was sitting in a room by myself on a Monday afternoon, snorting cocaine after being released from jail for being drunk and high. This wasn't the life I envisioned, this was so far from the life I wanted and grew up with that I struggled to figure out how I had gotten there. The disappointment in myself brought me to tears and after a few blubbering minutes I realised that I had to get out of this place and I had to do it now. I called a friend.

Liam was one of my best friends and had been like a mentor to me during our Army service together. He was in Australia and most likely asleep but he picked up immediately and I told him about the situation I was in. I told him that I needed to go somewhere to get myself clean and refocus on my life. He told me about a place in Phuket, Thailand called Tiger Muay Thai, a Thai boxing training camp in the jungle. He had been there once himself, said it was the hardest training he had ever done and that it would be a good place for me to pull myself together. In the condition I was in it sounded perfect and after hanging up I immediately opened my laptop and booked a one-way flight to Phuket from London, leaving that day.

I was still high while packing my bag, I was still high when the taxi turned up to take me to the airport. I finished the last of my cocaine in the car on the way to Heathrow and it wasn't until going through customs that the drugs were wearing off and I began to feel the sickness creeping up inside me. I started to doubt my decision to leave but managed to fight off the desire to flee the airport until I had boarded the plane and the door was closed.

I was going to go cold turkey from alcohol and drugs in a Thai boxing camp in the jungles of Phuket. I couldn't fight, I had never been to Thailand and I was on my own. What the hell was I getting myself into?

CHAPTER 5

THAI MEDICINE

...

The flight from London to Phuket was fourteen hours and after the first two hours of paranoia about leaving I managed to close my eyes and fall asleep. Sleep while coming down from drugs isn't a pleasant sleep, it's restless, twitchy and for me is accompanied by nightmares. I woke up many times throughout the flight dying for food and water. I hadn't eaten or drunk fluid that wasn't alcohol for four days. I'm sure I looked like an absolute mess but I wasn't concerned about my appearance at all. In my head I was thinking over and over about what the hell I was doing; I had nowhere to stay in Phuket and only had the name of a Muay Thai training camp to go off. I was disappointed, scared and feeling sick but deep down I knew this was the right decision.

The plane touched down mid-morning in the tropical paradise of Phuket, home to 600,000 Thai locals and visited by millions of tourists every year. As soon as I stepped off the plane I was enveloped by the inescapable humidity and I was already sweating while waiting in line to clear immigration. I collected my bags and made my way from the carousel to the hustle and bustle of the exit. The front sliding doors of the exit opened and I was engulfed by Thailand.

The tropical heat mixed with vehicle exhaust and a hint of some waste-management issues overwhelmed the senses. As I stepped outside there was a wall of locals staring back at me holding signs for hotels, bungalows and taxi services. They were all in chorus trying for my business, yelling over the top of each other, creating an intimidating scene being amplified by my fragile state. Not knowing any streets, provinces or landmarks I simply said 'Tiger Muay Thai' to a taxi vendor and his eyes lit up. He knew exactly where I wanted to go and for 600 baht he would take me there. Grabbing my bags and ushering me into his cab we were away at rapid speed towards my destination.

After a nerve-racking, high-speed transit along Phuket's highway we pulled up forty minutes later at Tiger Muay Thai, a Muay Thai and mixed martial arts training camp in Chalong province, at the southern end of Phuket. Stepping out of the taxi, the first thing I was drawn to was the sound of shins kicking pads accompanied by grunts and yelling from those doing the kicking and the trainers holding the pads. I paid the driver and made my way to a small office building at the front of the camp to get some more information about training at Tiger. Kicking my shoes off and stepping inside to much needed air conditioning, I was greeted by friendly faces, one of which told me to take a seat.

I was very tired and was not looking like I was ready to train at a Muay Thai camp but I told the lady I had an open-ended ticket, I had nowhere to stay and wanted to train. She smiled and said no problem, like she had heard it all before. I could pay for monthly all-inclusive training and have access to every class on the timetable. If I wanted private sessions with the Thai trainers that would be extra. I could stay at a place called Tony's just down the road that had rooms available and was very cheap when staying monthly. I could buy my mouthguard, wraps and gloves from the office when I was ready to start and if I needed a scooter I could also rent one off them. This was all working out just fine. I was in need of sleep and told her I would start the next day and paid for a month of training up-front.

Before setting off to find my accommodation I decide to have a walk through the camp to get my bearings. Directly behind the office as I moved inside was a boxing ring, raised up onto a metre-high platform, surrounded by a dozen men, all partnered off and sparring each other. Inside the ring were two other pairs doing the same with four Thai trainers moving through the group yelling commands and holding pads. The training area was covered by a tin roof with no walls, just a few banana trees and plants creating separation from the outside. It was sweltering hot and sweat was pouring from their shirtless bodies and pooling up on the floor around them. There was no air conditioning or fans, it was all open-air, and I was sweating simply walking through watching the group kicking, punching, throwing elbows and wrestling each other. I would find out later that this was the pro fighters training area. These guys trained and fought in Thailand all year round and took their Muay Thai very seriously.

Further into the camp was the intermediate training area, it looked the same as the pro fighters' ring at the front except this group were striving to get promoted to the professionals. Pro fighters could fight for the camp and earn the rewards that came along with winning fights. The rewards were nowhere near western standards but they could earn enough to live and train comfortably in Thailand. Close to the middle of the camp was a small restaurant that served the clients daily and behind that was the beginner training area. This was the biggest area and had the most trainers working with guys and girls to teach them the art of Thai kickboxing. There were toilets and shower blocks located in the middle of the camp and right at the back was a small weights gym for everybody to use.

At the back left corner there was a small caged ring surrounded by another training area. This was the mixed martial arts section where Brazilian Jiu Jitsu and striking for cage fighting were taught. The men training in this area were all wearing long shorts and tight tops and were ferociously wrestling each other on the ground and not holding back with the intensity of their punches. I was blown away by this camp already; I could feel the energy of the place, smell the scent of sweat and Tiger

Balm and hear the effort of everyone trying the improve themselves. I was intimidated yet excited to start my training, but first I needed water and sleep or I wasn't going to last another hour.

The front office had pointed me in the direction of Tony's, a short walk away from the camp. The street was lined with a rubber tree plantation and jungle. Along the way to Tony's were a few small Thai restaurants, some other bungalow accommodation and a pharmacy. I knew I had arrived at the right place when I saw the sign saying 'Tony's' at the front and out walked a short Thai man with a pot belly yelling 'Hello sir, I am Tony, you stay here, yes?' I said 'Absolutely' and his face was all smiles. We negotiated a monthly rate of about 220 Australian dollars for a nice little bungalow with air conditioning, no TV and a rock-hard bed. Tony offered me some dinner, which I couldn't refuse, and after a chicken fried rice, a pad thai and a belly full of water I retired to my bungalow for a cold shower and a much needed sleep. The following day would be day one of my training and my first step in a new direction.

• • •

I had a semi-restless night's sleep while getting used to the solid bed and still cleaning out my system from the London toxins, and arrived at Tiger early the next morning. I purchased the Thai fighter starter pack from the front office, consisting of a mouthguard, hand wraps and boxing gloves, and made my way over to the beginner area for my first session. The class started at 7 am and the Thai trainers arrived and gathered all of the beginners together in a circle facing inwards. With no hello or welcome introduction the head trainer gave his command and the warm up began with the group running in a large circle left, then right, then left again. Doing various knee-up drills, side shuffles, push-ups, sit-ups and shadow boxing, we were twenty-five minutes into the class and still warming up.

Sweat was pouring from my body and I was light-headed from the humidity. Finally the command was given to drink water and pair up. Rushing to my bottle I gulped down half of it and knew I had made a mistake in only bringing one. I was partnered up with a big European guy; no names were exchanged as I think those pleasantries were lost during fight training. For the next two hours we completed round after round of sparring, bag work, pad work and endless push-ups. I was out of water and sweat was cascading from my body onto the floor around me. Before starting the session I knew I wouldn't perform to my best ability but I set myself the goal of just not giving up, no matter what.

Two and a half hours into the session the command was given to stop, take off our gloves and complete 200 sit-ups and 200 more push-ups. I was totally exhausted and on the brink of collapse by the time I'd finished the sit-ups and had started on the push-ups. I noticed the push-ups of the other guys – in the military we had to get our chest to touch the ground and then return to a full locked-out arm position at the top for a push-up to count, here, I noticed most people were doing half reps. I knew this would make my sets easier but something in my head wouldn't allow me to concede to half reps, even while doing 200. Throughout the session every punch I threw, every kick I landed and every drop of sweat that hit the floor was a small step in cleansing the shame of drink and drugs from myself. It wasn't the police washing the filth from me this time, it was me.

The reps were completed and the trainers had us back in our circle stretching down. When the final command was given for the end of the session we had been going for three hours. I was a zombie and staggered out, back towards my bungalow. How I was ever going to be able to do this again in the evening I didn't know. I gulped down as much water as my belly would hold, showered, ate a huge lunch of fried rice, eggs, chicken breast and a coconut then collapsed into my bed and was asleep before my head hit the pillow.

I woke up four hours later and my body felt like it had played back-to-back games of rugby, every single muscle fibre was sore. Just sitting up in bed was an effort and I had two hours before the 4 pm session was due to start, which I knew was going to be another gruelling three hours. I had to eat to get energy or I wasn't going to make it, so sitting at Tony's little restaurant I consumed rice, scrambled eggs, fruit salad, a protein shake and coffee. I felt slightly better after eating, and taking two big bottles of water with me I started the walk back to Tiger.

The afternoon session was in the same format as the morning and I wasn't feeling too bad until we had about an hour to go and I began to run out of energy; I was exhausted. My sit-ups and push-ups at the end were dismal and the trainers decided to throw in 300 knees to the bag to make up for it. Stumbling home afterwards I was so tired all I could think about was sleep but I knew I had to eat if I had any hope of sustaining this intensity. I forced down as much food as little Tony could cook for me and collapsed into my bed. I had just completed my first day of Muay Thai training, six hours of exercise in my first day of getting clean. I hadn't performed well, I knew I could do better but I was also proud that I hadn't quit and that I was actually here doing it and changing the course of my life. I set my alarm for 6 am and when my head touched the pillow, before a single thought could be conjured I was asleep.

My routine for the following few weeks was one of survival and progression. I was definitely getting fitter doing six hours per day of training and my mind and body were slowly coming back to a place I had known before: one of performance, confidence and limitless energy. Tiger camp became my home and with it came a family of friends from all over the world. On any given day at one of the tables at Tiger I could be sitting next to fitness freaks, fighters, alcoholics, drug dealers, millionaires or a sheik from Dubai. It was an amazing place that attracted people from all over the world, from all segments of society and cultures. The common denominator was we were all there to make a change in our lives and that's what bound us together each day, a survival instinct and a desire for something different.

I met a guy named Randy at Tiger, he was an American Marine veteran, around forty years old, who was there training and fighting Muay Thai. One thing that he thought the camp was missing from its schedule was some pure fitness-style classes. Randy said one day that he could take us for a class he called BodyFit. I immediately liked Randy. His no bullshit attitude and his confidence were refreshing, so along with a handful of other guys we turned up for Randy's first session. He did not disappoint, dealing us a ninety-minute smashing that I hadn't experienced since the military. It almost broke me. Burpees, squats, kettlebell swings, all mixed in with multiple tyre drags and runs, it was a nasty yet perfect relief from the monotonous punching and kicking I had been doing for weeks.

Randy continued to run his class from that day forward and it became a permanent fixture in the camp schedule. I really enjoyed BodyFit; more than anything else, it gave me a taste of the military training from years before. It was really tough and focused on many different aspects of my training that were lacking. His classes grew from the five of us in the beginning to twenty, thirty and forty people some days, with an equal mix of guys and girls. This balanced out my training week perfectly. I'd do BodyFit every morning, Muay Thai every afternoon and every second day I would be in the weights gym working on my strength. My desire to party was destroyed by my desire to be the fittest and strongest I could be. My mind was clear, I was focused on my goals and I was happy.

At the southern end of Phuket there is a mountain that has a big Buddha statue and a temple at its summit. The Buddha is 45 metres high and 25 metres wide, could be seen from our street and looks incredible around sunrise and sunset. I made running up to this temple part of my weekly routine, as a test of my fitness and simply to take in the pristine surroundings. Running has never been terribly hard for me and I enjoy the way my mind wanders when I run, contemplating the various issues of the world. One thing I realised once I was sober was that while I was drinking and partying I was never thinking about anything of substance or importance. It was great to have an active mind again, to be reading and writing and, at least in my own mind, solving the world's problems.

The little street that I called home seemed like an oasis in a turbulent world. The street had its own life force and a vibrant energy, however it also had its fair share of drama. After staying for over a month I named the street Ramsay Street, after the hit TV show in Australia called *Neighbours*. Every day it seemed like there was another funny story or another drama circulating to keep me entertained, from the 'who's sleeping with who' to the constant scooter crashes, there was never a dull moment.

Ramsay Street was twenty minutes away from the party district of Patong and on any given Sunday, while having breakfast at Tony's, I enjoyed watching the walk of shame procession that followed a night out in sin city. As I was now avoiding the party scene I was privy to the aftermath of the night before, and as I sipped away on my coffee and ate my scrambled eggs the show would begin. Leaving Tony's bungalows I would see a western girl with deeply ingrained make-up from a night of sweating and dancing. As she walked past the restaurant to the taxi rank down the street I would offer a smile of support. Tony would come and sit with me sometimes and we would giggle away together. Often there would be Thai girls following, appearing a little bit less energetic than I'm sure they were a few hours before. On one occasion an absolutely stunning, tall Thai lady walked past and Tony leant in closer and whispered into my ear 'Lady Boy'. I said 'No way', she couldn't possibly be, but he was right. On closer examination, the bigger hands and slightly masculine frame gave it away. Thailand was famous for the beauty of its trans community but until you see them up close you can never appreciate it.

Tony was known as the little godfather of the street. Not to be fooled by his 4-foot stature, he carried some heavy weight in the community. Whenever travellers got into trouble with the local police Tony was always their first call; he was known to get you out of a serious incident before it was too late. For tourists, the consequences of getting involved in an altercation in Thailand can be brutal, and I heard of a fair few horror stories while I was there.

The most brutal story I heard about the Thai world was when Russian businessmen were venturing into Phuket buying up all of the nightclubs. The Thai mafia seemed to be okay with letting this happen and did nothing to hinder their purchases. Then, however, the Russians wanted to get into the tuk-tuk (taxi) business. This was a bad decision by the Russians – the taxis were extremely lucrative and belonged to the Thais, leading to an underground war. It culminated in three Russians having their heads cut off with a machete and their bodies hanging out the front of their nightclubs. Tuk-tuks stayed in Thai ownership and the war was over.

This was the world I had come to know and love; as chaotic as it was, it all seemed to make sense to me. I was thinking clearly again, training like a machine and making plans for what came next. I was reading adventure books and my mind started to drift towards a question that I had asked myself many times before. Do I have what it takes to be like the explorers I am reading about? As I glanced over a list of the biggest mountains on each continent I believed I did.

I had come to Thailand to escape the London scene and begin a new chapter in my life and Tiger Muay Thai had given me more than I could ever have imagined. This place had cleansed my soul, through sweat and pain, giving me a chance to think and analyse my past and show me a world outside the drink and drugs. I met people in Thailand who would become lifelong friends, and in helping myself get clean, I could help others who turned up every week in a similar condition to what I was in on arrival. It had been two months of glorious transformation and I was ready to immerse myself back into the 'real' world.

• • •

As I hadn't worked for so long and had minimal savings when I arrived, I was rapidly approaching broke and I needed to get myself back into the workforce fast. I was very fortunate to learn that my mum had started working for a company back in Australia that trained people to work in the mines. Mum, being the resourceful people person that she is, had talked to a small company working in the underground coal mines who had agreed to give me a job if I was willing to live locally. 'Local' meant flying home to Australia and making my way out to a small town in central Queensland named Emerald. After careful consideration and weighing up all of my other options, of which there were few, I agreed to the job and booked my flight for home. I said goodbye to my Tiger family and said farewell to Ramsay Street knowing in my heart that one day I would be back there again, training in the heat of this amazing country.

Emerald is a town built on the back of a mining boom that has sustained the Australian economy for decades. Coal was being extracted from the earth in ever-increasing quantities and nobody forecast a decline in the world's need for the black gold. Working in mining can earn upwards of $150,000 dollars a year with no experience, and that's what I was there for. One week after departing Thailand I found myself in a classroom sitting through five days of endless slideshows and exams covering every aspect of operating in a dangerous underground environment. I had a clear mind and a brain operating at the necessary level to blitz all of the testing and the following week I was ready to start my first shift as a miner.

I was employed as a contractor which meant I was not a full-time miner and could be let go at any time. This suited me fine as I wasn't looking for a career I was just after the money. Travelling underground for the first time was intimidating and after learning about miners getting trapped and dying from cave-ins during the course, I didn't know what to expect. I was wearing overalls, a helmet with a light so I could see in the pitch-black of the tunnels, a belt holding a battery for my headlamp and an evacuation mask. The mask would allow me just enough time breathing clean, filtered air to evacuate the pit in case of an emergency. Our biggest dangers underground were poisonous gases and cave-ins, which apparently were a rare occurrence.

I loaded into a specially designed vehicle that looked like a steel-plated dune buggy out of the *Mad Max* films. These vehicles were powered by diesel, with built-in scrubber tanks to filter the exhaust so they didn't pollute our air with dangerous fumes; all that exits the exhaust pipe is air and water. Seconds later we were heading towards the rectangular tunnel entrance, 6 metres wide and 4 metres high. Once through the opening it was pitch-black, only the vehicle's small headlights illuminating the way forward. The roof and walls of the tunnel are the earth's crust and protruding out from every angle were large steel bolts that I later learnt get drilled into the walls and ceiling to help prevent their collapse. Steel mesh was pinned on with the bolts and the entire scene looked like a tetanus infection waiting to happen.

I was the new guy and because I had no idea what I was doing I was a possible danger to those around me. Like all new miners I wore a yellow hard hat instead of the standard white, informing anybody working with or around me that I should be watched and double-checked for safety. It took thirty minutes of driving through tunnels and pressure doors to get to the bottom of the mine where I was going to be working. When the headlights finally turned off it was a full blackout; I literally couldn't see my hands in front of my face. Turning on my headlight brought the harsh environment back into vision and even though it wasn't a powerful light on the surface, down at the bottom it was a lighthouse. The battery pack on my belt was supposed to last an entire twelve-hour shift and had to be put back on the charger at the end of the day.

The temperature underground could fluctuate from being comfortable and cool in the intake air tunnels, to humid and extremely hot in the tunnels where air was returning to the surface. Air was sucked through the mine from the surface and when it was on its way back to the top it was full of coal dust, fumes and was hot as hell. I was a new guy in a contractor company, which meant a majority of my jobs were to be conducted in the areas where it was the dirtiest, hottest and most uncomfortable. A shift was twelve hours in length and depending on the work I was doing it could be the longest day of my life.

I had a lot to learn but I was keen to work and attacked the job with the same vigour I have with training. My jobs included hanging pipes and hoses for the air and water supplies, putting in roof and wall bolts, using big water and air powered drills, building structures for the massive coal belts to run along and building walls to re-channel the ventilation of the tunnel system. Most of it was manual work and almost always ended with me being soaking wet from head to toe and as black as midnight from all of the coal dust. I wore a face mask, glasses, gloves and ear plugs, which as well as being safe was stifling and added to the uncomfortable nature of the job. At times it was really hard physical work and the only thing that would keep me going was the thought of that fat pay cheque coming in. Every hour I worked was $55 to my savings, overtime hours were $110 per hour and I was grabbing every overtime day I could get my hands on. My first week's pay totalled $2200 and as my skills improved and the overtime became more readily available, my pay got bigger and bigger.

One of the benefits of mining work was that you received free accommodation and free food. I lived in a big hotel/village of miners that had its own kitchen serving first-class food from 4 am to 10 pm every day. They also provided all the food I needed for my work day and transport to the mine was via a free bus that departed in front of the hotel. All of my work clothes were provided along with the washing of them. This allowed me to save nearly all of my money with my only expenses being a gym membership and the occasional meal out in town. I had even found a way around the need for a car by finding an old pushbike at the back of the hotel and getting it working again. The gears wouldn't change, it was rusted beyond repair but it moved when pedalled and got me from A to B.

I maintained my training routine while mining in Emerald as I didn't want to lose the fitness focus I gained in Phuket. I would ride to the gym at 4 am before work and then again at 8 pm after work and I enrolled in an online personal trainer course to continue my education in the health and fitness industry. I also finished a security course which allowed me to work as a security guard. I did this for two reasons: one was because on my days off when I had no work at the mine I could get a second job to keep the dollars coming in; and the other was that I didn't want to drink at the pubs in town, I wanted to keep a clear head, but I also wanted to meet girls and catch up with friends. So by being the bouncer at the best pub in town it covered all of my bases; I could talk to everyone and have a fun night while also taking care of them. I wouldn't be drinking and at the end of it I was paid. Perfect result.

I was in great physical and mental shape, and even though the work hours were tough I was loving life. The other miners thought I was slightly crazy, especially on occasions when I asked to get dropped off the bus outside of town to run the rest of the way home. I was always a good runner and was starting to put in longer and longer distances. One of the guys at work said to me, 'You're too big for running.' I said, 'That's not true, I could do a marathon if I wanted too.' At 94 kilograms I was a lump of a man and they all laughed thinking I was delusional. I wanted to prove them wrong but I had never run more than 15 kilometres in my life.

At 4 am on the following Saturday morning I had a friend drive me 42 kilometres out of town, making him stop every 10 kilometres so I could put down some water on the side of the road. As he was about to drive away he asked me, 'Are you sure about this bro?' I said, 'Don't worry, I'll be fine,' and he just smiled, told me I was nuts and drove away. It was still a while before dawn as he drove out of sight and the surrounding bushland was pitch-black. It was time to run a marathon.

I was alone in the bush as I set off at my usual pace, with the crisp, fresh morning air nudging me along. The sun started to break through on the horizon sending orange and deep yellow beams of light penetrating through the trees and shimmering off the road in front of me. The first 10 kilometres were easy and my confidence soared as I stopped at my first water drop for a drink. Setting off again I thought to myself, I'm going to smash this, as my naive confidence was bursting at the seams. Reaching the second water drop at the 20-kilometre mark I had slowed down slightly but was still making good speed. The sun was up by the time I was searching for my 30-kilometre marker and I had decreased in speed substantially.

The mid-morning heat was affecting me, my legs were on fire and everything was starting to fatigue. The last 12 kilometres as I searched the horizon for town were absolute hell. My feet ached with pain, my legs were weakening by the second and my pace was almost walking speed as I rounded the corner home. I collapsed onto the front lawn gulping water from the garden hose and trying to dissipate the burning sensation in my legs. I had just run a marathon in five hours twenty-five minutes and it almost killed me. My body was shattered and it would take me a week to recover, however when I rolled into work on Monday and told the guys I finished a marathon on the weekend I was bursting with pride and had a smile from ear to ear.

• • •

Working underground is a dangerous job and after six months it became a reality when we had a cave-in at work. I was working down on the main coalface with the full-time miners who specialise in cutting the coal. It's a dangerous place to be because the coal and rock are exposed and we hadn't placed in any roof or wall support at this stage. As I was clearing away a broken drilling rig I heard calls for help coming from further down the tunnel. I dropped the drill and raced down to see what was happening and came across a miner trapped under a slab of rock with his leg pinned. The more experienced guys turned up and started the rescue operation and I jumped in to help where I could. We lifted the slab of rock off him and placed him onto a stretcher. It was clear to see his lower leg was shattered and we had to get him out of the mine as quick as possible. My days in the military once again came in handy as I carried one corner of the stretcher over the rock and rubble and down the tunnel. A vehicle had been organised and we placed the stretcher inside, it sped away towards the waiting ambulance on the surface leaving us all in a semi–state of shock.

It was a big wake-up call for all of us and for me especially. It set in motion thoughts of finishing up in mining and getting back on the road travelling and having adventures. It wasn't due to the danger or the fear of dying, it was the fear of getting hurt or dying down there because of my quest for money. If I'm going to die I'd like to go out my way doing something I love doing, not dying or becoming seriously crippled for $55 an hour.

I showered up after work, washing off the black coal dust from every pore of my skin, coughing up phlegm tainted with grey specks from the dusty air. I had made my decision, it was time to leave and I knew exactly where I wanted to go.

I had been reading adventure books my entire life. I was given a Wilbur Smith book when I was a kid and devoured the stories of explorers in deepest Africa and voyages on the high seas. While mining I was engrossed in mountaineering sagas. *Into Thin Air* by Jon Krakauer was a favourite even though it was written about the 1996 tragedy on Mount Everest that killed eight climbers. *Touching the Void* was an amazing story of survival and the books on Sir Edmund Hillary and his siege of Everest made me wish I was born a century earlier. The adventurers of old seemed to be made of steadfast stoic bravery that inspired me, captured my imagination and made me believe that I could be made of the same stuff if I was to endure similar extremes. I began to search for an adventure that would test me and when I came across a familiar list I knew I had found what I was looking for.

The Seven Summits is a list of the highest mountains on each continent and is a lifetime mountaineering goal for many climbers. I made a decision to attempt to climb these seven peaks all in one year: Aconcagua, 6961 metres in Argentina; Denali, 6194 metres in Alaska; Kilimanjaro, 5895 metres in Tanzania; Carstensz Pyramid, 4884 metres in West Papua; Mount Elbrus, 5642 metres in Russia; Vinson Massif, 4892 metres in Antarctica; and Mount Everest, 8848 metres in Nepal. I had no experience apart from what I had learnt in the military, no climbing equipment and no idea how to go about planning this ambitious goal. I set myself to task and researched every single detail over the following month. I was like a man possessed and nothing was going to stand in my way of achieving this dream.

I needed a logo to represent me as I attacked this adventure and also to help me recruit sponsors. I was in need of funding to offset the mountain of costs associated with climbing on the seven continents of our big world. I sat down with a pen and pencil and started brainstorming ideas. After lots of scribbles and many crumpled pages I called Mum; she was always great with ideas and I knew she could help me out. I called her up and when I told her I was stuck for a logo, she immediately mentioned the tattoo I had on my forearms, One Life One Chance, 'Why not OLOC' she said, 'OLOC Adventures.' My mum was a genius, it was a perfect fit to my persona, values and life ambitions.

I was sitting in the mess hall of the mining camp as I sketched the words OLOC Adventures onto paper. I placed two crossed ice axes around the text and in the middle of the logo I sketched a picture of Ama Dablam, the most beautiful mountain you will ever lay eyes on. Ama Dablam is located in Nepal and I first saw her while on a hiking trip to that amazing country during one of my first summers living in Europe. From the moment I saw her exposed summit no other mountain, not even the majestic Mount Everest, could cast a shadow over her beauty. I sent my sketch away to a graphic designer friend of mine who sent back what you now see on the back of this book. OLOC Adventures was born.

I found a company online based in New Zealand that specialises in guiding people up the biggest mountains on earth and they sounded like a perfect fit to help me achieve my goal and teach me the much needed skills to survive climbing the seven summits. Next I came up with a list of equipment that was essential to climb mountains above 6000 metres and I sent this list to a local climbing store a few hours' drive away to order in from America for me. It was a big list and when I handed over the cheque for A$12,000 it was the biggest payment the little shop had seen before. Boots, ice axes, harness, snow shoes, sleeping bags and much more.

After weeks of emails, phone calls and face-to-face conversations I was starting to get some sponsors for my adventure. The Coalfields Lodge mining camp that I was living in was the first to come on board and I will be forever grateful to them for doing so. I was beginning to think I wasn't going to get anyone at all before they handed over a $1000 cheque. A week later I received a cheque in the mail for $2000 from Dick Smith, a successful Australian businessman, who didn't even reply to my constant emails and just sent the money, a true Aussie legend. I wanted to get a supplement sponsor to help me sustain myself with powdered protein while in the mountains. The biggest company I knew of was ASN (Australian Sports Nutrition) and I sent an email to everybody in the company outlining my seven summits challenge. I finally received a message from Simon, the owner of the company, who said I was annoying everyone with my emails but asked how he could help. He is a great guy who has been a constant sponsor of my trips and a good friend to this day.

The final cost to accomplish the seven summits was going to be upwards of A$150,000. I had no idea how I was going to raise that kind of cash but I set my sights on one mountain at a time and I was sure something would come along to help me get there. I had one more week of underground mining to go before I departed, firstly back to Thailand for a month of build up training over Christmas and New Year, then onwards to Argentina and my first mountain Aconcagua. I was the fittest I had ever been, my mind was clear and I was focused on my goal. My training routine had increased my overall fitness and prepared me physically but I still had no idea how my body would handle the high altitude or the freezing temperatures I would be facing. I was searching for a challenge that would test me to my core, forcing me to a place where I would find out exactly what I'm made of and capable of.

In the Army I was pushed to breaking point and in that moment I discovered who I really was; I wanted that clarity again. This would be the biggest challenge of my life and push me to my absolute limit both physically and mentally. Would I be made of the same stuff as the great explorers that came before me? Or would I be left wanting? As I boarded my flight I contemplated these questions and in the end I came to one conclusion: we only have one life and one chance so let's go find out.

CHAPTER 6

ACONCAGUA, ARGENTINA

• • •

Aconcagua is the biggest mountain in the Southern Hemisphere and the biggest mountain outside of Asia, standing proud at 6961 metres. It's located in the Andes mountain range of Argentina and is 112 kilometres from the city of Mendoza. While researching my first big mountain, some reviews rated Aconcagua as a safe trekking peak suitable for all aspiring mountaineers. Others warn never to underestimate the biggest peak in South America as the weather is unpredictable, can change in minutes and trap climbers on its exposed face. The mountain has a 60 per cent success rate and kills on average three climbers per season making Aconcagua the deadliest mountain in Argentina and given a nickname by the locals, 'Mountain of Death'.

I landed in Mendoza on 31 January 2011 and was ready to test myself against the mountain of death. I was joining a team of climbers from all over the world as part of an Adventure Consultants expedition led by a local guide and support team. Mendoza is one of the world's nine great wine capitals and sits in a region that is the largest wine producer in Latin America. It has tree-lined streets, friendly locals and some of the best meat, bread and olives I had ever tasted. After checking into the recommended team hotel I threw my bags onto my bed, washed my face and went to find everyone on the team at our pre-arranged meeting.

We had a mixed bag of international adventurers making up our expedition team. Our head guide was Matias from Chile, who had ten years of guiding experience on Aconcagua and before leading expeditions worked as a porter ferrying loads. Matias came across as a friendly guy, down to earth, who knew every little detail about his beloved mountain. He had two assistant guides, Leonardo and Juan, who both beamed big smiles when introduced to the group. The team consisted of Petros, Warwick and Michael as my fellow Australians. Richard and Simon were from our closest neighbour, New Zealand, Johanne and Knut were from Norway, Richard from the USA, Brian from Canada and Dody from Indonesia. Eleven excited members in total including myself, with ages ranging from twenty-six to sixty-one years old.

After we had met each other and shared our short stories about who we were and where we came from, Matias proceeded to tell us about that season's attempts to climb the mountain; the reports were not very encouraging. Most teams had hit extreme winds and cold and hadn't had more than a couple, if any, of their team members summit. One team in December had most of their tents blown clean off the mountain at camp three and had to return home. Although the weather had been terrible up until now Matias assured us that it was time for it to change, with the utmost confidence he told us, 'It cannot stay this bad all season.'

Matias had confidence yet wasn't cocky, he respected the mountain and his assistant guides respected him. He had a wealth of knowledge and answered endless questions and queries from the newly formed team. We ran through a full gear check to ensure every member of the team had all the necessary equipment to summit safely. We were all dismissed shortly afterwards to enjoy the afternoon and evening in Mendoza. Anyone who was missing equipment would have time to find and purchase it and everyone else could enjoy the famous hospitality of this Argentinian city.

It was a cool afternoon as I wandered around the tree-lined streets, being careful not to trip on the uneven pavement, where the roots from the enormous trees had burrowed underneath and forced it skywards. The locals were all very friendly, smiling as they passed by, and the local restaurants and street vendors were all doing their best to entice me in for a wine, beer or food. I wandered for the best part of the afternoon and met up with a few members of the team, who invited me along for a drink and dinner. Sitting at a local restaurant I wasn't going to drink but I did order the local dish, *bife de chorizo* (steak). It came with warm bread rolls and a dish of butter, I'm a simple man when it comes to cuisine and I was in heaven.

As I listened to the two Richards and Simon talk about their mountaineering achievements and hash over the details Matias had given us about our attempt on the mountain, I daydreamed about the first big ascents on the great peaks and in whose pioneering footsteps we would be following. We would be climbing Aconcagua expedition style (siege style), meaning we would set up multiple camps as we ascended the mountain, using local porters to carry the extra equipment, and spending as much time on the mountain as necessary to complete the job. This style of climbing was famously used by Sir Edmund Hillary while laying siege to Mount Everest in 1963. He was part of a team comprising over 400 people, 362 being porters, 20 Sherpa guides and a staggering 4500 kilograms of equipment.

We were due to depart the following day by bus to a ski field called Penitentes, which was to be our staging area, 180 kilometres west of Mendoza. After dinner we all retired to our rooms early and I made a final gear check before packing everything away and getting to bed. I slept well and after a quick breakfast at the hotel and some very strong coffee we all loaded into the bus and weaved our way through the narrow streets and onto the road heading west. The countryside around Mendoza is endless wineries with some cattle paddocks dotted throughout the orchards. As we travelled further away from the city and into the low-lying mountain ranges it transformed into grassy fields and cattle grazing farms. Argentina is the third biggest exporter of beef outside of Brazil and

Australia with Argentinians eating on average 60 kilograms of beef per person each year.

We arrived into Penitentes after lunch and settled into one of the ski fields lodges, almost entirely vacant due to it being summer and there not being a flake of snow on the ground. Matias wanted to get us up to the top of the fields that afternoon for an acclimatisation hike. I'm sure he also did this to check how everybody moved while hiking and if we had any injured or unfit members in our team. It was a nice steady hike, two hours up to the top of a series of gondolas that in winter would be loaded with people but now swung idle. With a quick break at the top, it was back down in forty-five minutes with no signs of weakness from anybody. We had a solid team and were all eager to set off the next day.

• • •

The expedition gear was broken into mule loads the following morning. The mules would carry 60 kilograms per animal and stay with us for three days until we reached our base camp. We had ten mules, and it was great to mingle in and load up these sturdy creatures. The noble mule featured in many of the adventure books I had read, assisting men and women across arduous terrain and into the mountains for centuries. The main trail towards Aconcagua started just outside of Penitentes at a ranger outpost, where we had our permits stamped by a friendly guy who wished us all the best. As soon as I turned away from the outpost and took my first step along the trail I knew this was it, my first big adventure, my first big mountain and my first big test since the military. I wondered to myself whether I would have what it takes to stand on the summit.

It was a slow and silent walk that first day, everybody seemed to be deep in their own thoughts about the days to come. We paralleled a stream for the first hour and passed a few small lakes that provided water to the cattle in these low-lying hills. Mountaineering isn't a race, it's actually some of the slowest hiking you will ever do. A slow approach while gaining altitude is the best way to let the body adapt and acclimatise safely. To rush into a big expedition is asking for altitude sickness at best and severe cerebral or pulmonary oedema at worst. After six hours of steady progress we arrived at what looked to be some old ranch stables, and our camping spot for the night, at 2800 metres elevation.

We unloaded the mules who were taken away to be watered and fed and set up our tents close to the stables. Once the mules had been tended the mule drivers cooked us an Argentinian barbecue, a tradition for the first night in the mountains. The smell of the meat cooking over an open fire was mouth-watering and it tasted absolutely amazing. It could easily have been one of the best barbecues I had ever eaten; coming from an Australian that's a big compliment. I washed down dinner with a locally brewed herb tea called *mati*, which had an extremely strong flavour and an overall pleasant taste. I slipped into my sleeping bag early and fell into a deep sleep of the overly fed.

• • •

At 6.45 am the following morning Matias was eager to get on the trail in the cool early hours. We had our tent down and gear packed up within thirty-five minutes, which is fast and easy to do when you have perfect weather conditions. When we got up high with big winds and colder temperatures it was bound to take us much longer. It was 5 degrees Celsius overnight, which should have made me cold, but I was sweltering inside my sleeping bag. I checked the tag on my bag and it read 'rated to minus 67 degrees Celsius'. It became clear my sleeping bag purchase was perfect for Antarctica but was going to give me a greenhouse effect any other time.

As we started onto the trail with the mules following close behind, I settled into the same slow and steady pace as the day before. The first couple of hours after leaving the stable camp were nice and cool for trekking, with a slight breeze sweeping down through the valley. As the sun rose above the mountain range to our east the temperature skyrocketed. We were having regular breaks to hydrate and take in food and by the middle of the afternoon the heat had really set in. The breeze had disappeared and as the trail wound around to the west the sun was directly in our faces. Beads of sweat were dripping from my nose and even at this snail's pace I could feel my back beneath my pack slowly soaking through. Just as I was thinking about needing another break the peak of Aconcagua poked up on the horizon and all my worries disappeared.

The scene in front of me was stunning with low mountains in the foreground and the snow-covered summit of the biggest peak in South America towering over it all. The snow glistened in the afternoon sun and the black rock of the windswept summit ridge gave it a rugged and daunting contrast. As I gazed up and stumbled due to not watching my footing, it dawned on me how far we really had to go and how much work it was going to take to reach the top. Shortly after my humbling reflection on the task at hand, we arrived at our second camping site, and as the mules wandered in we were setting up tents and kicking our boots off. We had been going for six hours and forty-five minutes, which was slightly longer than the day before, yet I felt energised after laying eyes on our goal. Our altitude was steadily rising and I crawled into bed at 3200 metres above sea level.

• • •

Crossing rivers in mountainous country or around snow and glaciers should never be taken lightly. I remember crossing rivers in the jungle and in the outback while training with the Army back in Australia and never thought of it as much of a challenge. It wasn't until crossing a river like the one we crossed the morning of day three that I understood people's concern. The rivers in these areas are created from glacial melt and often contain silt that gives it a light brownish tint. The crossing we had to make was only knee deep and after removing my boots and socks I strolled in boldly but when the icy water made contact with my skin it felt like my legs had been set on fire. The water was so cold it went beyond freezing and sent a shock wave up through my body. I shuffled onwards trying not to show too much concern on my face as I lost all feeling below the knees.

Reaching the other side I dashed away to a large rock bathed in the morning sun and started to rub some sense back into my legs. My feet were white and frozen to the touch, I immediately thought I had frostbite and then dismissed the idea before vocalising it and embarrassing myself. As I dried my feet and the sun warmed new life into them, the others made their way across one by one. It would be near impossible and borderline life-threatening to swim a river like that and I hoped I would never have to try. We carried on for the remainder of the day making our slow progress towards base camp. Aconcagua slipped in and out of view throughout the day and seemed to be watching and judging us, deciding whether we were worthy.

Our arrival at base camp late that afternoon concluded our three-day approach and gave me a small sense of achievement. I knew it was only the beginning but I was feeling physically and mentally strong, especially after the day's gain of 1000 metres in altitude. Base camp was called Plaza de Argentina and sits at 4200 metres above sea level, 2000 metres higher than Australia's highest mountain. Our tent sites at base camp needed to be bombproof, as we were now in an area prone to very high winds and extreme swings in weather. Matias warned us again about the team in December losing their tents and having to abandon the expedition. While piling rocks around my tent and tying off support ropes I started to feel light-headed and had a pounding headache. I was in acclimatisation mode and according to Matias this was totally normal after such a big gain in altitude. A strong drink of flavoured cordial and a piece of cake eased my symptoms and I fell asleep thinking of the adventures ahead.

It was cold at night and my sleeping bag was starting to earn its place in keeping me warm. There is nothing worse than getting out of the tent at night to use the toilet, especially when it's freezing, so I used a spare Nalgene water bottle as my nominated pee bottle. Afterwards I just had to make sure I didn't get mixed up with which one I was drinking from. Throughout the night I had stages of thumping headaches and shortness of breath as my body adapted to less oxygen in the air. Day four was a scheduled rest day and all Matias wanted us to do was eat, drink lots of water and relax. We also had to get checked by the base camp doctor to make sure we were fit and healthy enough to continue up the mountain. This screening process is an initiative designed to limit the number of deaths on the mountain each year. To get stopped at this point by the doctor would be heartbreaking but if it saves lives then it's well worth it.

When it was my turn for the check-up I made my way over to the medical tent and sat down in front of the doctor. He was a lean and mountain-hardened Argentinian who spent weeks at a time at base camp looking after all of the climbers. He stuck a small device on my finger to check the oxygen saturation levels in my blood and it registered great with a level of 91. Next was my heart rate, which was normal and then my blood pressure; as the doc released the air from the pressure band on my arm I was expecting the thumbs up but instead was told your pressure is up. I was sitting at 160/80 and he told me this was at the limit for letting someone continue. I was slightly pissed off at the situation because I was feeling great but I calmed down knowing he was just doing his job and keeping me safe.

I awoke the following day and was due to see the doctor again before breakfast. He had given me some pills to take after our last consult to bring my blood pressure down and he wanted to check their effectiveness. To my surprise it was now worse than before. I was at 180/80 and started to worry that he might send me down. I pleaded my case saying I was feeling fit and strong, and after a few minutes he agreed to let me do the day's load-carry up to camp one but wanted to see me that night. He gave me a new batch of pills and I was out of the tent before he changed his mind.

Load-carries are part of mountaineering; we had mules to get our equipment to base camp and now we had to separate it all equally between the team and start moving it up the mountain. We would do our first load-carry and then come back down to sleep as part of the acclimatisation process. Gaining elevation in the day but then allowing the body to recover back down lower is a tried and tested method for adapting to altitude. Matias brought some local porters over and told us that for a small fee they would carry our extra expedition gear up to camp one for us. A few of the team members opted to use the local porters and save their strength for the summit day but I wanted to carry mine myself. It was just a personal choice and a goal I set myself, to climb the mountain under my own power as much as possible.

The first load-carry was a tough one, and gave me my first taste of hiking at elevation. It was an 800-metre elevation gain up to 5000 metres where camp one would be located. When trying to ascend a steep slope, the most direct route, straight up, is usually far too hard to attempt and when this is the case the path will start to switch back. First moving diagonally across the face then turning sharply to go diagonally across the other way. It takes slightly longer to reach the top but saves a lot of energy in getting there.

Scree is a hiker's worst nightmare; a scree slope is made up of tiny fragments of stone larger than sand but smaller than a box of matches. We crossed over one glacier that was covered with dirt and scree and then hit endless switchbacks up a scree field that was literally three steps up and one step back for what felt like an eternity. It was tough going with the extra weight but not impossible and we reached camp one in seven hours and forty minutes, where we rested. We stayed long enough to cache all of the equipment under some rocks, get pounding headaches and take in the amazing view. Then it was back down the scree field in a much more direct fashion, sliding semi–out of control all the way to the glacier.

When I had pictured glaciers before the expedition I imagined beautiful ice structures shining blue and dusted in white snow like scenes from Antarctic documentaries. In reality a moving body of ice descending a mountain like this one becomes covered in the surrounding dirt and rubble and the glacier we were crossing looked like nothing more than a dirt field to the untrained eye. On closer inspection, I could dig down a few centimetres below the dirt and see the ice. It's an amazing natural wonder and its sheer size and power baffles the mind.

We all arrived safely back to base camp after a great day and with all the extra supplies securely cached up high. I consumed my body weight in chicken and rice and was then due back to my friendly doc for another check. My blood pressure was 170/80, better than it was in the morning but still not low enough to put the doc at ease. He gave me another handful of pills and told me to come back again in the morning. I was starting to get nervous about the whole situation, with the chance of being sent down becoming a real possibility. The following day was another scheduled rest and acclimatisation day. Everyone else in the team was relaxing while I made frequent trips to the doctor's tent. First before breakfast with the same result and again before dinner with no change. The doctor gave me a new batch of pills and told me that if by the morning my blood pressure wasn't down to at least 160 he wasn't going to let me continue on with the team.

In the meantime, Warwick decided to abandon his attempt on Aconcagua; he was our oldest member and wasn't adapting to the altitude or physical stress our bodies were under. He was a great guy to have around and it was a morale blow to all of us to watch him break down his tent and pack up his gear. It seemed as though we had only just started to gel as a team and we were already losing a teammate. I respected his decision. It's always better to turn around and have the option to come back another day, rather than push on and risk your life. Without knowing it at the time, I would soon have to make the same tough call in my adventure career and it's an incredibly hard thing to do.

I was in stress mode and as I lay in bed that night, thoughts of all my hard work and training being wasted due to one doctor's decision consumed me. I took all the pills I had left over and thought I'd either get the result I wanted or slip into a coma; it was worth the risk. The next morning I tried to stay as calm as I could while making my way to the doctor's tent at a snail's pace. I lay down on the bed and went into zen mode as he wrapped the pressure pad around my arm. The doc did his thing and when I heard the air release from the pad I opened my eyes and looked square in his. He smiled and said '145'. I yelled in excitement, gave the doc a hug and raced from the tent before he changed his mind or realised he had botched the test.

The rest of the team applauded the result and we all started to gear-up for the day's work ahead of us. We were leaving base camp for good and moving up to camp one with the rest of our equipment. I knew what was in store for us that day as I pulled on my pack, which felt heavier than it had on the load-carry day, knowing it was going to be a tough slog up to 5000 metres. A few of the team opted for porters again and once we were all ready to move, Matias stepped off in the lead. It was a cooler than average day, which made the hiking more comfortable and the scree field switchbacks less of a heartbreak. Halfway to camp one it started to snow, a light dusting of beautiful white flakes descending upon us. It was such a beautiful scene, with the snow turning the brown and grey scree into a thinly veneered snowfield. We finished our day in a shorter time than our load-carry and everyone was feeling great as we settled into camp and bombproofed our tents for the coming days.

It was a bitterly cold night and for the first time on the trip I needed to zip my sleeping bag almost fully closed. My water bottle, which was normally secured firmly inside my bag, had fallen out during the night and was now a snow cone. It was a bad start to the morning when I woke up desperate for a drink of water and grabbed my bottle, only to be greeted by something resembling crushed ice. My pee bottle was in the same state of affairs and I needed it to defrost in the morning sun before I could empty it.

As we moved higher and the temperatures dropped, getting ready in the morning started taking longer. I'd sleep in my long thermal pants and top, then I would pull my trekking pants on and add a second cotton layer to my upper body. I'd also wear a fleece vest over those two layers and a shell rain jacket over the top of everything. If it started snowing or if we had rain I'd pull on my waterproof pants. For summit day I had a down jacket and down pants to go over everything again. On my feet I first had thick socks, then a foam-layer inner boot that fit inside my big, double layer mountaineering boots with built-in gaiters that covered halfway up my lower leg. Crampons could be fitted to my boots when we hit the snow and ice. On my hands I had thin liner gloves then thick mountaineering gloves over the top, and if it started getting really cold I had down mitts to pull on as well. On my head I had a buff to cut the wind and protect my face, a beanie and UV glasses or goggles to protect my eyes. It was a mountain of clothing to pull on every time but once I had a system in place it became much easier.

For breakfast that morning I consumed cake dipped in warm water; my throat was dry from breathing deeply throughout the night due to the lack of oxygen and the cake soothed it perfectly. After some strong coffee and morning rituals Matias wanted to crack on with a load-carry up to camp two. Camp two was uncharted territory and sat 500 metres above us at 5500 metres, which is slightly higher than the base camp of Mount Everest. We divided up the loads as we had done previously and those opting for porters palmed off the extra weight onto the hardened mountain men. We stepped off with Matias in the lead and I could immediately feel the effects of the altitude on my performance. An hour into it I was panting like I had just run a 100-metre sprint yet I was moving at a snail's pace. It was steep scree and rock fields most of the way, with a cold headwind blasting down the trail. As hard as it was, when I took the time to rest and look out at the surrounding mountains and valleys it was an amazing view. The incredible, snow-capped peaks stretched for miles; this was something not many people would ever get to see and it made all the effort well worth it.

We arrived at camp two in three hours and forty minutes. A layer of snow covered the flat area where our tents would go and we buried the equipment there and piled rocks on top to stop it from getting blown away. As we started our descent the wind picked up and it began to snow, first just a light dusting and then a heavier fall, with the wind at our backs. The weather slowly intensified and chased us all the way back to camp one, where we were quick to scramble inside our tents to keep warm. It was a tough day overall and as white-out conditions settled over the camp, we huddled to warm ourselves in our bags. One of the porters brought us a hot drink each, with a big smile. I smiled back as my morale skyrocketed, and I thought to myself that this was living.

The storm had cleared by the morning and the rising sun was quickly melting the snow that had become stuck to the outside of my tent. It was day nine and another scheduled rest day before we moved higher. I had a very restless sleep, needing to pop headache tablets at midnight to ease the jackhammer behind my eyes. I've read many accounts from climbers who say the hardest part of climbing big peaks is adapting to life at altitude and staying fit and strong enough for a summit bid. I was beginning to understand what they were talking about. As we proceeded higher and higher sleep was getting shorter and more restless – constantly waking up gasping for breath. The altitude made me less hungry but I needed to eat and drink more than normal to acclimatise well. The endless hours inside the tent waiting for the weather to clear can be like torture if you don't have books or journals to occupy your mind; too much time thinking negative thoughts is never a good thing.

• • •

On day ten, Petros and Johanna decided to quit the expedition. They each had their personal reasons and were evacuated by helicopter that afternoon. Maybe the first taste of bad weather was enough to make them second-guess their decisions or maybe the tougher slog to camp two was an eye-opener as to what summit day would be like. Either way, they left the team healthy, and as the helicopter echoed away down the valley towards Mendoza, we became a team of eight.

I still remember vividly the strong bond our team had, regardless of our ages, experience, religion or where we called home. We were all there for the same reason, and especially after we had lost three teammates, the remainder of us pulled together even more. There were plenty of funny stories shared during tough times high on the mountain and a whispered word of encouragement from one of my team while I struggled for breath and was swamped in negative thoughts was enough to push me forward and finish the day. Little moments like that gave real meaning to the term teamwork.

A light snow began to fall again in the evening but the weather report for the following day was good and with conditions improving, our plan was to move permanently to camp two the following day and repeat the load-carry process all over again. Temperatures dropped to minus 10 degrees throughout the night and I made sure to keep my water and pee bottle inside my sleeping bag. Hiking a frozen pee bottle up to camp two was not going to happen. As the sun brought its glow into the valley the winds were blowing steady and the sky was clear, so Matias made the call to push us on to camp two. As I pulled my pack onto my back I had to stamp life into my feet and keep my hands under my armpits. It was still well below freezing and my down jacket was staying on for the first part of the climb. An hour into the ascent it started to snow, steady at first and then it was thicker and heavier. The slopes were getting blanketed and we were pushing through knee-deep fresh powder as we came to the final turn before camp two.

It took us four hours to reach camp two and as we arrived the wind turned gale force and it was white-out conditions. The horizontal pelting snow was stinging my face as I grabbed the tent from my pack and wrestled it open. Leonardo raced over smiling under his goggles and mask to help me get the poles into position and tie the tent down with rocks. The conditions that were crazy and exhausting for me were second nature to him. We both helped the rest of the team set up their tents and then everyone crawled inside to shelter from the storm that was getting stronger by the second. I was totally spent, it had been one breath per step all day, with ice forming into long strands from my beard and the wind howling; it was pure Hollywood stuff. The storm raged on throughout the afternoon and at dinner time there was a shake on the tent and Matias handed in a cup of soup and a hot drink. These guys were absolute legends and made our lives so easy at times I almost felt lazy.

Our meals were all prepared by the guides and not having to worry about food prep was one of the biggest bonuses in joining an organised expedition. Years later on trips that I'd organise and execute myself, I would understand how good I had it on my early adventures. As we rested, Matias and the guides would be procuring water, boiling it, preparing our food, making hot drinks and sharing out snacks. Our meals would be as high in calories as possible, filled with oil, rice and sugar-rich local produce. My favourite meals were always ones that were easy to devour like rice and vegetable stir-fries. Breakfast was typically oats with dried fruit and coffee, quick and easy and perfect before a big day. Snacks were chocolate, nuts, muesli bars and preserved cakes, all high in good fats, sugars and calories. Our team would eat together whenever the weather allowed it and we would all cram into the cook tent and share our feelings and thoughts of the day we had endured or the one still to come. If anyone sat quietly it typically meant they were feeling sick or struggling mentally and we would all make an extra effort to cheer them up.

...

The weather grew in intensity and was fierce by the middle of the night. I was suffering badly from headaches while watching the tent strain under the wind, convinced it would tear apart at any moment. I managed to get to sleep in the early hours of the morning as the winds eased. The storm died down by dawn and the snowfall had stopped, so the team came together for breakfast under the main tent where we shared our storm stories and Matias gave us an update on weather and conditions. He dropped a news bomb on us, reporting that a team of Spanish climbers who were making a summit bid the day before were caught in the storm and were now missing out on the Polish Glacier. Then he told us an English team had also been caught in the open and one of their teammates had slipped into unconsciousness and died from exposure. We were very lucky to be low on the mountain when the storm hit, the teams up high and those on summit bids got caught in our worst nightmare. Rescue teams were now out risking their lives searching for the missing climbers.

I thought about the missing climbers a lot throughout our rest day and into the night. To be trapped out in the storm, exhausted and freezing, would be terrifying. I ran scenarios through my head about how I would react in that situation and then hoped I'd never have to be tested like that, finally succumbing to sleep around 10 pm. I noticed while I was using my pee bottle after midnight, trying not to spill a drop into my sleeping bag, that it was now calm outside. The winds were gone and it was eerily quiet. As I zipped the tent open at dawn I was met with an incredible view of the valley below us, fresh thick snowfields all around and the sun beaming down on it all.

The conditions were perfect for our load-carry and acclimatisation climb up to camp three, the 6000-metre mark on the mountain. We were the first team to hit the route after the storm so we needed to break trail through almost a metre of snow the entire way. I had never seen snow in this volume before nor had I broken trail, making day twelve a day of firsts for me, and a tough, gruelling one. Altitude's effect on the body is a dominant force. If I was sitting and resting I was not breathing overly hard and all was fine but as soon as I took a step to go higher I had to gulp air into my lungs in order to get the oxygen I needed, then it would be one step, one breath the whole way up. The 500 metres of elevation gain took us five hours to complete in the tough conditions, and we cached our equipment and enjoyed a rest on an exposed and beautiful perch high in the Andes.

The descent back to camp two was without incident and Matias pulled us all together for another round of weather and updates. The weather for the coming days was holding clear and if this stayed the case our plan was to move to camp three the next day and push for the summit the following day. Matias told us that two of the missing climbers had been found and had sustained severe frostbite to their hands and feet, the third was still up there somewhere. He then lowered his head before telling us that two more bodies were found higher up. The climbers had been making a summit bid when the storm caught them and they died of exposure. The bodies were still so high on the mountain that it would be very hard to move them and they would stay there until a fresh team could be organised to bring them down.

This was devastating news and the team's morale was definitely affected and it was hard to process all the information and the current climate on the mountain. It was stacking up to be one of the worst seasons on record for fatalities. I thought to myself that the climbers who had perished could have been professionals with loads of experience, and yet they died; what the hell was I doing on this monster as a total beginner? I consoled myself that I'd trained very hard for this expedition, I was the fittest and most mentally capable I'd ever been and I wouldn't be taking any chances with my life. I had total faith in Matias to guide us through the unknown scenarios as well. I could tell by the way the news had affected him that he had great respect for the mountain and the utmost compassion for all the climbers trying to climb it.

As forecast, the weather was perfect the following day and as soon as I unzipped the tent I knew we would be going for the summit the day after. We shouldered all of our equipment and stepped off towards high camp shortly after breakfast. The conditions were perfect and with better acclimatisation and no trail to break we were sitting in camp three, three hours and thirty minutes later. We set up camp and settled into an afternoon of hydration, food and rest. Matias came around to each individual team member asking us if we were ready for the summit bid the next day. When he came to me and asked if I was good to go I didn't hesitate in saying, 'Absolutely mate, I'm ready.' He smiled at me and said, 'Perfect, we will step off at 5 am so get a good rest. Tomorrow will be a very big day.' The reports of the dead and missing climbers were my last thoughts before drifting off to sleep.

It was day sixteen and the day that we had all been working towards since our first hike around Penitentes. The alarm on my watch beeped at 4 am but I was already lying awake in my sleeping bag and waiting for it. I was instantly alert, switched on my headlamp and began my preparations for summit day. It was bitterly cold outside so I decided to leave three layers on under my down jacket until sunrise. I filled my water bottles, packed a few snacks and a camera into my pack and pulled on my boots. Sitting with my legs out in the vestibule I strapped on my crampons and then crawled out into the dark frosty morning.

As I stood tall and stretched out my back I could see a line of headlamps making their way up the start of the trail towards the summit. It was another team that had gone out before us and were making very slow progress up the dark slope. I looked around at our team tents and could see everyone getting ready. It was close to 5 am and I began stamping my feet and waving my arms around to keep warm as I waited. The first stage of our summit bid was to make it from camp three to a ridge line called Independencia, then from the ridge, stage two was up to a rocky outcrop called the cave, and from the cave, stage three was to the summit.

I didn't want to focus on the entire route; just like everything else, I broke it down in my mind into short manageable sections and I'd just plug away.

Once everyone was ready we moved off in a single file to begin one of the biggest days of my life. We moved slowly and methodically, the last thing we wanted on a summit day was for anyone to slip or fall and hurt themselves. The route was covered in a thin veneer of ice mixed with rock and scree. An hour after we stepped off I was in a slow, steady dreamlike state when a children's song that I hadn't heard since I was a boy started to repeat itself over and over in my mind. The song was from the *Roger Ramjet* cartoon and it was funny to hear it at first but after another thirty minutes I thought I was starting to go slightly insane. I tried to block it out as best I could as we trudged on upwards.

We reached the ridge line of Independencia just as the sun was showing itself on the horizon. The rest break on the ridge timed with the glorious morning sun over the beautiful mountain range below gave me a warming recharge. There was a very small ruined wooden hut just back from the ridge and I wandered over and poked my head inside to see what was in there. I was ripped back to reality by a dead climber wrapped in a silver foil blanket lying in front of me. This was one of the climbers who had died of exposure a few days before and was yet to be recovered from where he lay. As I looked up from the body Matias made eye contact with me and I knew not to mention the body's presence to the rest of the team. This was the reality of what can happen when things go wrong and morale would not be helped by everyone knowing he was there.

I hadn't seen a dead body since my time in the Army and it definitely had me questioning my choice to be on the expedition. In the end I came to the same conclusion – life is for living and yes, adventures are a risky way to explore that life, but with the right training, ability and decision making, adventures can be enjoyed in relative safety. This is what I convinced myself as I shoved my down jacket into my pack and pulled on my goggles to protect me from the sun's strong UV rays. We departed the ridge, traversing up towards a second ridge called the Windy Pass. I'm sure you could guess from the name that it's renowned for hurricane-force winds. This section had been a road block for many teams in the past, forcing them to turn back. I pushed the image of the dead climber from my mind and steadied myself for this next challenge.

As we turned a corner to enter the Windy Pass I was expecting to be hit by a wall of wind but instead we were caressed with a gentle breeze and a clear trail. The sun was bathing us in all its glory and my spirits were high as we made our slow progress, one step, one breath at a time towards the next checkpoint at the cave. Halfway across Windy Pass, Matias made a tough decision to turn back one of our members who was showing extreme levels of fatigue. It's a really tough call to make for a guide but a very important one to ensure the safety of the team. If one of us collapsed up high we would put the entire team at risk, and they would have to abandon their summit attempt and conduct a rescue. Matias turned Dody around, who I could see was upset with the decision. After a few minutes of consolation he began to make his slow progress back down with one of the guides towards camp three.

It had been a tough six hours since we departed high camp when we made it to the cave and stopped for our second break of food and water. Matias mentioned to me in private that the other English climber lay dead close by somewhere but he thought that his friends had hidden the body out of respect. I imagined giving that same level of respect to one of the members of my team if we were placed in that situation. It would be incredibly hard to move past it mentally and as I guzzled some water, washing down a biscuit, I hoped again to never be put in that position. The final stage to the summit lay ahead of us, a steep rocky section made all the more difficult by the altitude and our level of fatigue. I guzzled one more mouthful of water to help down a headache tablet and we moved off towards the top.

An hour after leaving the cave, we were moving at a crawl and needing constant rest breaks to keep everyone together. I was having fake-summit syndrome like I used to get years ago while hiking mountains in the jungle with the Army. It's not a real illness, but as I came up over one rise and I was absolutely sure that this was the top and it couldn't possibly go any higher I would then see the next steep slope in the distance going up. Every time it happened I would need to stop, take a few big breaths to calm myself and continue on. There was no other choice; I wasn't turning back.

I let my mind wander for an unknown period of time and when I looked up I saw some other climbers coming down the route towards me. They were smiling as they passed and looked energised and I knew where they had come from. As they passed one climber gave me a thumbs up and I latched onto this small sign as acknowledgement that we must be almost there. As I crested the next rise, expecting to see another slope continuing on higher, there was nowhere to go. Stretching below us in the distance were mountain tops as far as the eyes could see, I was standing on the summit of Mount Aconcagua.

A feeling of accomplishment overwhelmed me and a few tears fell from my tired eyes. The team were all in a celebratory spirit, giving high fives and hugs to each other. It had taken us just over eight hours from camp three to be standing on the summit, six of our starting eleven team members having made it to the top. The summit was a rocky field about the size of a basketball court, a small smattering of snow lay on the ground but most of it was blown off due to the intense winds and storms. As we sat down to recover, the weather was changing, clouds began to block our view and a light snow began to fall. Matias reminded everyone that we had only done half the job and the most dangerous part was getting back down. He was right – statistics show that most deaths and accidents in mountaineering occur during the descent.

I pulled out the sponsors' flags and took some pictures for the media before we all shouldered our packs and began the slow process of getting back to the safety of our tents. I took one last look at the summit I had worked so hard to achieve and then looked up at the growing cloud cover, immediately thinking about the English climbers who were caught out in the open by the storm on their summit day. This thought triggered an alertness in me and I refocused all my remaining energy and attention on the climb and getting down safely. There was no way I was going to be another statistic wrapped in a silver blanket, motionless, on top of a mountain.

As we descended, two of the team began to stumble and were starting to look very tired. Matias made the decision to short rope them to Leonardo and himself in order to help them get down safely. If they stumbled on any of the ridge lines during the descent they would fall thousands of feet to their deaths with nothing to stop them. By roping up, their lives were now linked to the guides and it was a brave call for Matias to make. Our progress was very slow and the gathering clouds and snow were following us down the mountain as an ever-looming possible worst-case scenario. Four hours after departing the summit, we stumbled back into camp three like a line of zombies.

It was a physically and mentally brutal twelve-hour summit day, and as I untied my crampons, pulled off my boots and crawled into my tent I finally let myself relax. A smile crept onto my face and I was overwhelmed with total happiness and a sense of accomplishment. I lay back to give my back a rest and instantly fell into a deep sleep with the cheeky grin still glued to my face.

The following morning my body was feeling 100 years old and Matias was adamant about getting us up and going early. We were still high on the mountain and had over 4000 metres of altitude to descend. After a very hearty breakfast and some strong coffee we shouldered our packs and started our journey back to civilisation and home. In the two and half days that followed we covered 40 kilometres of winding trails and I was beginning to have flashbacks of some of the death marches we were made to endure in the military. As we descended the air became rich in oxygen again, my energy grew and my strength returned in abundance. Early on the third morning of descent, and day nineteen overall, we made it to the edge of the national park and to an intersecting roadway where, parked in the distance, we noticed a glorious bus waiting to drive us back to Mendoza.

It was hugs and smiles all round for the team; taking off our packs for the last time and loading them into the bus was the concluding act of this unbelievable experience. It was a three-hour drive back to civilisation and although I thought we would all fall asleep on the bus immediately, instead we were talking and smiling together like hyperactive children. The sense of relief at accomplishing our goal was energising, especially after the tragic events and the loss of life in the past week. We had a great team and amazing guides who didn't hesitate in making tough calls for the safety of the rest of us – I will be forever grateful for their support. Weighing in at the hotel I had lost 9 kilograms in body weight, had blisters on my feet but had escaped any serious injuries. Standing in my bathroom and staring at my sunken eyes in the mirror I smiled and said to myself, 'Well done mate.'

Successfully standing on top of one of the seven summits had given me a massive confidence boost and solidified my belief that I could successfully achieve anything with the right training, mindset and preparation. It was six weeks until I set off for the next big challenge. I had stood on top of the biggest mountain in South America, now it was time to attempt to stand on the biggest in North America, Mount McKinley in Alaska. I was going to recover, eat, train and prepare my mind for what was soon to be the most intense and terrifying moment of my life.

CHAPTER 7
DENALI, ALASKA

...

When I think of adventure and stories of survival one place comes to the forefront of my mind – Alaska. It's a wild frontier where only the boldest hunters and gold miners made their claim during the gold rush era of the 1890s. Reading Jack London novels as a boy, my head was filled with the wild remoteness of Alaska and his famous stories *The Call of the Wild* and *White Fang* swelled my head with a yearning to endure the hardships of these early settlers and test myself against the untamed land. It's a place that today has spawned a catalogue of reality TV shows like *Deadliest Catch*, *Ice Road Truckers* and *Gold Rush* in order to give the normal person a glimpse into one of the harshest environments on earth. Yet as much as people admire its remoteness, very few ever venture into these wild places and of those who do, even fewer return unchanged.

Mount McKinley, or Denali as it's known to the locals, is the highest peak in North America, soaring 6190 metres above sea level and is the centrepiece of the Denali National Park and Preserve. The native Koyukon people who inhabit the surrounding areas have referred to the mountain as Denali for centuries and in 1896 a gold prospector renamed it Mount McKinley after the then presidential candidate William McKinley. The name stuck until 2015 when the Department of the Interior announced the official change back to Denali. Naming rights aside the mountain is awe-inspiring and is renowned in mountaineering circles for being a cold, brutal mistress with a 50 per cent summit success rate, and has claimed over 100 lives.

I flew from Sydney into Anchorage, Alaska, arriving in peak physical condition and mentally prepared for what was going to be my first time in extreme cold, snow and ice. I was anxious and excited to get started and after checking into the hotel I went searching for my teammates. We had a prearranged meeting and after everyone had come together the room was full of talk and laughter as we all got to know each other. Aiden Loehr, our head guide, was an American in his forties who was supremely fit and had a lifetime of experience as a mountain guide. He had summited Denali many times and led first ascents of remote peaks from China to the Andes. He was also a pilot who flew bush planes throughout the Alaskan wilderness delivering climbers or ferrying scientists, clocking up over 16,000 hours in his craft. We got along instantly and he was going to be a wealth of knowledge and a pillar of confidence on our expedition.

Aiden had two assistant guides, Andrew and Erin, both in their mid-twenties and up-and-coming professional guides with their own wealth of experience from an upbringing in the mountains. They were full of energy and seemed as excited as we were about the expedition. There were eight clients including myself and we were a mixed bag of nationalities and experience. Richard and Alan were from the UK, Anna and Bill from the United States, Kevin from South Africa and Chok, Simon and myself from Australia. We all had our own interesting life stories to share and an equal desire to stand on top of the biggest mountain in North America.

Aiden and the guides ran through a thorough gear check and assessed each of us in turn. Denali is a very different climb to Aconcagua. It's totally covered in snow, we would need to cross large crevasses to reach our designated camps and temperatures have been known to plummet to minus 30 degrees Celsius with wind chill, even in summer.

Where Aconcagua had night and day, Alaska during summer can have up to twenty-two hours of sunlight, adding a totally new environmental factor. I was jumping out of my skin to get going; this was the stuff I had been reading about in books for years and I was so close to doing it, I couldn't wait.

The following day we were all up early and loaded into a bus to take us north towards the Denali National Park and the town of Talkeetna. This tiny place has a local population of around 1000 people and is located at the merging point of the Susitna, Chulitna and Talkeetna rivers. Founded in 1916 when the area was chosen as the headquarters for the Alaskan railroad, it is now a tourist town and the start point for all the Denali expeditions. We arrived in town at 10 am and pulled up at the K2 aviation hangar and started to weigh and prepare our gear. The plan was to get two small de Havilland Beaver planes from Talkeetna to our base camp. These specially designed bush planes could land and take off on snow, making them ideal for getting climbers up into the mountains.

The winds for the afternoon were not looking favourable for our departure so while we waited for conditions to improve we all made our way to the Denali National Park office to pay our entrance fee, pick up our permits and watch a short video on the park's many dangers. If I wasn't intimidated by Denali before the video I certainly was afterwards. Extreme cold, crevasses, avalanches, hurricane-strength winds, snow blindness and sunburn were just a few things we were to keep in mind once we were on the mountain. Back at the K2 hangar while we waited for the clouds to clear at base camp, I did my best to suppress the negative thoughts and fears swimming around in my head. I began to think about all the training and effort I had put in to reach this point – I may not have all of the required mountaineering skills yet but for mental and physical preparedness, I was ready.

It was summer in Alaska and even at night the sun does not go down totally, it stays low on the horizon dropping slightly below only to rise again. This leaves a twilight glow in the sky throughout the night, and it was under this amazing yellow glow that we received the call that base camp was clear of bad weather and we were to depart immediately. We were all buzzing as we loaded the small red planes with our gear and taxied to the end of the short runway. As the plane's wheels left the ground it was almost midnight and I watched Talkeetna drop away below us and looked up to see the Alaskan mountain range for the first time, rising proud on the horizon.

The flight into the mountains was breathtaking; the snow-covered peaks and jagged formations surrounded by glaciers were the realisation of a dream and all of the documentaries I'd watched were now becoming reality right before my eyes. I could see the dark, bottomless crevasses crisscrossing the glaciers. We would soon be walking across some of the very same terrain and the fear and excitement was building inside me. The pilot began to circle and pointed down at the glacier below and I could make out tiny tents up on its left slope. This was the lower Kahiltna Glacier, our landing strip and our base camp. As the plane came in to land I couldn't judge our height due to the whiteness of the snow covering the glacier and it wasn't until the wheels and skis buried into the snow that I realised we were landing.

The pilot gunned the engine as we bounced up the glacial runway towards the tents. We were skiing along the snow in a tiny bush plane in the middle of the Alaskan range and a big smile came across my face as I thought to myself that this was so damn awesome. We pulled up close to the tents and the pilot asked us to make it snappy in getting out and unloading, as he needed to get reloaded with climbers departing the mountain and get back into the air before the weather conditions changed. We all piled out into ankle-deep fresh snow and dragged our gear clear of the plane, as the waiting climbers, looking beaten and tired, climbed on board and closed the door.

The pilot gunned the engine again and bounced along to a higher point up on the glacier, spinning the plane around, and without hesitation opening the throttle and surging down the slope. The plane was bucked left and right and when it hit a small mound of snow it launched into the air never to touch down again. The skis lifted clear and they were airborne, climbing to safety. If all went well we would be back at this very location in under three weeks, looking beaten and tired after standing on the summit. I watched the plane disappear down the valley and it was then I took notice of where I was.

I was standing on a glacier at 2200 metres of elevation. Around me rose Mount Hunter at 4442 metres and Mount Foraker at 5304 metres and it was only once the plane had vanished that I noticed the stillness and felt the cold. From now on we were totally dependent on ourselves and each other to get back down to Talkeetna safely. It was almost as if a switch flicked on in my head from happy holiday to survival mode in this remote and dangerous place where conditions can change in an instant. Aiden called us together and we made our way up the small slope to flatter snow that had recently been used for other tents. We set up our cook tent and sleeping tents and came together for our first meal, excited to have finally made it to base camp and the start of the expedition. Everyone was tired and after a hearty meal of Thai noodles we crawled into our sleeping bags, zipped them up tight and slept.

The following morning we began to get organised for our first move higher to camp one. We were broken into rope teams and had to organise our sleds that would be carrying all of our supplies. I was part of a rope team of four. Teams are mainly for safety and if one of us fell through a snow bridge into a crevasse the other three were to quickly drop to the ground, burying their ice axes deep into the snow. This would stop the rest of us from being pulled into the crevasse and halt the fall of the other climber. Once we had arrested their fall we could conduct a crevasse rescue that would see them hauled out of the blackness within thirty minutes. Timing is crucial with a rescue because even though it's cold above ground, as soon as you fall through into a crevasse, the temperature plummets well below zero. If we weren't quick enough with the rescue drills, hypothermia and frostbite would become a real concern.

For most of the day we practised moving as a rope team up and down the glacier next to our tents, witnessing small avalanches on both Mounts Foraker and Hunter as we did so. Moving together safely required constant focus. If we were moving down a gradient my sled wanted to slide down from behind me and knock me over; it was up to my teammate on the rope behind me to keep the rope tight enough to stop the sled from touching me but not tight enough to pull me backwards. If one of us tripped and fell from getting tangled in the rope or sled it could pull all of us down the mountain. The person at the back of the rope has the hardest task while heading down hill, as they must control their teammate's sled in front of them, and also control their own sled which slides in front as well. Having two sleds pulling you forward while moving down hill is a tough position to be in, as I was to find out in the days to come.

Our training day was also important to help us acclimatise to the elevation. I had no headaches yet but remembering Aconcagua, I knew I would. We conducted the final rigging of our sleds – they were between 50 and 60 kilograms each, which was hard to pull up a hill but felt very comfortable while on flat snow. A few of my teammates were worried about the physical aspect of pulling the sled but to me that was going to be the fun part. My fear was falling into a crevasse. I weighed more than 90 kilograms, and although I had faith in my team, I didn't want to test out their new-found rescue skills so early on. After our evening meal we cached some food supplies and equipment for our return to base camp and made a plan to get some sleep and be ready to step off at 3 am, when it would be cold and the snow safest to travel on.

After a few restless hours of sleep I woke at 12.30 am on day three ready for our move to camp one. We packed the sleds with our tents and equipment, broke into our three rope teams and set off. The first section was a 300-foot descent, which tested our sled handling skills immediately. Once we cleared the first area and had a short rest at the bottom, we turned up the Kahiltna Glacier and with my big snowshoes attached to my boots I started marching. The feeling of exposure was electrifying, excitement and nerves pulsed through my body as we stomped along dragging sleds in this untouched and intimidating environment. Beauty was everywhere I turned, from the perfect white snowfields high on the peaks, to the dark menacing rock exposed on the wind-blown ridges. On my left a crevasse opened up to reveal opal-blue ice and a black void at its bottom, their menacing presence ringing warning bells to me every time, 'Don't get complacent, Luke, and stay alert.'

We stopped every hour for a sip of water and a snack; the best way to combat altitude sickness is to stay hydrated and keep eating while moving higher. We had covered 8 kilometres by the time Aiden called out that we had arrived at a good spot for camp one. On Aconcagua there were specific locations for set camps, but on Denali, camp one was on the middle of the glacier, anywhere that was crevasse-free. The rope teams waited while Aiden and Andrew probed a safe area for the tents by shoving a long PVC pipe through the snow, searching for cavities or crevasses beneath. The area was clear and as a light snow began to fall we broke out our gear and started to set up.

The team had done really well on the first physical day with 8 kilometres covered in four hours, and for a few of the team, including me, it was our first time in snowshoes and dragging sleds. It was 1 pm by the time the camp was organised and we enjoyed a hot meal together in the cook tent. Aiden told us he wanted to push on that night to camp two with a load-carry that we would cache, descending again to sleep at camp one. Camp two was 975 metres higher than our current position at 3400 metres. This would be my next physical challenge, and as we settled down into our sleeping bags in the afternoon glow I started to mentally prepare myself and drifted off to sleep.

Toilet protocols on the glacier were something new for me. I'd use a pee bottle at night to avoid getting out of my sleeping bag and immediately after using it my pee bottle became my hot water bottle as I fell back to sleep. If I needed extra bodily functions we were using WAG bags, which have become the standard issue for mountaineering expeditions around the world due to the impact mountaineering has on the environment. The WAG bag is a large plastic bag containing some odour eradicating chemicals and absorbent crystals. Predominantly used for number twos, the big plastic bag is then wrapped up and placed in another zip lock bag for storage and reuse.

We were up early again at 5.45 am, ready and loaded with provisions to be cached up high. It was a slow steady haul upwards on a slight gradient, nothing backbreaking but enough to get a sweat going. Working physically hard in extremely cold environments must be managed correctly. Getting too sweaty can be very dangerous as the sweat will freeze against your skin and can cause hypothermia. The key is to layer clothes and always be slightly cold and never at the point of sweating profusely. When we were standing around I had four layers on and a big down jacket over the top. Right before we took our first step I removed my big jacket, shoved it in the top of my pack and started moving. If I started to warm up too much I'd unzip my wind-breaking layer and the fly on my pants to cool me off. As soon as we stopped, even for a drink break, the big jacket would be back on again. It's irritating at first to always be putting on and taking off layers but once I was in the swing of it, it was easy and just became part of life in the mountains.

We had hauled for six hours and made it to camp two where there was already a few caches set up by other expeditions. There was solid snow the entire way and anytime we would stop for a drink the scenery would mesmerise me. It was postcard views in all directions, and even though I had never been one to take many photos, I was stopping all the time, pulling out my waterproof Olympus camera and snapping away. We dug a deep pit in the snow for the cache and stacked our supplies of food, fuel and spare equipment inside. We then refilled it and built a big pyramid of snow blocks on top. We needed to be able to find our supplies even in stormy and white-out conditions so the bigger and higher the better. We planted a flag on its summit with our team details written on it so that anyone who came along didn't make the mistake of digging up our cache.

It was a nice easy descent back to camp one but on arrival we had the bad news that Anna had decided to leave the expedition. It must have been a tough decision after all the hard work, training and preparation, but she wasn't able to keep going. It's always sad losing someone from the team but for me always slightly motivating as well. It's like running a marathon, and even though I'm hurting on the run, if a runner next to me drops out it gives me a boost. I know it must sound egotistical and selfish but I reaffirmed with myself that I was ready for the expedition, and as Anna joined the rope of a descending team bound for base camp and a flight home, I tried to delete it from my mind and focus my attention back to the mountain.

· · ·

I slept soundly that night, and in the morning, after all the rituals and duties were performed, I was raring to go back up to camp two. From the moment of waking to stepping off it was taking us almost two and a half hours to get ready, longer if it was colder. In such a remote and dangerous place everything takes time, from melting snow for our daily water, to putting on extra layers before exiting tents to the exact science of packing a sled so it's balanced and easy to slide. We arrived at camp two in four hours, feeling much stronger than during the previous day's six-hour journey. I helped dig in the cook tent before setting up my tent, bombproofing it for any bad weather we might encounter. As we moved higher the weather would become more intense, and soon we would be building huge snow walls around our tents. The clouds had descended over camp as we enjoyed some of Aidan's freshly cooked burritos and shared funny stories in the cook tent.

Our plan for the following day was our second load-carry for the trip, up to a place called Windy Corner. As the name describes, it is renowned for formidable winds, and where there's wind there is extreme cold flying along with it. Aiden informed the team that when we reached camp three at 4250 metres we could really settle in and spend some decent rest days acclimatising, but for now we had to push on while we had a good weather window. I settled into my sleeping bag with my water bottle and empty pee bottle tucked in with me and fell asleep in the twilight of an Alaskan summer.

It was absolutely freezing on the morning of day six and we were up at 4.30 am to begin our preparations, but a call from Aiden saying to take an extra hour of sleep due to the cold was well received. My pee bottle had slipped out of my sleeping bag during the night and as I viewed the yellow ice block in the bottom I cursed myself and drifted back to sleep. An hour later I could hear the other members beginning to get ready and with the temperature mildly improved I began to crawl out myself. I needed to keep my pee bottle inside my big jacket for a while to thaw it out so that I could tip it out and not carry the extra weight all day. To help warm us up Aiden prepared some bacon bagels with extra cheese, soaked in bacon grease, for our breakfast. They were the tastiest treat I had devoured in a very long time and morale soared immediately.

We departed at 8 am in our rope teams, carrying packs and dragging sleds. It was an extra cold morning, which bothered me in the beginning but not after we passed over some really big crevasses. The colder it was, the safer the frozen snow bridges were that we were walking on and as I was staring down at the bottomless black mouth of one particularly intimidating crevasse I wished it was colder. We passed underneath the granite face of the West Buttress just before reaching Windy Corner, four and a half hours after departure. Windy Corner didn't live up to its reputation, which we were very okay with, and a strong breeze cooled our bodies as we dug in our cache 15 centimetres below the snow and marked it. This cache didn't need to be as deep as the other one because we would come back down to collect these supplies in a few days after reaching camp three. From our position we could make out camp three at 4250 metres and if the great weather conditions stayed with us we would be up there the following day. Turning around from Windy Corner with the breeze at our backs and no burden of weight we were back down at camp two in 47 minutes.

It was 11 June on day seven, and it was my birthday. I had turned 27 while climbing Denali in Alaska; what an incredible place to have a birthday. We followed the same route up as we did the day before and made it to Windy Corner without any problems. As we were passing the Corner on a narrow section of the path, our sleds slid off to our side and down the slope towards a few thousand feet of oblivion. It was a very tense time as we plodded forward while being pulled sideways down the sheer face of the mountain. Later that night we all agreed that if any of us had fallen at that moment it would have meant disaster for us all because stopping a slide on that part of the buttress would have been near impossible.

We passed some of the biggest crevasses so far on the mountain and crossed some of those monsters on snow bridges that I just hoped were solid. Some were 15 metres across and while peering down into their black depths and seeing no bottom in the vastness, I remembered some of the adventure stories I had read leading up to the trip. Stories of climbers falling into these chasms while travelling alone or unroped and never being seen again. Entire dog teams dragging huge sleds disappeared into them in seconds during the early days of polar exploration. A classic story of Joe Simpson ending up inside one in Peru then crawling out and down the mountain with a broken leg over the following three days. This story became the international bestseller *Touching the Void*. These were the thoughts floating around in my head as we moved past, and I wondered if I would have the same mental and physical fortitude that Joe had if I ever found myself in a similar position.

We arrived at camp three and 4320 metres, staring at dozens of tents already set up and surrounded by snow walls, creating a mini adventure city high on Denali. Luck was on our side because as we started searching for a suitable place to dig in our camp we found a recently departed site, perfect for us to move straight into. A descending team had departed the day before leaving tent sites with fully erected snow block walls still standing and a large pit perfect for us to erect our cook tent. This little stroke of good fortune saved us many hours of labour and, as I popped some tablets for the headaches that were starting to set in, I was very grateful. We had made it to camp three, a big milestone on the expedition, and we were looking forward to a sleep-in the following day and a few days of semi-rest and acclimatisation. As the weather conditions changed and the snow began to fall I crawled into my sleeping bag and fell asleep in seconds.

I had slept for what felt like an eternity and my back was killing me, forcing me to get up and walk around at 8.30 am. It was a rare sleep-in for the team who all started to show themselves shortly afterwards. As we tucked into breakfast together in the cook tent, Aiden gave us our mission for the day, which was to retrieve the cache from Windy Corner and bring it back to camp three. He then delivered some very bad news. Up above us at 5180 metres, a fellow climber had a cardiac arrest and died during the night. He didn't know any more details at this stage except that his body was still up there and plans were being made to get him down at a later date. To me it felt like the Aconcagua trip all over again, and it brought back feelings of vulnerability and the dangers of trying to summit big mountains. I tried not to dwell on the situation too much instead I went to prepare my gear for our back carry; I was feeling energised after a full night's sleep and was eager to get moving.

The descent to Windy Corner with empty packs was easy. We dug up our supplies buried shallow in the snow and divided it all up evenly between the team. We then set off back towards our new home at camp three. I had a slight headache on the way back up but nothing to cause any great concern, I knew it was just part of my body adapting to a new altitude. I rested for the afternoon, drank plenty of fluids and prepared myself for the next stage of our climb. The following day we would do an acclimatisation hike over to the base of the fixed lines and practise moving as a team. The fixed line section leads from a spot 400 metres higher than camp three, up to a ridge on which our high camp is located at 5180 metres. It's a very steep ascent that would test our fitness and requires good crampon skills. Moving as a team is safer but only if everyone in the team knows what they are doing, so the following day we needed to make sure that everyone was on the same page before we started the ascent.

We set off in rope teams towards the fixed lines after another sleep-in and a big breakfast of pancakes and coffee. Once at 4720 metres and the bottom of the lines Aiden gave us a brief on moving safely with communication being our number one priority. A fixed line is a rope anchored into a section of a route that typically has a high chance of fall associated to it. In today's climbing world lines are getting used more and more to help inexperienced climbers ascend mountains that they ordinarily couldn't climb. Traditionally however, they protected a climber from a dangerous section of the climb, especially a dangerous section that needs to be climbed multiple times, such as the one on Denali.

To use the fixed line correctly I had two small lanyards fixed to my climbing harness each one about an arm's length. Attached to the end of one lanyard I had a carabiner that would slide along the fixed line up or down, and to the end of the other one, I had an ascender. The ascender is locked onto the fixed line and can only go up; if I were to fall at any time, the ascender would bite into the rope arresting my fall. The ascender is shaped like a handle and can also be used as leverage when pulling on it. The need for two lanyards arises when reaching an anchor point on the fixed lines, and I would unclip my carabiner lanyard first and move it past the anchor before re-clipping, then unclip the ascender and do the same. This ensured that if I fell at any stage while moving past an anchor I'd still have one point connected to the line to arrest my fall.

The practice drills all went well and I was a lot more confident in our team's abilities as we made our way back to camp. Once we arrived, Aiden needed help to build snow walls around the cook tent. He had been keeping a close eye on the weather and wanted to be prepared for any storm system that might be coming our way. Our sleeping tents were all protected but the cook tent still stood exposed to the wind. To build a snow wall we needed snow blocks and to cut these out of the hard snow required a great deal of physical effort. Using a small plastic snow shovel and a small saw we worked away and built a barrier around the cook tent, thick and high, something I'm sure the Egyptians would have been proud of. I had a pounding headache by the time we had finished and decided to retire to my tent for a nap after lunch and some headache tablets.

I had made the mistake of not protecting my lips with sunscreen and they began to crack and start bleeding. The sun, especially when reflected by the snow, can be unforgiving and I wasn't used to the conditions. Any time I'd smile or try to eat, droplets of blood seeped to the surface and I cringed with discomfort. I had to stop talking and smiling as much, which is a lot harder than it sounds, and take tiny sips of fluids, especially hot drinks, to protect them. I would not be making the same mistake ever again and as part of my morning routine I'd apply copious amounts of sunscreen to any exposed areas.

The afternoon was used for rest, some frisbee, and preparing our gear for a cache-carry to camp four the next day. The weather reports were not looking the greatest and overnight the temperature plummeted. We unzipped our tents early in the morning of day ten to total white-out conditions and snow falling. The call was made for a rest day and we all returned to our tents for more sleep followed by eating, drinking and possibly some more frisbee later. So much of what happens in the mountains depends on the weather. Some expeditions have perfect conditions and summit with sunny skies, others get snow and wind the entire way and are forced off the mountain from camp three. As I wrote in my journal that night I hoped for clear skies the following day and I also thought about the deceased climber who never got to stand on the summit of Denali.

The following day conditions had improved enough to make our push to camp four and cache supplies. After a breakfast of bagels soaked and fried in fat we geared up and moved off in our two rope teams. I was feeling fresh, slightly nervous yet confident in my abilities to get the job done. We made the bottom of the fixed lines in no time and once clipped onto the rope we started to ascend. My rope team moved well and we were keeping a decent pace considering how steep the slope was.

Shortly after we started the climb I had to unzip my jacket and pants to get cold air to cool me and stop me from sweating profusely. It was hard work on such a sharp gradient but with every gruelling step the view below me was getting more incredible. Our camp and tents looked like a few tiny yellow dots in a vast expanse of snow, ice and rock. It was a scene that humbled and inspired me in the same moment and one that will stay with me forever. The steepest section of the fixed lines was a 240-metre-long section named the head wall. It was just under 50 degrees, which on normal terrain wouldn't have been that great a challenge, but up here at 4870 metres in icy conditions it was very tough going. I settled into a steady pace, closer to that of a snail, yet slowly and surely I was making my way towards the ridge above.

The weather started to turn as we made it to the top of the head wall and onto the relative safety of the ridge. We unclipped from the fixed line and took a rest break. As snow started to fall, the wind picked up and white-out conditions were looking imminent. Aiden made the call to send down most of the team and take Allan, Erin and myself to high camp with the food and supplies. We quickly repacked the team's supplies into our packs and as the rest started down the fixed line the four of us turned to go up. The snow was getting heavier and forty minutes after leaving the fixed lines, and seconds after hearing the distinct rumble of cascading snow, Erin and I were hit side-on by an avalanche. I dove onto my ice axe burying it into a hard section of snow as quick as I could to stop myself from being swept away. Erin was lucky to be clipped into a section of rope close to an anchor point and she was buried up to her waist in fresh powder but didn't get taken away either. Aiden yelled out, 'Is everyone okay?' We called back that we were fine and helped each other back to our feet. We moved on with a few nervous laughs, and I was trying to act like I had seen it all before in front of the more experienced climbers, but that was my first avalanche and I was terrified.

Ten minutes later Aiden and Erin were discussing the worsening conditions and decided to abandon our attempt for a cache at camp four and to cache at a place called Washburn's Thumb instead, a rocky outcrop not far from our position along the ridge. It wasn't our ideal location but we needed to start descending and get out of those conditions straight away. We made it to the jagged exposed rocks of the Thumb in ten minutes and started to dig in the cache immediately. Once the cache was secured and marked we didn't waste any time putting our packs back on to move back down.

Aiden, who sounded slightly more urgent in his orders, told us to move fast but safe and keep an eye on each other. We traversed back to the fixed line and once we clipped in we made our way back down, step by step. Another small avalanche broke away to our right and slid down beside us, the heavy snowfall was making the route very unstable and we needed to get off the slope as soon as possible. There was less wind once we dropped below the ridge but the storm stayed with us all the way down the head wall, to the bottom of the fixed lines, and followed us back to camp three.

It was a full white-out as we all settled into the cook tent for a hot drink and watched the heavy snow fall outside. Aiden said we might be waiting a day or two for this weather to clear and also that he was very happy with how the team had performed up high that day. As I lay awake in my tent after dinner the snow was still falling and I could hear the sound of avalanches all around us. If I was high on the mountain right now I'd be terrified by what I was hearing, yet snuggled into my sleeping bag I was content and exhausted, falling asleep to the humbling power of Mother Nature.

I opened my eyes on day twelve to sunlight and silence, there was no snowfall and a dead calm all around me at camp three. It was a late rise for the team, enjoying brunch at 11 am, where Aiden informed us we would be having a cautionary rest day. Due to the amount of snow that fell the previous day and night, the avalanche risk was very high. It was also a case of being fresh and fit enough for a summit attempt in the next few days. If we pushed to camp four breaking new trail through thick snow, it would be exhausting and that lack of energy could be the difference between standing on the summit or turning back.

Andrew wanted to take the team to a place called the 'edge of the world', a view point not far from our camp that is renowned for a spectacular view of the Alaskan range. It would be a nice hike, give us something to keep our minds occupied and also help us acclimatise. Aiden stayed behind to prep our food for the move to high camp and the rest of us followed Andrew to the edge. We were roped up for safety and it was a short, fifteen-minute hike to what must be one of the most incredible view points on earth. The edge of the cliff narrowed up onto a big overhanging rock only allowing one of us at a time to climb out and sit right at its edge. The drop was 2100 metres down onto the north-east fork of the Kahiltna Glacier with Mount Foraker standing proud in the distance. We had a perfect clear day and as I took a seat on the very top posing for a photo, the sight was awe-inspiring. Nature continued to take my breath away with her incredible beauty. I'd done plenty of travelling in Europe and although cathedrals and the architecture were nice, in my eyes they have nothing on what the natural world creates.

Late that afternoon I was resting back at camp three watching the small avalanches break off every few minutes around us on the peaks, cementing Aiden's decision to stay put today. I heard the helicopter before I could see it, picking out its dark shape on the horizon against the white backdrop of snow. But it looked slightly different. It had something swinging below it on a pendulum and at first I thought they must be ferrying food up the mountain for a climbing team, but then I realised what it was, a body bag. This was the mountain rescue helicopter bringing down the climber who had the heart attack earlier in the week. Since the weather had finally cleared they were evacuating him off the mountain. The body swung above me on a rope as the helicopter came down to land at camp three. Without shutting down the engine, the body was repacked and placed inside the cabin of the chopper. Lifting off again the pilot flew back down the mountain towards Talkeetna and to the waiting family of the deceased. The sound of the rotors slowly faded and the scene had left a dark mood over the camp. The realities of mountaineering were exposed in front of our faces just a day before we were scheduled to move up to high camp, the very same place this climber had died. I tried not to think of myself ending up swinging below a helicopter in a body bag but in a way it was good to see it right before our summit attempt. I knew with that image burned into my consciousness that I would be watching every foot placement and every clip on the fixed line to avoid the fatal reality of making a mistake.

After dinner that night we were told that the weather for the following day was expected to be good, so we would be moving to camp four and needed to be ready for an early departure. I slept soundly on our final night at camp three, my body had acclimatised well and I felt strong and confident for our push to high camp. After breakfast and packing away our tents and equipment we moved off in two rope teams. We retraced our steps to the base of the fixed lines and seamlessly transitioned into climbing the steep slope towards the head wall and onto the ridge. We were taking rest breaks every ninety minutes and the team was looking strong; the forced rest day had paid dividends. We passed Washburn's Thumb where we had buried our extra supplies two days before and continued up into uncharted territory.

The ridge continued to narrow as we progressed higher until we were traversing a knife-edge section with drop offs of thousands of feet on both sides. The views rivalled even those from the edge of the world the day before, and even though I was in robot mode, focusing on every single step, I couldn't help but stop and be blown away by my surroundings. The wind had picked up slightly and it caressed my cheek with a below freezing temperature. The overnight weather report from camp four was minus 15 degrees Celsius before the wind chill so this was not a place to get caught outside of a tent in a storm. With the wind beginning to chill me, I prised myself away from the scenery and started climbing again. The ridge took a turn to the east and as I came around from behind a large boulder I could see the tent city of camp.

It had taken us seven and a half hours of climbing to reach camp four. We had all arrived safely, and even though we were tired and my headaches were kicking in again, I was excited to be there. The only place higher from our position was the summit. We were lucky again with our camp site, finding a newly built weatherproof site, freshly vacated and waiting for us to move into. The snow walls were thick and high allowing us immediate rest instead of hours of intense work cutting blocks. The teams that had descended that day leaving us our new home had waited in extreme cold and wind for four days for a weather window, eventually deciding to abandon their attempted ascent and head down. Aiden and Andrew went back down the short distance to Washburn's Thumb to retrieve our extra food and supplies letting the rest of us hydrate, eat and get ready for the summit.

The weather report for the coming days was not looking great and the best day out of the next few for a summit attempt was the following day. It had a likelihood of being cold and windy but it was our best shot. Aiden asked us if we were ready for a shot at the summit and remembering the teams who waited days for the good weather that never came, we all agreed we were. He told us to take some Diamox, the medication that assists with adapting to altitude, sleep well and be ready to move by 10.30 am for the summit. It took me longer to fall asleep than usual as the altitude was taking its toll, but I was also very nervous. I had the same feelings as I lay in my tent on Aconcagua hoping I had what it takes to reach the summit and get back down safely without incident or letting the team down. Fatigue eventually overtook me and I slept soundly in a cold minus 12 degrees.

...

I was up early and preparing my boots, crampons and clothing layers; we were going to travel light with minimal food, water or unnecessary equipment. My pack was going to be the lightest it had been on the expedition but with the added altitude and difficulty of the terrain this would not be an easy day. The summit team of Simon, Bill, Allen and myself with guides Aiden and Erin stepped off at 10 am towards a flat section of glacier heading towards Denali Pass. Chok and Richard had decided that they were not strong enough to attempt the summit. They were both having trouble adapting to our new altitude and decided to be safe and stay at camp four. It was a tough call to make this close to the summit but I respected them more for their decision – in my eyes no mountain was worth getting killed or injured for.

The first challenge of our day was a 340-metre elevation gain on a 45-degree traversing slope up to Denali Pass. This section, known as the 'Autobahn', has claimed the lives of many tired climbers descending from the summit in poor weather. It was given its name after a team of German climbers slid to their deaths on the steep slope, unable to arrest their fall. I put my head down and fell into a steady rhythm of heavy breathing and slow progress upwards. We were heating up quickly and a short rest to take off our down jackets was needed. I unzipped my shell jacket and the fly of my pants for ventilation and continued on with the hypnotic crunch of crampons on snow.

Two hours later I reached the top of the incline and stood on top of Denali Pass at 5550 metres, puffing hard and nursing a pounding headache. We stopped for water and I inhaled some headache tablets and some chocolate to help me recover. The wind was blowing a steady 20 kilometres per hour, which wasn't very strong but it did drop the temperature to minus 15 degrees Celsius. The team seemed to be doing well and after a short rest we proceeded up the ridge over rocky outcrops towards our next landmark, a large plateau called 'the football field'. We stopped every hour for a quick sip of water and to check on each other's condition – we were all beginning to show signs of fatigue. By the late afternoon, we had reached the end of the football field and come face to face with our biggest obstacle before the summit ridge, Pig Hill.

Pig Hill was a 40-degree slope which at sea level would be a lovely afternoon hike but up here, above 5790 metres and after six hours of climbing, it was a serious challenge. We dropped our packs at the bottom of the hill and tied our down jackets around our waist. We would make the last push up as light as possible, taking the bare necessities. We started up the hill and I knew after the first few steps this was the make or break point. I was taking three deep breaths for every two small steps and I couldn't catch my breath. High altitude robbed the body of oxygen and made physical work near impossible. I set small goals telling myself, 'Make ten good steps then have a few extra breaths, now make twenty to that small chunk of snow.' These little goals gave me a small sense of achievement every time I made it and ever so slowly I was chugging my way up the hill.

Ninety minutes later I felt light-headed and had a pounding headache as I crested the top of the hill and stood on top of the summit ridge. In between panting breaths I looked across and laid eyes on the summit of Denali. I knew I wasn't there yet and the dangerous summit ridge still had to be crossed, but just to make it this far and be within an hour of the top filled me with confidence and the pain didn't feel so bad. We rested at the top of Pig Hill, throwing on down jackets to protect us from the freezing wind.

It was the last leg and we stepped off from the top of the hill onto the knife-edged ridge to the summit. We had to stand aside as two other climbing teams were descending from the summit. A few smiled and gave us a thumbs up as they passed but most of them were in their own worlds and seemed to be fighting to get back down. We traversed across large hanging build ups of snow called cornices, that have been hanging strong for decades, but if they ever let go while we were all on the top I doubt our bodies would ever be recovered. I was watching every foot placement as we made the traverse and as I looked up to take in another deep breath Aiden was staring back at me from the highest point of the ridge, the summit.

I took small steps up onto the summit and put my fists in the air, the pain went away and the joy and excitement overtook me as I stood tall at 6190 metres, on top of the tallest mountain in North America. I pulled out my sponsors' flags and had Aiden take some photos of me and then I let one of the others take my place to do the same. We were all ecstatic to share this moment together and as I sat down to drink some water and watch the others on the summit, I was beaming.

We had the entire summit, to ourselves and after fifteen minutes my mind started to refocus on my environment. We were now at a halfway point, and the most exposed section of the mountain. I needed to get ready for the climb back down to high camp – most of the deaths and injuries in mountaineering occur during the descent when energy and focus are low and exhaustion is setting in. Once we had all taken some pics and we had a group photo together it was time to start our descent. I was feeling good with only a slight headache and the added surge of adrenaline from summiting pulsing through my veins.

We traversed the summit ridge carefully and made it back to the top of Pig Hill, welcoming a short rest. I started to descend the hill treading carefully and making sure to not get my crampons caught in my pants or trip myself. A fall at any stage on these steep sections would put the whole team in danger. Descending was far easier than going up but with every passing minute I could feel my body getting tired and I started to realise how hungry and thirsty I was. With minimal food and water all day my body was running on fumes and adrenaline, my legs were getting heavy and my head was starting to pound. We reached the bottom of the hill in a third of the time it took to ascend it, arriving at our backpacks where we had another short rest. I inhaled a chocolate bar, the last of my food and drank some water I had left behind in my pack.

We set off again down and across the football field. It was physically easier during the descent with less hard breathing and no need to set myself little goals to reach. However this ease was allowing my mind to drift away and as I lost focus I was snapped back to reality as a crampon caught on my boot causing me to stumble. I scolded myself for the little incident and tried to stay fully alert as we reached the other side of the football field and began to descend the rocky outcrops towards Denali Pass. I could feel the air thickening as we descended and breathing was becoming easier with each passing hour. We slipped beneath Denali Pass along the Autobahn, using the fixed lines as protection. The team was very tired and our clipping and unclipping drills along the fixed lines were taking a long time to complete. The light was fading to a twilight in the late evening and the amber glow set the scene for incredible views as we descended. I was too tired to pull out my camera, instead I visually absorbed this amazing place that in all likelihood I'd never see again.

We stumbled into camp four and the safety of our tents twelve and a half hours after departing. I was exhausted and as the excitement and adrenaline of the day dissipated I felt my body shutting down and begging for rest. We ate enough hot food to feed a small village, drank copious amounts of water and tea then crawled into our sleeping bags. I fell asleep within seconds, proud of what we had accomplished yet knowing that we still had many miles of descent to make it off the mountain. The job wasn't done yet.

We slept in late and after a quick breakfast of oats and coffee we loaded our packs with all of our tents and equipment and departed camp four. My body was very sore from our summit day but my mind was alert and I had a smile on my face thinking about the day before. We descended the ridge, past Washburn's Thumb and rested at the top of the fixed lines. Clipping into the fixed line we took it very steady descending. Freezing temperatures overnight had left the route icy and dangerous and extra care needed to be taken with rope management and foot placement. From the bottom of the fixed lines we had an easy hike down to camp three; it had only taken us three hours to get back down to where we dug up our cache of sleds and remaining supplies.

While we ate a hot meal together in the afternoon Aiden gave us a weather update and a decision to make. We could stay the night at camp three and start our descent the next day or we could load up and push down the mountain all night back to base camp. He said there was a good weather window for the next twenty-four hours where a flight out of base camp back to Talkeetna was possible, after that we could be waiting out a few days of bad weather for another chance. As a team we decided to push on – it had been a tough trip, filled with extreme weather and physical challenges, so one more big push to finish the expedition sounded like a great final test to me.

After dinner we moved off, roped together, to start our descent. It was late afternoon and the early evening twilight was starting to blend itself into the background. As we made our way out of camp three, past the same huge glaciers that had filled me with dread a week earlier, I felt confident and able to handle myself in this harsh environment. We fell into our standard routine of taking short breaks every hour as we skirted Windy Corner, which once again wasn't overly windy, to our relief, and went down the slope to where we had our original camp two. It was late evening by this stage and everyone was sleeping in the small community of tents at the camp. Aiden knew one of the guides and teams sleeping there and with a few whispered words he was able to get us some rest time in their cook tent and a hot brew. The temperature had dropped to well below freezing and this little respite was a big bonus.

We stayed long enough in the cook tent to get warm and comfortable and I knew that starting our death march to base camp again was going to be hard. As we were roping up I had my big down jacket on to combat the cold and I remembered I had a heap of caffeine chewing gum in the top of my pack. Knowing they would be ideal for our current situation I fumbled them out and gave them to Bill and a couple of the others as I shoved two into my mouth. We would be needing the extra kick as we descended through the twilight hours and into the following day. My down jacket came off as we started our descent, moving quicker in the beginning to warm up and get the blood flowing back into my numb feet.

We fell into rhythm again and the hours ticked by – moving through this rugged environment in the twilight with nothing but the sound of crunching snow and sliding sleds was truly amazing. The colour changes in the mountains as the sun crept up from the horizon again were incredible and as we stopped for a break at our original camp one, I thought to myself, that this was one of the most beautiful places on earth. We had been going for almost twelve hours straight and as much as the caffeine was giving me a much needed boost my body and mind were starting to fatigue.

The sun was up and starting to warm everything and some clothing layers were removed before we stepped off again down the Kahiltna Glacier. This was our last push to base camp, the only issue was we had left our trek across the lower glacier a little too late in the day and the snow was beginning to turn to mush. We had originally crossed this section during the evening when the snow was frozen and the snow bridges were solid, now I could see the gaping holes of the crevasses and the mush snow covering them; I was getting very nervous. It wasn't long after this my foot broke through the snow into the black void below, I jerked it out quickly staring into the foot-sized dark hole with my heart pounding.

As we continued on I could see the others having similar experiences and it wasn't long before I broke through again, this time up past my knee. By this stage I was terrified. I hadn't expected this at all and the thought of falling into the crevasse as I pulled my leg free pumped adrenaline into my blood. We were roped together and I knew that if I did fall through completely that my rope team could stop my fall but the protection did very little to ease my fear as we continued on. We were caught in the middle of the crevasses and had no choice but to keep moving through to get to the solid land on the far side.

Walking across the glacier in these conditions would have to be the closest simulation of going through a mine field. Every time I placed my foot down I was expecting to break through, or for the snow bridges to give way completely. Another thirty minutes of this constant anxiety had passed when I looked across to Andrew on the other rope team, who was smiling. I thought to myself, that he was having a great time, right before he disappeared completely below the snow. He had fallen straight through the snow bridge and as the rope pulled tight on his other three teammates they dove onto their ice axes burying them into the snow to arrest his fall. He was suspended in mid-air below the snow bridge inside the crevasse. The rope connected to him cut into the snow a few metres back from the hole he had vanished into.

Aiden took charge yelling at the team 'hold firm on your axes', before bringing our rope team over to attach onto theirs, acting as more anchor support and more power to pull him out. Before we could haul him up Aiden moved to the very point where the rope cut into the snow and used trekking poles to build a ledge for the rope to pull against. If he didn't do this when we started to pull the rope would cut deeper through the snow and could get caught or cut on protruding glacier ice. At this stage Andrew was hanging in open space with a black void underneath him but he was an experienced mountain guide and knew he was in safe hands. He stayed calm and managed to take a few photos while we were getting organised – the pictures he showed us later that night were incredible. Once the edge was prepared, together both rope teams applied our weight and we slowly brought Andrew back to the surface and into the light.

The entire rescue only took fifteen minutes, if we didn't have two rope teams and the extra bodyweight it could have taken a lot longer. Once everyone was separated we had a small rest to refocus our minds on the job at hand then continued our descent. We were only a couple of miles from solid land and when I finally placed my foot onto snow that I knew had ground below it, the sense of relief was overwhelming. The final push to base camp was an uphill sled drag that had been our first downhill section when we departed two weeks prior. A few of the team were totally exhausted so Aiden attached their sleds to his and took the extra weight. No way was I going to let someone help me, especially this close to the end.

I bent into my harness, leant on my trekking poles and hauled up the incline, panting and sweating with the effort. It was a short distance but in my physical state it took all of my strength to keep going. Finally I could see the tents of base camp ahead of me, and inside I cheered with relief. I hauled until the trail flattened out in front of some tents and I let the sled come to a complete stop. We had done it! A solid descent from high camp to base camp in a non-stop fourteen-hour death march. My eyes teared up as we gave each other high fives and hugs, with the wear and tear of the expedition showing through on our faces. We unloaded our sleds like crippled old people and set up our tents. The plane was due to arrive early the next morning and we were going to be the first team out.

I can't remember falling asleep that afternoon; I was sitting upright in my tent and woke up many hours later with my legs and back so sore I could barely sit upright. My body had finally given in and I had slept like the dead. It was twilight outside and the camp was quiet so it must have been late in the evening. I unzipped the tent to stare out at the incredible sight of the mountains one more time, knowing that in a few hours a little red plane would be coming to take me back to the real world. Living in the harshness of an environment shrouded in such incredible beauty is a humbling experience. It has made me even more grateful for having the opportunity and ability to be out there doing what I love to do. I pulled out a hand-held mirror from my bag and studied my dry cracked lips and skin, my dishevelled appearance and my tired blue eyes. I smiled into the mirror and stared into the eyes of the guy looking back at me, trying to understand the man I was becoming. Unable to figure it out just yet I whispered to him, 'Well done mate.'

CHAPTER 8
THE CHICKEN-STICK EFFECT

...

I regularly get asked how I managed to afford all of the expeditions I have been on in such a short space of time. When I think about it I have been very fortunate, and when I trace my good fortune it goes all the way back to one thing, a chicken stick.

I was training at Tiger Muay Thai again after finishing in the mines and getting ready for my first summit, Aconcagua, and was in a mindset focused on my goals and preparing for the first of the seven summits. While I was at Tiger there were people from all over the world training for their own reasons. Whether it was for weight loss, preparing for a fight or cleansing their bodies of addiction; it was a great place to mingle with people of all ages, from all classes of life and from every corner of the globe.

One morning I noticed an older guy training in one of the BodyFit sessions who was giving it his absolute all. He looked to be in his fifties, was heavily overweight for his height, and his face was red with effort and pouring sweat from the humidity. No matter how hard the session became he hung in with the young guys until I was certain he was going to keel over and die right there on the mat. He had a friend with him who looked to be in his mid-thirties and was also giving it his absolute all. At the end of the session I went over to say hello and shook their hands. The young guy was Michael and the older guy, who took my hand and looked me straight in the eye sizing me up immediately, was John.

John was fifty years old, born and raised in Sydney with a Lebanese background, and I liked him from day one. He had a great presence, a big smile and was on a mission to lose weight and change his life. During the previous year his wife had successfully fought off breast cancer while suffering from Addison's disease and the stress on him during that time was easy to see. He had packed on the weight and had made a last-minute decision to come to Thailand in order to try and halt the heart attack he was destined for. Flying to a martial arts training camp in Asia to save his own life and help get his family back on track – I admired his courage and determination.

John and Michael didn't have any idea of how to go about their training or what to eat to lose weight while in the camp, so after meeting them briefly I said I'd drop by their hotel pool later that day to give them some advice. I went home, showered and then hopped on my scooter to go and buy barbecue chicken from my favourite street seller, five minutes away. Every dollar I had saved while mining in Australia was put aside for the expeditions so I was on a shoestring budget while in Thailand, which meant eating local street food every day. I had been going to the same Thai guy for weeks and his chicken was amazing. I ordered my usual snack of two chicken sticks then thought I'd get one each for John and Michael. For the grand total of 80 baht ($3) I rode away with a whole chicken skewered on four sticks in my left hand.

I arrived at the hotel where the boys were staying and found them sitting on the edge of the pool. I sat down and handed over a chicken stick each. 'Welcome to Thailand lads, have a chicken stick.' John said, 'Thanks very much mate,' and offered to give me the money. I protested, 'Don't worry, it's my treat.' We ate together as new friends and then chatted about training, nutrition and how to get the best result out of their time in Thailand. John had plenty of funny stories about his life in Sydney while running cafes and small businesses. Michael seemed to be the new, up-and-coming guy, learning as much as he could from the man who had been there and done it all. John and I became good friends after that first chat together, spending every breakfast, most lunches and many dinners talking and solving all the problems of the world. John would recount to me years later the moment I handed him the chicken stick and described it as a selfless act of kindness from a guy who didn't want anything in return. That gesture secured our friendship from that day on.

Over the following month John trained like a man possessed and lost 12 kilograms of body fat, changing his entire physique and gaining back a healthy glow in his skin. His energy was limitless and he tackled every session like a twenty-year-old, often leaving the younger guys in his dust. For a special New Year's Eve session a few guys and I planned a massive test of endurance and invited everyone to come and join in. The session contained hundreds of reps of varied exercises, a 6-kilometre tyre drag and a run to the top of big Buddha mountain and back, 12 kilometres away. Many who started didn't finish the session yet John came stumbling in 5 hours and 45 minutes later, looking like a broken man but beaming a big smile.

I was due to depart for Argentina the week following New Year and after a farewell dinner with my close group of training buddies I was ready to go. While shaking hands with John he said, 'Thanks for all the help,' and 'When you get back to Sydney after your climb give me a call and we will go for a beer.'

After successfully climbing Aconcagua, I touched down back in Sydney and made my way to a friend's house in Newtown. I remembered John and wanted to track him down, say hi and see if he had kept up his training. Finding the scrap of paper with John's number written on it, I gave him a call. He picked up immediately and in a formal voice said, 'John speaking.' I told him who it was and his tone changed as he asked how and where I was. I told him I was in Sydney staying at a friend's place and he replied, 'Great, be ready for lunch tomorrow and I will pick you up.'

I slept under my friend's staircase that night on a comfy mattress and the following day I was waiting out the front of the house for the midday pickup. A Porsche sedan rolled up with tinted windows, and as the window came down I saw John looking like a million dollars, sitting in the front seat with his son Luke driving.

He was wearing designer slacks and a very impressive shirt pressed to a pristine quality. His shoes were shining, as was his buckle and the massive watch hanging from his wrist. His hair was freshly cut and styled to the latest trend and the best thing was he had kept the weight off. Luke was similarly flawless in his appearance, and as I was the guy wearing a T-shirt and jeans I felt like the odd man out. I climbed into the back onto the soft leather seats and settled in. I began to think there was more to John than what he had let on in Phuket, and as we drove into the city I recounted to them my climb of Aconcagua.

Luke dropped John and I off in Darling Harbour, a waterfront area of Sydney's central business district, and I was feeling the shock of civilisation. I walked uncomfortably through the crowds of tourists and corporates in suits when only a few days earlier I had been standing on a remote mountain summit in Argentina. John's phone was constantly ringing and it was glued to his ear as we walked along. We arrived at a restaurant called Meat and Wine Co and as he reached for the front door a server opened it and said, 'Hi John.' We entered and made our way upstairs through a beautifully decorated restaurant to a private room on the third floor, where a table was set and waiting for us. The servers were buzzing around John and settling him into his chair and started to bring out snacks and drinks before I had even seen a menu. John finished a call and then turned to me with a cheeky grin; he must have picked up on my confusion at the situation and he said to me, 'Just relax mate, I know the owner.' I began to think that John might have been playing down his 'few small cafes back home' when we used to talk in Thailand.

I had lost a lot of weight on the expedition and John was taking it upon himself to fatten me back up again. I had two plates of food in front of me minutes after sitting down and the flow of food didn't stop, no matter how much I protested. John had arranged a lunch meeting with a guy named Grant who he was about to do a deal with for another 'small restaurant', and when he finally arrived I had already gorged myself on the first course.

Grant was another businessman of impeccable appearance and arrived moments before one of John's associates, 'Chris the Greek'. I swear that is exactly how he was introduced, and I started thinking I was caught up in an Australian version of *The Sopranos*. Everyone was seated and the wine started to flow. I didn't drink, as I was in training mode and wanted to stay focused, so I became the adventure-story relief during the meeting. Whenever negotiations hit a stale point John would ask me a question and I'd tell a story about the expedition, the army, Thailand and anything that was of interest. Once I was done the meeting would resume and I'd settle into another plate of food.

The afternoon carried on with tense moments of discussion, bouts of laughter and plenty of food and drink. It was close to sunset by the time negotiations were slowly starting to finish up. I couldn't follow who had the upper hand in the deal but John looked happy as more wine was ordered and I told another story about our time together in Thailand. We moved from the dining table to the lounge bar upstairs and settled into a comfy antique sofa, where desserts were waiting for us to snack on. I was having a great time watching the boys in action. In my mind I always thought business was conducted in sterile offices with stacks of white paper and striped ties; here I was witnessing how deals were really done, with long lunches and fine wine.

I had eaten myself into a food coma by the time the lunch had stretched to nine hours and I was yearning for bed. The meeting was concluded and it was handshakes and back slapping all round as we said our goodbyes and made our way downstairs. I had given John a $1 chicken stick and he gave me nine hours of fine dining at one of the best restaurants in Sydney in return. We exited the front door and made our way to the street where Luke was waiting with the car. I was dropped off back in Newtown with John saying he would call me the following day.

My sister and I dressed up as beer cans for a fancy dress party. My creative mum made them all by hand.

One of the baby freshwater crocodiles we kept in our bath for two weeks until Mum had had enough and wanted her bathroom back.

My gypsy parents, Mandy and Clive. They flip their lucky penny to decide which road they will travel next.

In the jungle of East Timor at eighteen. Serving my country on my first deployment in 2003.

The small hut that contained the dead climber during our summit day on Aconcagua, Argentina.

Descending Aconcagua, Argentina after celebrating on the summit.

The summit of Denali, Alaska.

Departing Denali base camp bound for Talkeetna and a beer.

Inside the container at the Freeport mine, West Papua, with Dean sitting up next to me.

Standing on the summit of Carstensz, West Papua holding a picture of the king of Thailand.

Locals waiting outside of the chief's house in Sugapa. Eighteen would be selected to work with our expedition as porters.

Valentine and I after our close call on Mount Elbrus, Russia.

One of our captors in West Papua, a good bloke just doing his job.

Dad and I during our ascent of Mount Kilimanjaro, Tanzania.

Moving to high camp on Vinson Massif, incredible Antarctica stretching to the horizon.

Slowly making my way up Vinson Massif.

In the middle of the Atlantic it was time for a selfie while the crew scraped the bottom of the boat clean.

Inside the tiny cabin that Jake and I shared for 55 days during our Row2Rio campaign.

I lost 14 kilograms (31 pounds) during the Atlantic crossing, my largest weight loss on any expedition.

I was human bait in the middle of the Atlantic. I shot a proposal video for Elise while trying not to drown.

Learning to throw myself from cliffs in Moab, Utah. Freedom was a simple leap away from the edge.

No church for us on our wedding day, just a balloon and a priest in Las Vegas. That's Dylan (Jimmy) James on the right, who filmed the day and mentored me into BASE jumping.

The rest of the house was quiet as I took a quick shower and slipped into my little bed under the stairs.

The following day John called, telling me I wasn't going to sleep under the stairs anymore and that I was going to come and live with him. I didn't even have to think about it before saying yes, and made my way to the suburb of Parramatta to meet up. I arrived at his building and met his other son Nathan, and John's brother George, who all worked in the family businesses. George was a little older than John and Nathan was my age. They were both impeccably dressed, minds sharp as a razor and very friendly. They were eager to hear about training with John in Thailand and about climbing Aconcagua, so once again I was the storyteller at the coffee shop, with John egging me on and encouraging me to talk. As we departed Nathan pulled me aside to say a heartfelt thankyou for helping his dad lose weight in Thailand. I told him it was my absolute pleasure but that his dad did all the work and deserved all the credit.

John and I arrived at his home shortly before dark. His house was amazing, a huge brick place nestled in a really nice suburb with front gardens looking as if every leaf and blade of grass was in its perfect place. I entered through the large wooden front door to a reception from John's wife Robyn. She had a big smile as she hugged me and made me feel right at home. To say the bedroom I was given was an upgrade from the bed under the stairs is a massive understatement – I had my own huge double bed, cupboards, drawers, full-length mirror and enough room to do a training session. On my bed Robyn had bought and laid out a toothbrush, toothpaste, shower gel, deodorant and a towel; I'm not sure if she was trying to tell me something but all I felt was grateful and slightly overwhelmed by the generosity. Robyn was Australian, which explained why Luke and Nathan had more European features than Lebanese and she had only recently beaten breast cancer, which John told me took a huge toll on the entire family. She was now in remission and doing well and her energy seemed endless when I first became a full-time guest of the family.

Living in the house with John and Robyn were their two stunningly beautiful daughters, Carly and Taryn. They both had long-term boyfriends and were soon to be married and moving out with their husbands. It was Lebanese tradition that the girls live at home until they were married. My daily routine from that point forward involved training with John and the boys every morning and then joining him at work. I sat in on all of his meetings, drove with him into the city for lunches and never had to put my hand in my pocket once in the entire time I was with him.

Every morning we trained at a gym called Revolution X, not far from John's house. It was a CrossFit and strength and conditioning warehouse owned and operated by a guy named Rob. I had never done CrossFit before but I took to the training like a duck to water. It was exactly the style of training I loved – hard sessions utilising kettlebells, weightlifting, gymnastics and running in killer circuits, racing the clock and each other. It was a great atmosphere and through John and the boys I met tons of new people, who thought what I was trying to achieve was incredible, offering me their support any way they could. I started training twice a day at Rev X and after two months Rob offered me an assistant coaching position. Following on from that and with some external pressure from John I'm sure, Rob let me move in and live upstairs of the gym. It was a perfect deal for me, training all day for the next expedition, learning to coach and drinking as many free protein shakes as I could stomach.

My training routine involved a lot of functional movement; over the years I have tried many different styles of working out but no other training program has gotten me as fit or as strong as I was with CrossFit. It must be performed safely with the right technique and weight for your ability, but it works. I blended in pack marches to keep up my pack fitness and also some hypoxic training at the local pool. At the pool I'd drop to the bottom holding onto a 20-kilogram deadball, then while holding my breath and carrying the ball I would try and run as many sprints as I could. I repeat this over and over until what started as one lap holding my breath, turned into three, four and five. This hypoxic technique is utilised to try and force the body to create more red blood cells, the very same cells

I needed while in the mountains to carry oxygen around my body in the super thin air at altitude.

By the time my second expedition, to Denali, came around, I was in incredible shape and champing at the bit to get to Alaska. The entire RevX family had wished me luck and off I went to do my best. After successfully summiting I returned to the gym, was given my job back again and my same bed upstairs. I was so fortunate and grateful to be able to get straight back into training and pick up where I left off. I was officially broke by this stage with no idea of how to fundraise big amounts of money besides going back to underground mining, but when I caught up with John he had a plan ready and waiting for execution.

John had put together a full fundraising event for me to try and raise the money I needed to keep going with the seven summits. I would learn that he had plenty of experience doing this and used to hold charity events and fundraising galas for the Penrith football club, where Luke and Nathan had played rugby league. He also owned his own function centre called the Waterview inside the beautiful Sydney Olympic Park that could hold up to 700 people. What I have come to realise more and more in business and in life is that it's all about your network, which can make impossible tasks very possible. John had built a network over forty years in business that fanned out across Sydney, Australia and the world. He had called in a favour for 400 bottles of wine from Queensland, free printing of flyers, posters and tickets in Sydney, organised guest speakers, a band, DJ, film crew and five-star dining to bind the night together. His business partner Chris the Greek took me around his community for weeks to meet people, tell stories and sell tickets for the night. John's other friend Jamie gave me a $2000 cheque to buy a car so that I could get around while in Sydney. The generosity was endless and overwhelming.

The night came together bigger than we could have imagined and almost 400 people dressed in their best turned up for the night. I had plenty of my Newtown friends there and my parents flew down from North Queensland for the occasion. I had to deliver my first ever public speaking performance and I was nervous standing on stage looking out across the sea of people all staring back at me. A week before the event a lovely client from the gym named Cathy told me her brother Andrew was a public speaking coach and after hearing what I was trying to do offered to coach me for free. His sessions were invaluable; it's one thing to tell a few stories around a meeting table or over lunch but a different thing all together when delivering a speech live. He helped me pick my best stories, mould them and then present them in an interesting and professional way. I practised my speech over and over again leading up to the big night and when the moment finally came I didn't miss a beat. Once I started speaking the nerves fell away, I relaxed and the words flowed out perfectly.

To raise money John had organised items to raffle that he had pulled in from everywhere – football jerseys from the Parramatta club, year-long theatre passes, coaching clinics for kids' football teams, guest appearances from rugby league stars and all-inclusive nights at some of John's best restaurants. The tickets were selling like hotcakes and a number of the ladies from the gym jumped in to help us sell all the tickets on the night, doing an amazing job. The raffles alone pulled in almost $10,000 in a few hours.

As I was floating around during the night, John's business partners from his various ventures would pull me aside and shove cheques into my hand saying 'Best of luck on your next trip' or 'Go conquer those mountains.' It was an unbelievable show of generosity. At one point in the night one of John's associates stood up yelling, 'I will give you $50,000 for Mount Everest if you take off your shirt and do 100 push-ups on stage right now.' I immediately jumped up onto the stage and started taking off my shirt in front of 400 of Sydney's elite. Everyone was applauding and laughing as I dropped down and started pumping out the push-ups with the MC counting every single rep. I think it was the adrenaline and the thought of standing on top of Everest that allowed me to pump out 100 straight, collapsing to my knees to the roar of the room. It was one of the most ridiculous and incredible moments I have been part of. The band were cranking, the comedians kept us laughing all night and the DJ kept it all pumping 'til the end when everyone started departing for home.

The final tally of funds raised was $57,000 from the raffle tickets and tickets to the gala event. On top of it all was a pledge of $50,000 sponsorship for Mount Everest. I had never seen so much money in my life let alone that amount of money collected in one evening. It was enough to finish the remaining five summits. I was totally blown away. John and I sat back to have a Scotch after the event and he smoked a cigar. He had a look of benevolence on his face and I thanked him for everything he had done for me from the bottom of my heart. He said, 'Don't worry about it, Richmond, just go climb your mountains.'

It was only two months before I was due to depart for Carstensz and my mind had already started to focus back on training and preparation for what lay ahead. With the burden of financing lifted I could now work and train at the gym and depart for my expeditions with the freedom of knowing my bed and place at Rev X would always be waiting.

Thinking back years later on the chain of events that had led to my success, and following it all the way back to the beginning, it had started with a smile, the shake of a hand and a chicken stick. Never underestimate the power of a single tiny gesture of kindness. Just as the flapping of a butterfly's wings could cause a tornado, the chicken-stick effect could take you to the top of the world.

CHAPTER 9

CARSTENSZ PYRAMID, WEST PAPUA

...

I thought I had seen thick jungle before while at the jungle training wing in Tully, North Queensland during my Army career, or patrolling on peacekeeping missions in East Timor. Yet it wasn't until I arrived in West Papua that I finally discovered what a thick jungle was and how unforgiving it can be. I was on my way to attempt my third summit, Carstensz Pyramid. At 4884 metres it is the biggest peak in Oceania, also known as Puncak Jaya to the locals. I flew out of Sydney and landed in Bali where I would meet the rest of my team and then fly on to Papua.

Papua has been part of Indonesia since 1969 when an independence vote by Papuan elders, under rumours of coercion, was held with a resulting decision to remain part of Indonesia. The vote was riddled with corruption allegations and rejected by Papuan nationals, who in their opposition created the Free Papua Movement. This movement started with peaceful protests and international pressure but has since descended into guerrilla warfare against the Indonesian administration. West Papua has a population of 800,000 people who spread themselves across some of the most inhospitable terrain on earth. Tribal culture still dominates the jungle regions and I was en route to see first-hand how primitive some of the tribes still were.

The mountain itself would be a different climb to the two peaks I had summited already. The relatively low altitude, under 5000 metres, would mean very little altitude sickness and much less time needed acclimatising. We were hoping to summit and be back out of Papua in under two weeks. The first stage is a six-day trek through the jungle to base camp at 4330 metres and then one big summit day, which is predominantly a rock climb all the way to the top. There would be no snow on top even though it would be cold and any overnight ice on the route should melt away with the sun. Following summit day there would be a six-day journey back out through the jungle and a flight back to Bali. That was the general plan for the expedition, although reality turned out to be a whole lot different.

I had signed on to a team organised by Adventure Indonesia, and our head guide's name was Meldi, a young Indonesian guide based in Jakarta who was all smiles and big welcomes when I met him at the hotel in Bali. The rest of the team consisted of Chris, James, Roy, Susan, Nicole and Dean from the United States, Thomas from Germany, Vitidnan from Thailand and Edward as the other Australian. Ten members from different parts of the world all with the same desire to stand on top of Carstensz and claim one of the seven summits. At the team briefing, Meldi gave us our itinerary for the following few days and then we all went through a thorough gear check, shared our stories and got to know each other. I was fresh off my Denali expedition, still with limited experience compared to some of the other team members, but I had plenty of stories to keep everyone entertained.

Meldi recommended we wear gumboots for the initial approach through the jungle; it was extremely wet and muddy and according to him gumboots were the best way to try and keep the feet dry. I had no experience in the jungles of Papua and even though I have been in similar environments before and worn normal military boots my feet were always soaked, so I ventured out to buy some rubber boots to give his advice a try. We were partnered up with a tent buddy and I was matched with Vitidnan. He was a very friendly guy and was on his own journey to be the first Thai national to climb the seven summits. He had already summited Everest, the hardest of the seven, and was filming his entire trip for a documentary. We got along great and I offered to help him with his filming any way I could.

We departed Bali on a commercial airliner and landed in Timika, West Papua. The town's airport acts as the main gateway for the Grasberg Mine, the largest gold mine and third largest copper mine in the world, located close to the mountain ranges that we would be trekking towards. The mine employs 20,000 workers, many of them Indonesians, and foreigners to Papua. It is largely owned by Freeport-McMoRan Inc., an American corporation and has come under constant pressure and guerrilla attacks from the Free Papua Movement. They view the mine as a violation of the Papua national interest and accused the company of not distributing jobs or profits to Papua, as well as causing large-scale environmental impact. The mine employs Indonesian special forces units to secure the area against attacks but in the years since 2002 roads have been blocked, miners have been shot travelling to and from work and in 2011 two employees were burnt alive in their vehicle after being fired upon by hidden gunmen.

In Timika we transferred to a small propeller-powered bush plane and took off over the jungle towards a small village called Sugapa, our starting point for the expedition. The dense green jungle below mixed with splashes of red dirt roadways was a big contrast from the white glaciers and snow on route to Denali base camp. We descended towards Sugapa and landed on the tiny, rough gravel runway that was longer than the assortment of buildings that made up the village. We came to a stop at the end of the strip and through my small window I watched as a crowd of locals swarmed the runway and surrounded the plane.

Stepping off I was engulfed by local Papuans who were all smiling and keen to lend a hand carrying our bags to where we would be staying for the night. The locals were short, averaging maybe 5 foot in height, dark skinned with thick black hair and very lean. While some wore western clothing, more than half of the crowd were semi-naked and wearing traditional dress. Most of the elderly men wore a long wooden tube tied to their waist that had their penis hidden inside. This display of wooden endowment was matched with a spear and machete that seemed to be in every set of male hands above teenage years. It was a confronting scene and I could see that a few of my teammates were not sure how to handle it. After my time in Timor I had gained a good understanding of village politics, and felt at ease after shaking hands with a few of the bravest from the crowd.

Our bags were unloaded onto the ground and the mob of villagers all crowded in to grab something to carry. We were about to employ a number of them to act as porters so I'm sure they thought if they got in early and started working they would secure a job. We walked off into the village following our baggage, that a short time later was deposited in front of the village chief's house. It was nothing more than a poorly built western-style house with multiple colours of panelling used on the outside walls, and it was our home for the first night. It was late afternoon by the time we moved inside and found ourselves a space on the floor. The largest front room was immediately occupied by the village elders who were going to be discussing who should act as porters for our expedition.

A job as a porter for western climbing teams not only offers opportunity to earn western dollars but also has a level of prestige in the community. We would be hiring eighteen porters for the six-day trek through the jungle to base camp and with each porter planning to bring their wife and kids along we were going to be an entourage of forty-five people by the time we departed the following morning. To get to that point however, hours of discussion and many heated arguments needed to take place. Meldi had completed this process many times before and wasn't too worried by the elevated voices in the front room. He said by the morning all would be arranged and we would begin our first day.

We ate a simple dinner prepared by Meldi and his newly employed expedition cook and settled down for an early night listening to the villagers debate late into the evening. Mosquitos kept me awake for a while as I lay with half my body in my sleeping bag, trying to find a balance between getting eaten by mosquitos and sweating profusely inside. I reflected on how lucky I was to be able to be standing on top of a mountain in Alaska one week and then be sleeping in the Sugapa village chief's house in the middle of the West Papua jungle the next. We are so very lucky in the western world and have no excuse to not achieve absolutely everything we want to do. We have no roadblocks or limits on what we do in life, it's only our own conditioning and doubts that hold us back. I finally drifted off to sleep as rain started to patter the tin roof above me and drowned out the front room meeting that raged on.

A combination of rain, mosquitos, porter debates and a creaky old house made for a restless night and by morning I was ready to escape to the jungle. I picked up a local greeting, *A-Muk-A-Knee* which means hello and good morning, and as we exited the chief's house to the waiting crowd of locals I was saying it to all the smiling faces staring back at me. We were told that people from all the surrounding villages had arrived to be selected as porters for the expedition and it was the chief's job to choose who would be going. There was lots of politics involved when selecting porters equally from each village, and making sure no village missed out was essential to avoid unnecessary conflict between the tribes. This process of careful objective selection took two full hours and when the chief was finished we had eighteen porters plus their extended families ready to leave immediately. They rushed forward grabbing our bags, knowing that once one was on their head and heading to the jungle, the chief couldn't change his mind.

We were finally ready for departure and our first challenge was a 500-metre elevation drop down from Sugapa to the start of the jungle trail. Meldi had organised the locals who owned scooters to give us a ride down the hill to the trail head in under fifteen minutes. A shirtless villager rolled up in front of me beaming a big smile and gestured for me to get onto the back of his bike. I thought 'Why the hell not?' saying 'Amukaknee' as I shouldered my pack and climbed aboard. The engine of the scooter sounded ancient and I was sceptical it would even make it down the hill but he gunned the throttle and I gripped onto his lean body realising I was mistaken. We shot off at breakneck speed and I was second-guessing my decision to take the easy way down. As my driver dodged potholes and muddy sections like a professional, I started to relax and enjoy myself, realising that this guy knew his local trails like the back of his hand.

Ten minutes after leaving Sugapa we stopped at the end of the dirt trail at the point where it entered into the jungle. Travelling by foot was the only option from here on in. I thanked my scooter driver, slipping a few American dollars into his hand and wished him farewell. He swung the bike around and flew off back up the hill and out of sight. I waited at the edge of the trail for the rest of the team to be dropped off from their motorbike shuttles, some looking a little white knuckled. Once we were all together Meldi took the lead and we made our first steps into the jungle. I was wearing my new gum boots and with thick socks they actually felt fairly comfortable – when it started to rain, turning the ground to slop, I was happy with Meldi's recommendation. I pulled my trouser legs over the top of my boots to keep the water from pooling inside. After an hour of constant drizzling rain all but my socks were totally soaked.

I hadn't felt the discomfort of jungle travel since leaving the Army and most of my team had never set foot in anything like it before, so the first day being wet, muddy and uncomfortable was a big 'welcome to Papua' for all of us. A few hours after departing we came across two men in tribal dress blocking the trail. They had machetes and spears and told us we couldn't cross into their land. First I thought we had done something wrong to offend the locals but after the first exchange of words between Meldi and the villagers, and hearing money mentioned, I realised they were simply trying to cash in on westerners passing through their territory. A few rounds of negotiations concluded with a small cash payment and us being able to carry on down the trail. I was soon to learn that this was one of many negotiations to be had with the Papuans for the right of passage.

Travelling through heavy jungle can be uncomfortable at best and soul destroying at worst. While trekking along the trail, no foot placement was secure and I was stumbling around and tripping over constantly. I knew my body would adapt to the new environment eventually but on day one I was getting frustrated and slightly embarrassed in front of the locals every time I fell over. The path was overgrown with branches, leaves and vines at about western face height – the porters passed happily underneath with their shorter stature leaving the silly, overgrown foreigners to get slapped in the face. Overlay this scenario with soaking wet clothes and sweltering humidity and you have a recipe to test the limit of anyone's patience.

By the time we had stopped for a lunch break that first day we had encountered two more trail blocks by locals, one guy claiming he actually owned the mountain yet was happy to rent it to us after a small cash payment. Then another tribe was upset about none of their people being hired as porters, only to find out after a name check that there were three of his tribe already with us so we were okay to proceed once more. Our eighteen porters had brought along their kids, wives and whoever else wanted to come for a walk with them and when we were all caught up for lunch at a small village we counted forty-six in total. The sun was out for a short time over lunch, allowing me to dry my clothes and bathe in the morale boosting warmth. When we were ready to depart the rain started to fall once more and the porters wanted to renegotiate their wages before setting off. One more round of negotiations had concluded and as we made our way back into the jungle I smiled at Meldi and congratulated him on his patience with the locals. He smiled back and said, 'Just another day in Papua.'

The rain poured all afternoon turning the trails to mud; in some parts I was sinking up to the top of my gumboots and hoping it didn't spew over the top and fill them up. Waterfalls were forming along the trails and the terrain was getting steeper and more densely covered as we moved further and further away from the villages. It was close to dark when we stopped beside a river that had a partial clearing next to it and a small wooden structure built on its bank that looked like it was once a cabin. The porters all piled into the wooden shell and lit fires in the centre to warm themselves. We set up our tents in the pouring rain and tried to crawl into them without saturating the inside as well. The only way it could be done was to get naked outside leaving my clothes in a wet pile at the entrance, then crawl inside and dry myself quickly with a towel from my pack.

Part of the team was travelling slower than us up front and they didn't arrive until after dark. I could see their head torches coming through the jungle and making their way along the river to the camp. The team's cook made us all a hot meal for dinner. He was a local Papuan who had a smile on his face at all times and I was feeling guilty as I took the steaming hot food from him as I sat warm inside my tent. I thought to myself that I could easily make my own food to save him the hassle but then I remembered that this was probably one of only a few small jobs he would have this year and the small amount he would earn could see him and his family through with a year of food. The guilt evaporated as I took a mouthful of the noodle and stew combination on my plate. The heat from the food fogged up the air inside our tent so I couldn't see Vitidnan sitting less than a metre away from me.

• • •

I was awake early after a solid sleep and had a very stiff body; my legs were sore and I was fairly battered after all of my falls the day before. It was a cold night and a chilly morning as I contemplated the day ahead. The rain had stopped for a while and I could hear the porters talking among themselves in the old cabin a few metres away. I crawled out of my tent and went through the bone-numbing process of pulling on my wet pants and shirt, praying the sun stayed out so they could dry off. I walked over to the cabin, keen to see how all forty-six of our entourage slept in there. They had fires lit early in the night but now it was just smoke pouring out of the structure's many openings. I entered through the old doorway and was hit in the face by a wall of thick smoke that burnt my eyes and scorched my lungs as I took a breath. I dropped down trying to get below it and opened my eyes again but still the smoke was too strong for me. I could make out human shapes in the dark interior but had to turn around and exit before I was overwhelmed.

Somehow the locals had grown accustomed to the smoke and it didn't seem to bother them, it actually kept them warm and fought off the mosquitos and other creepy crawlies inhabiting the jungle. The team sat down together for a breakfast of fried chicken, noodles and snails, all washed down with a 'three-in-one' coffee, which is a small ready to mix packet of coffee, milk powder and loads of sugar. While a few of the team shied away from the snails, I thought they were actually quite nice and polished off my plate. We were ready to start our trek after breakfast but the porters hadn't budged from the cabin. Meldi entered into another round of negotiations with them and without too much delay a deal was struck and we were off again. I had tightened a pair of gaiters over my gumboots, which is a piece of canvas that covers the top of the boot to stop water or mud from getting inside. It was fortunate that I had because ten minutes after departure I sank knee deep into mud and had to drag myself clear using my trekking poles as leverage.

The trail was in worse condition than the day before and mud patches replaced the path where landslides had torn away the trees, leaving bare earth and rocks. Two hours further on we came across a river that was a raging torrent of white water spanning 15 metres across. Apparently there was supposed to be a bridge here from last season but it was plain to see that the floods had torn it out and carried it off down the river. The porters gestured for us all to take a seat as they dropped all of our baggage in one place and ran off to inspect some trees close to the bank. I didn't immediately understand what they were doing but as they pulled out two small axes and started to chop into a big, tall tree standing close to the river edge I realised what they were up to and couldn't believe it.

The porters took turns chopping the bottom of the tree and within thirty-five minutes they had carved it down to a precariously thin base and then took smaller more precise chops at the side facing the river. The sound of splintering timber sent the porters running for cover as the big tree trembled and hung in the air for a split second as if suspended in time. It then began to fall, slowly at first, and then building up speed it fell across the river and shook the ground under our feet as it struck the earth and settled deep into the muddy bank on the other side. I was looking at a man-made tree bridge, half a metre wide and stretching the entire length over the river. A porter scrambled across first and behind him he dragged a few lengths of a vine. The vines were twisted together and tied off at waist height across the span of the bridge to act as a handrail.

This resourceful scene made me think about the West Papuans' close neighbours in Papua New Guinea. Similarly to our porters, they could adapt and overcome any obstacle the jungle would throw at them. In 1942 during the Japanese campaign for the Pacific the local tribes of New Guinea saved countless Australian soldiers' lives on the Kokoda Track. They evacuated our injured soldiers on stretchers across seemingly impassable jungle and obstacles and never left a patient's side until they were delivered to safety.

I climbed up on top of the fallen tree and tentatively made my way across, smiling at our porters who beamed with pride and smiled back. I was offered a helping hand on the other side, which I took, and once down I stood back to watch the rest of the team make the crossing without incident. Once we were all across and before we got too cold from standing idle, the march started and we were off.

We stopped for lunch at a small clearing and the porters lit fires for us to keep warm. We were all soaked to the bone and the cold temperature that day was adding to the risk of hypothermia. I stood inches away from the smoking fire as we rested. The sun came out for a short time before the clouds closed again and the sizzling splatter of rain began to fall on our fires. After a short break, long enough to eat some snacks and guzzle some water, we were off again, but not for long. We hadn't gotten far when the porters decided they had worked enough for the day and wanted to camp. We didn't have much choice in the matter but to be honest I wasn't too upset about the early end to the day. It had been a gruelling six hours of mud, vines and rain and I was happy to set up my tent, peel off my wet clothes again and crawl inside to get warm. The porters had performed well, and even though we halted two hours earlier than planned, there wasn't much protest from the team; we were all battered and needed the rest.

I awoke on day three to blue skies and a slightly warmer morning. The rain had stopped halfway through the night and hadn't started again by the time breakfast came around – another delicious meal of fried chicken and noodles washed down with some of the sweetest coffee I'd ever tasted. With no protest from the porters we were off early and breaking trail into the jungle. We managed three hours of sun before the clouds closed in and the heavens opened up, dumping torrential rain on us and leaving me soaked to the bone yet again. The jungle we passed through was the thickest and muddiest of the expedition; it was unforgiving. Knee-deep slop full of branches, vines and leaves mixed with countless inclines made it physically and mentally frustrating. Every few minutes I'd hear a member of the team either fall over or curse out loud as they were caught up on vines. I was trying my best to not get overly frustrated but as the hours ticked by and the terrain remained extremely challenging I was on the edge.

At one point we came to a section where the earth had eroded leaving a few metres of exposed roots from the enormous trees above. The roots were covered in a light green moss and small jungle flowers. We had to descend into the roots and pick our way through the damp labyrinth like a scene out of the *Lord of the Rings*. It was a beautiful moment and I had to stop and take a picture of the amazing root formations, knowing I'd probably never see something like it ever again. The day came to an end eight hours after beginning and we had covered the most distance so far – we had gained 700 metres in elevation through some bad-arse jungle and seen some incredible nature. I was ready for bed immediately following a hot meal. My legs were stiff and sore but I could feel my body slowly starting to adapt. I had only fallen over a handful of times throughout the day and I was determined to remain standing from sun-up to sundown the following day.

By 10 am on day four the rain was pelting down again and the environment had changed drastically. We had crossed from the thick jungle to muddy marsh land where grass and shrubs densely covered the ground. Every step forward was a struggle; the terrain was draining us of our energy as we were sinking shin deep into the marsh. We were all finding it difficult and the progress throughout the day was slow. By early afternoon we had a break in the weather and the clouds were beginning to clear. As they parted, up ahead on the horizon I could make out some grey jagged cliffs of a mountain range, and as they cleared I made out the tallest, most imposing peak: it was Carstensz Pyramid. The excitement of seeing the mountain for the first time gave me a surge of energy as we trudged onwards. I was continually stumbling while trying to keep my eyes on the summit for the remainder of the day.

We decided to camp after only six hours due to how tough it was going through the marsh land. The porters erected themselves a log shelter with some tarps over the top and then lit their smoky fires underneath for warmth. We set up our tents and sat down to an early dinner with the mountains still visible on the horizon. The peaks were still two days' hike away and I knew we were a long way from the summit, but I couldn't tear my eyes away from the view. The sharp edges of the rocky summit stood proud with the fading sun casting light onto the steep grey slopes leading to the top. I was daydreaming about climbing those ridges and was starting to shiver from the cold by the time I pulled myself away from the horizon and crawled into my tent. Vitidnan was already curled up snoring and as my head lay down on my small inflatable pillow I joined him within seconds.

Day five felt like groundhog day with endless marsh land and slow progress towards the mountains in the distance. Vitidnan asked me to do some filming for him so after a quick lesson in filmmaking I trekked beside him most of the day, trying to get the right angles and get some good footage. He hoped to make a documentary of his seven summits to inspire the people of Thailand to go out and have adventures. The more time I was spending with him the more I liked him. He was a humble and genuine guy who never complained; even when I noticed him hobbling with an obvious sore knee he simply replied 'It's no problem at all.' It was an eight-hour day of rain, swamp and frustration but every time the clouds cleared enough to see the mountains the frustration disappeared and I was grateful to be there suffering through the mud.

The porters didn't want to move an inch on the morning of day six. Clouds had descended onto the mountains and they told us it was a sign that the mountain gods didn't want us to go up that day. I think it could also have been because it was bone-chilling cold and they wanted a sleep-in for a few hours! Either way, after a round of negotiations and a ritual prayer to the gods we were on our way. The sun stayed with us for the morning but around lunchtime the rain began to fall and it didn't quit. We were ascending into rocky outcrops at the start of the mountain range, and following some exposed ridges, found a lovely cave to shelter us from the weather for lunch. I was trekking with Vitidnan again and it was late afternoon when we came over the top of a ridge and saw the mighty north face of Carstensz rising up from a small turquoise lake, next to which we would be setting up our base camp.

Upon laying eyes on the lake Vitidnan started to cry. He is a very spiritual man and he told me that as we were walking together he had been performing silent meditations. During one of his meditations he said he had seen a vision and heard a voice. He said the mountain had spoken to him saying, 'You will do this for your King,' and also that he and I would do something big together one day. Vitidnan carried a picture of his king to the top of Everest and the other mountains he summited and took these visions very seriously, so as we descended into base camp he was crying happy tears, while I walked beside him feeling slightly awkward offering up my Aussie words of comfort, 'We will be sweet mate.'

• • •

Our base camp was erected 20 metres from the lake on a flat, rocky surface and surrounded by exposed rock walls on all sides. The only place to go from where we were at 4330 metres was to start our climb up to the summit, or back down the mountain range to the jungle. The porters dropped off all of our bags and quickly descended to a big cave a couple of hours back down the valley where it was warmer, to wait for us to summit.

The team was feeling strong and we shared a hot meal together, congratulating ourselves on successfully finishing stage one. We decided to have a rest day the following day but be up at midnight for a 2 am departure. We would leave early to begin the climb in the dark during calm weather conditions, and hopefully be back down before the afternoon rain storms and clouds blanketed the area. Meldi told us there should be minimal ice on the route and that we would need to climb in gloves to fend off the cold. Climbing in gloves, especially on a technical rock-climbing route, isn't my favourite thing to do. To combat this I had modified my gloves by cutting off the tips of two fingers and my thumb to allow me to feel the rock better but also keep the majority of my hand warm. This was something we used to do in the Army when we needed to be able to feel the trigger pressures in cold climates.

We all slept late on our designated rest day and during the middle of the afternoon we came together to go over rope safety procedures and using the ascender in a similar fashion as we did on Denali. Everyone was on the same page after a couple of hours of practice drills, then we were told to rest and prepare our equipment for the early departure. Meldi told us that at one point on the climb there was a cable traverse that we needed to negotiate. This was a steel cable between two high ridges with a few thousand feet of air below that we must clip onto and pull ourselves across. I hadn't done a traverse like that before and I was excited to try it. I was going to climb light, knowing that every extra kilogram of weight added huge amounts of effort the more vertical it was and the higher we went. I planned to only take 2 litres of water, some snacks, a warm jacket and a spare pair of gloves. Light and easy instead of heavy and hard was my plan and as I settled into my sleeping bag for a few restless hours of sleep I pictured the climb in my mind and practised everything I needed to do to get back down safely.

Vitidnan's head torch burst to life and it felt like I had just closed my eyes; I thought it couldn't possibly be midnight, but it was. I could hear the others rustling around in their tents getting ready and as I watched my breath transform to fog in front of my face I knew it was going to be a cold start. It took us two hours to get dressed, eat some food, fill our water bottles and be ready to move off together by 2 am.

It was bitterly cold as we started our walk towards the base of the cliff – I decided to leave my big jacket on until I warmed up. At the bottom of the sloping face we organised our gear, packing away jackets and securing head torches for the first part of the climb that was still in darkness. When I first laid hands on the rock it was cold yet grippy to the touch and as I started to ascend behind Meldi I quickly fell into a smooth rhythm of climbing. Good footholds and handholds were abundant, making it an enjoyable scramble up the first cliff. My fingers were cold and going numb from the rock, forcing me to stop every ten minutes and shove them into my pants to warm them up between my legs.

Looking down I could see a trail of head torches following up behind me and in the windless morning all that could be heard was heavy breathing, the occasional clink of a carabiner against the cliff and the sound of shoes scaling rock. I was in the zone with acute climbing focus as the first light of dawn began to break on the horizon. We all came together at the top of the first ridge for a drink and a snack after three hours of solid effort. There were smiles on everyone's faces as we rested and watched Meldi lead the next steeper section of the climb, requiring a fixed rope for safety. Similar to Denali when we used the fixed lines up the head wall, I clipped into the rope with my ascender on a short lanyard and had a second lanyard with a carabiner clipped in as a back-up. The ascender also doubled as a handle I could pull on if I was unable to find good handholds on the more technical sections.

I really enjoyed the steeper section and I didn't need to use the ascender as a handle at any stage, finding decent hand positions as I went. It was a harder section to climb but the sun was up and it opened up my field of vision to plenty of possible footholds and handholds, and there were also good rest spots along the way. At certain points I found myself on fingertips and tippy toes with adrenaline surging into my blood. The fear of falling flashed to the surface and I had to control my emotions or it would lead to shaking, freezing in position and possibly falling. When I found myself in those positions I took a deep, slow breath, gripped with my fingers as if my life depended on it and forced myself to move. Freezing and not making a move is when things go wrong. It didn't matter if the move I made was the right one or not, I just needed to keep calm and keep moving and it almost always worked out okay.

The top of the fixed lines arrived at the top of the ridge, the same sharp grey ridge that I was staring at from two days away as we made our way through the jungle. While standing on its razor edge, facing up towards the summit ridge of Carstensz, I looked down thousands of feet to my right and thousands to my left. The formations of rock we were standing on were intimidating yet incredibly beautiful. Clouds that were surely to bring the afternoon showers were still many kilometres away in the distance, leaving clear skies and dry rock basking in the mid-morning sun. The temperature was warming up and I was climbing in my windbreaker, beanie and gloves, putting the extra layers away in my pack.

We scrambled along the ridge making steady progress towards the top. It was an easy traverse allowing some free-flowing conversation among the team. As we moved around a particularly jagged section of the ridge it came to an abrupt end where the cliff fell away beneath us exposing 1000 metres of rock face straight down.

We had arrived at the traverse Meldi had mentioned the day before, a fixed steel cable stretching 10 metres across between two high points of the ridge. This was our last big obstacle before the summit and it was going to take some time for us to navigate across it safely. We had to complete the crossing one at a time so we didn't overload the anchors of the cable. I wasn't feeling nervous or afraid as I stepped up but as I clipped my carabiner onto the cable and sat down in my harness letting it take my full weight, I was instantly anxious. I came from an old-school way of thinking that for something to be strong it needs to be big and tough so when I'm sitting on a lanyard that's 3 millimetres thick and 10 millimetres wide I instantly have doubts. I knew the science and I told myself the small lanyard could easily hold a truck but I still gripped the cable ready for it to fail at any moment. I eased back into my harness and took my first pull across the line, feeling my feet fall away from the edge and hanging in the void with a 1000-metre drop below me.

People always say don't look down but for fear of missing out I always do. Below me the cliffs fell away into the valley and I could make out the edge of the turquoise lake where our base camp was located. Slowly I pulled myself hand over hand towards the other cliff staying calm and keeping a firm grip on the cable. It felt like minutes but was only seconds before my shoulder nudged the cliff as I came tight to the other side releasing one hand from the cable and securing a handhold on the rock behind me. I scrambled up to a secure area and unclipped myself, feeling the rush of relief and adrenaline as I stepped away and took off my pack to await the rest of the team. Everyone managed the crossing well, a few slower than others, and only Nicole seemed to have a little freezing moment while in the middle of the cable but was talked around and finished the job to her credit. Conquering fears while in that sort of position is an incredible achievement and the rest of us were happy to see her safely across.

The final ridge to the summit was a scramble over sharp rocky edges with drop offs on either side, and eventually after another steady hour of moving upwards there was nowhere left to go. The ridge formed into the summit and as I pulled myself on top of the last boulder, noticing the ground falling away on three sides, I realised I was standing on top of Carstensz Pyramid. It had taken us almost eight hours of climbing to reach the summit and although I was physically tired, my mind was clear and my breathing was steady. We all hugged each other as we took turns on the top taking pictures for our family and sponsors back home. The view was incredible with grey rocky mountains all around us and small turquoise lakes filling the valley below. In the distance, from where we had come was the thick green jungle with the orange, grassed marsh land filling the space in front of it. Vitidnan cried as he held a picture of his king above his head and sung his national anthem. It was a moving moment and I asked him if it was okay for me to get a picture with his king as well and he gladly agreed. A final group photo of us all crammed onto the small outcrop of the summit concluded our time on the highest point of the Oceania continent.

The descent was faster than our climb up but still took us four hours of down climbing and rappelling to achieve. The traverse across the void was quicker the second time around but as I moved along I maintained total focus, knowing that any slip or fall from one of these ridges would be fatal. Clipping into the fixed line and rappelling down the steep section was great fun. The scary parts where I had been on fingertips and tippy toes, bounced past in seconds as I slid down the line. By the time I had unclipped from the last anchor point and climbed down the final section of the route I was totally exhausted. The last team member stepped from the wall just as the rain started to fall and we all cheered and congratulated each other for a safe and successful day. It had been twelve hours since departure by the time we filed into base camp in the drizzling rain, chatting among ourselves and settling in for a hot drink and dinner in the guides' cook tent. I ate as much rice and chicken as my stomach could hold and drank water and tea by the bucketful. When I rose to leave the group my body had stiffened up and I basically crawled back to my tent, utterly broken from an amazing day. Vitidnan was writing in his journal as I unzipped our tent, looking up at me with tearful eyes as he recounted the day's event in his writing. I congratulated him again on his success, cleaned my face with a baby wipe, brushed my teeth and pulled my sleeping bag on top of me.

• • •

The rain fell all that night and around midnight I woke up to shouting and arguing outside. I could make out Meldi's voice mingled with what sounded like the porters. There was lots of discussion as the rain continued to fall and I thought to myself they probably downed a few sneaky glasses of whisky and were just arguing about something unimportant, so I drifted back to sleep. In the morning I woke up very stiff and sore yet refreshed, and I walked down to Meldi's tent where a few of the team were gathered around looking very concerned. As I arrived I was told what had occurred overnight.

Down in the valley the rain had caused a slab of rock to come loose in the cave the porters were camped in, the rock had fallen and crushed one of the locals, a sixteen-year-old boy. It had struck him on the chest and head killing him, sending the rest of the porters into a frenzy. One of them charged up the valley to our camp with his machete and spear to claim the life of one of the westerners for the life of one of theirs. He was wild with anger, slashing his machete on the ground and demanding one of us come out of our tents and surrender to him. In their culture it was simple, a life for a life – it was our fault they were up in the mountains so one of us needed to die. Meldi managed to calm him down after a while with a promise we would come down the valley in the morning to see the body and sort everything out. The porter knew we couldn't go anywhere so he agreed to the terms and went back to the cave.

Meldi was nervous about the whole situation but he told us we had to go down and try to sort it out. As we were talking a porter arrived from down in the valley, a different one from the previous night. He was there to escort us down to the cave to see the body and discuss the problem. Dean and I volunteered to go down with him; we had no idea what we were going to say to them and the whole scenario felt like a trap but there wasn't another option. The team couldn't get back through the jungle without the porters as even Meldi didn't know the way back, and even if he did we had to fly out of the porters' small village. The porters weren't going to move until something was done about the death of the boy. We brought along a two-way radio and told the team we would try and keep them updated if we were within range and waved goodbye to the nervous faces of the others.

Meldi, Dean and I moved off down the valley with our escort. I had been in tense situations before with the military but this was up there with the best. I was running all of the 'what if' scenarios through my head, trying to come up with solutions to problems that could occur. Dean and I were both nervous but kept it hidden as we walked and chatted quietly to each other. An hour later I spotted another porter standing up ahead. He was carrying a rifle, and as my heartbeat increased I was on high alert for an ambush. As we came closer and he was within ten metres of us I noticed it was a harmless air rifle and I felt a sense of relief. I think the guy was there for theatrics more than actual security or attack and he fell in beside us as we continued our walk in silence. We were at a point in the trail that cut in towards an overhanging cliff and I guessed the porter camp was nestled in under there somewhere. Our porter escort began to whistle out to the camp up ahead to warn them of our arrival, and I was once again expecting an ambush.

We crested a ridge in the trail and before us lay a collection of small fires and shelters under a big, overhanging rock wall. As we walked into their camp it was a mixed reception with some of the porters crying, some smiling and shaking our hands and the younger guys staring at us with hatred in their red swollen eyes. We were led to the scene of the rock fall and to the body of the boy, which was being cradled in an older female's arms. The slab of rock that had fallen down was massive, at least a foot thick and the size of a coffee table, it would have weighed 100 kilograms at least. They gestured for us to take photos, which I thought was weird, but I did as they requested and took some photos of the rock where it now lay. Dean asked to see the victim. He was a qualified mountain rescue ranger in Utah and had seen plenty of avalanche and rock-fall victims in the past and wanted to assess the body.

The ladies laid the body down on the ground and Dean leant over to check his condition. Blood was coming from his right eye and he had some clear liquid seeping from his ears, showing clear signs of head trauma. He put his hand softly on the boy's chest and noticed a very slight rise and fall. He then put his ear to the boy's mouth and felt a very soft breath; checking the pulse he confirmed what he suspected and looked back at me saying, 'This guy's still alive!' I couldn't believe it; we could possibly avert a disaster if the kid was still alive but we needed to make sure he stayed that way. We had a quick talk among ourselves about what our options were and after realising the jungle was impossible and that we were within three hours' walk of the Grasberg gold mine, we made a snap decision. We organised the porters to build a stretcher for the boy. We were to carry the kid to the mine and hopefully get help from the mine doctor and ambulance that they surely must have with 20,000 employees. We knew it was a risk after everyone telling us to keep clear of the mine, but we were out of options and needed to save this kid's life.

The rough stretcher was assembled in minutes and with some porters running ahead to clear the way and to alert the mine of our arrival we followed up behind, taking shifts carrying the boy over the rocky trail. Hours later we climbed the steep dirt wall bordering the mine, and as we stumbled over the top there were security guards and military soldiers already waiting for us. We placed the boy at the feet of the heavily armed guards who were in immediate discussion with Meldi and the porters. I couldn't understand what they were saying but I could easily see they weren't happy about our arrival. After a few minutes of protest the head guard notified someone on his radio and twenty minutes later a mine ambulance arrived. I was over the moon as they loaded the boy into the back of the ambulance and departed for the mine hospital; I thought we had pulled off a miracle rescue. As the vehicle disappeared into the pit we sat with the porters for a discussion about what to do next. We were supposed to head back into the jungle so we wanted to know if they were happy to lead us out and back to their village. They agreed to start the next day so Dean, Meldi and I made the slow hike back up the valley towards base camp, proud of how we handled the situation, but also thinking about what could still go wrong.

We arrived back to our nervous team who hadn't heard a word from us all day, as we were out of range of the small radio. We called everybody together into the cook tent and recounted the day's events, up to the porters agreeing to take us back to Sugapa. We then brought up some possible scenarios to discuss: the porters had seemed okay with letting one of us die the night before and we were now going to go back to their local village minus one young porter; how would the boy's family react when we got there? What if the boy died in hospital while we were travelling through the jungle and we arrived at his village to an angry crowd who had found out about his death before we did? These were our two main concerns and Meldi seemed just as worried as we were. Meldi called his boss Ferdinand back in Jakarta and told him the situation, he then asked about a possible helicopter evacuation that we all had the insurance cover for. Ferdinand told us there was no possibility of a helicopter rescue and that we were best to head into the jungle. He did not seem very sympathetic to our situation. Our only other option was to risk everything on the mercy of the Grasberg mine security again, leave the porters to go home alone through the jungle and surrender ourselves to the mine for a possible evacuation on their helicopter.

We decided to leave our final decision until the morning and all retired to a restless sleep under the ever-present cliffs of Carstensz. The porters arrived shortly after breakfast ready to take us back to Sugapa. Meldi called a few of the senior porters together and asked them about our concerns and what could possibly happen if the boy died in the next few days. The porters were silent for a while and when they couldn't give us a straight answer, it heightened our concerns about worst-case scenarios. We then held a meeting as a team to make our final decision with the porters waiting patiently nearby. Dean ran through the possibilities of heading back to Sugapa which we all readily understood and then the likelihood of being arrested and held in custody if we tried to go into the mine. Together we decided on the option with less risk of injury and death – to abandon our porter team and walk ourselves into the mine and take our chances.

Meldi made another call to Ferdinand to update him on our decision. He was very angry and told Meldi that if he went with us he would lose his job and never work again in the trekking industry. Ferdinand was only concerned about the risk to his company's ability to operate in the area if we violated the mining company's rules of no trespassing, and from what I could tell he didn't seem to care about Meldi or our safety. I really felt sorry for Meldi who was crying as he hung up the phone and told us, 'I have to go back to Sugapa with the porters.' We consoled him as best we could and then borrowed his satellite phone to make a few final calls before we parted ways.

I waited my turn for the phone and dialled Mum's mobile number back in Australia. Dad picked up at work, having borrowed Mum's phone for the day; the country twang in his voice was a comfort to hear. I gave Dad the rundown on our current situation as well as our plan to head into the mine to face possible arrest and told him to relay everything to Mum. I told him to ask Mum to contact the Australian embassy and tell them of our predicament just in case things didn't work out in our favour. Dad comes from a tough country breed where no problem is too big and in signing off he simply said, 'No worries mate, chat to you soon.' I felt some relief that Mum would be straight onto the embassy for us, and as we said goodbye to Meldi and the porters we took our first steps towards the mine and to whatever fate awaited us.

Together in single file we made our way down the valley towards the Grasberg mine. Two hours later we scrambled over the edge to the very same outpost we were at the day before, this time however, it was abandoned. We dropped our packs next to a shipping container and Dean and I set off walking into the mine, leaving the rest of the team behind. Not sure what our overall plan was, we were just going to alert someone to our presence and see what happened. We walked for twenty minutes down the winding dirt road and heard the rumble of the dump trucks ferrying dirt out from the bottom of the pit. We saw one coming towards us and stood to the side of the road on a pile of gravel as this enormous piece of machinery rolled slowly forward. When it was close enough we waved to attract the attention of the driver who looked bewildered spotting two white people in bright Gore-Tex jackets standing to the side of the road. The young Indonesian driver didn't stop but we noticed him pick up the radio to tell someone what he was seeing. Moments later a small water truck came by and stopped to let us climb into the cab.

The driver looked confused and didn't understand a word we were saying while picking up his radio to talk to someone. He placed the handset back and gestured to us that someone was coming and we should stay inside the cab. Minutes later a security truck pulled up with two armed guys who collected us from the water truck and put us inside their vehicle. The head guard spoke English and we directed him back to the shipping container and our waiting comrades. When we arrived back to the team the guard looked baffled by all the white faces staring back at him. We gave him the full story of what had occurred up to this point, to which he simply replied, 'You cannot stay, you must go.' We thought there might have been a language barrier but after careful explanation of our scenario again his answer was the same, 'You must go.' We didn't budge and he wouldn't help us, which led to another radio call, this time to 'the Big Boss'.

Twenty minutes passed before two more vehicles arrived crammed with military-style armed security guards and an older man who was Mr Nolti, the Big Boss. We all nominated Dean to be our negotiator; he was the most experienced climber and in my eyes was a born leader who had stayed calm under pressure this entire time. Dean went through the details again with Mr Nolti, who listened patiently before dismissing us instantly and telling us all to 'Go back into the jungle.' He walked off under our protests, climbed into his vehicle and drove away. The remaining guards started to unlock the container door and it was obvious they were going to lock us inside. Thinking quickly Dean said, 'Follow me' and five of us snuck around behind the container and climbed into the remaining security vehicle. We weren't going to steal it, we just locked ourselves inside in protest. After realising what had happened, the guards came to the driver's window, where Dean was sitting with the keys, and gestured for us to get out. We didn't budge, asking them again to please just help us get through the mine so we could go home. The guard picked up his radio and called for back-up, and shortly, three vehicles pulled up loaded with security guards and soldiers. Mr Nolti appeared at the window holding a crowbar, he paused for a split second to see if we would get out before he smashed in the driver's window, where two guards grabbed Dean, dragged him out and threw him to the ground. We were all pulled out of the vehicle, shocked with the sudden escalation of the situation. Things were going from bad to worse, as one by one the entire team were shoved inside the container. The lock slid shut behind us with a metallic click and the vehicles departed one at a time, leaving a single soldier to guard the new prisoners.

There we were, ten of us, all crammed into a small shipping container that had one door and two small barred windows. The guard unlocked the door just on dark in order to let us perform bodily functions, knowing that we were stuck between a jungle we couldn't go into and a mine he would stop us from entering. He carried an F88 Austeyr, the very same rifle I had used in the infantry. These guys were not normal security guards, they were guns for hire who typically had no rules of engagement to stop them from doing what they liked. I lay awake on the floor, side by side with the others all night. We had multiple visits by soldiers on shift change, who would shine their torches through the windows and open the door to blow cigarette smoke inside to intimidate us. The door was opened at dawn again and as we crept outside to a chilly morning the guard was nowhere to be seen. I guess they were hoping we were going to just leave the way we had come but Dean and I simply asked each other how long do we wait until we venture into the mine again to poke the hornet's nest.

We didn't wait long before the cavalry arrived back but this time brought with them a medic who was tasked to check our health one by one, writing down all the details. They had also brought us some rice and chicken that seemed a couple of days old, but I was starving and it tasted delicious to me. After our meagre breakfast and check-up we were left alone once more, in the strange scenario of being left without a guard but having nowhere to go. An hour later another vehicle arrived, this time it contained two white faces, which smiled at us as they opened their doors and said, 'G'day guys, what are you lot doing here?' What were the chances of running into two Australian tradesman in a place like this? They were workers at the mine and were having a lazy day driving around the back roads of the mine and accidentally found us. The drivers names were Tony and Lance and they were blown away by our story, while filling us in on the missing information that the guards weren't telling us.

The entire mine was currently under a labour strike that had turned violent. Roads down to Timika were blocked with boulders and burning cars and a few miners had been killed. The Free Papua Movement had combined forces with the strike to blockade the airport in Timika and mine management were on high alert to a full-frontal attack by the free Papua militia. They told us we couldn't have picked a worse time to try and enter the mine and this new information sunk the team's morale to an all-time low. The two Aussies had to leave, fearing for themselves if they got involved in our situation, but they did take numbers and emails of our family and friends in order to send them word that we were alive and well. I handed Lance Mum's email and shook his hand saying, 'Don't forget about us!' before they drove away.

We stayed in and around the container most of the day. Mr Nolti returned to try to force us once again to go back into the jungle. We refused to go and he wouldn't listen to our pleas for help. He got into his vehicle to drive away and leave us but Dean jumped in front of his vehicle, with the rest of us following quickly behind him. We encircled him, blocking his departure as he revved the engine and mock charged us before braking suddenly. He wasn't going to run us down, he just radioed for the hired guns, who arrived minutes later. This time fifteen soldiers forced us off the road and threw us back into the container, where the metallic click signalled the end to another stressful day. The team was tense, morale was low and with nothing but uncertainty ahead of us, it was hard to keep positive. I always think about worst-case scenarios in situations like that. I was young, freshly out of the military, and the worst case for me was to seize one of the F88 rifles and take off into the jungle, as a last resort. I was sure I could get to the coast and over a couple of weeks make my way to safety. Perhaps I was naive, but while in the container my far-fetched back-up plan kept my spirits up.

Day three of detention began with the opening of the container for bodily functions and the departure of our guard. Lance dropped by mid-morning with a box full of noodles and junk food for us and some more news. He had emailed Mum who replied instantly, thanking him for his email and asking him to pass on her message to me that she was calling the embassy and pressuring them to help get us out. He told us that ·management has been made aware that we were there as up until the night before they had no idea we had even arrived. Apparently the hierarchy had no control over the security forces and information was never readily shared between the two. The bad news was that management were unable to assist us at that time and told us to sit tight and not to do anything to aggravate the soldiers. Apologising he couldn't do more, Lance said goodbye, promising to return with any new information and more supplies very soon.

The day ticked by with the team breaking off into smaller groups to go over all the 'what if' scenarios, the kind of talk that usually does more harm than good to overall morale. Every now and again I'd see one of the team crying, letting the pressure of the situation get to them. I busied myself writing in my journal, making video blogs or playing around with a fire I had started to keep us warm. I wasn't going to crack, no matter how hard our situation became. The guards dropped off some more chicken and rice, which a few of the team couldn't stomach, leaving ample supply of the nasty combo for myself. I knew that maintaining my strength was essential if my worst-case scenario ever eventuated. Early evening we had a visit from an American named Alec, who was the engineering manager at the mine and a friend of the general manager. He was asked by the GM to come and see how we were all doing and report back to him that night. He was a great guy who fully understood the situation but was limited in his ability to help us. He told us the strike was getting more violent and evacuations were being planned just in case the mine was overrun by the militia. He promised to pass on everything to the boss before driving away, leaving us to our little container on the edge of the jungle.

Alec returned the following day and offered to take one of us up to his office to use the phone and computers to contact family and embassies. Dean was nominated and after collecting emails and numbers from all of us drove away with Alec into the pit. This was to become routine over the following days, Dean travelling off to use phones to try to secure our own rescue, returning late with no new information and nothing to keep the team from spiralling into despair. I kept myself occupied as best I could, actually making friends with one of the soldiers who delivered our daily portion of food. He was a young Indonesian guy who spoke decent English and we found common ground as we talked about the Army and the weapons we'd used. He even let me pose with him for a photo, our smiling faces betraying our emotions and the situation. We had been in the container a week and the strike had escalated to 12,000 people with five murders committed. Apparently a violent group of 3000 people were parading a dead body around in the street in front of the Timika airport, the very spot we needed to get to if we were ever going to get out of this place.

During late afternoon on day seven our luck changed at last. Alec arrived to tell us that the General Manager wanted us out of the mine. The constant calls from embassies and loved ones must have done the job and he was worried we could be caught and killed in the violence, causing an international incident. Alec was tasked with our evacuation and he had to do it covertly – the security forces weren't to find out about it as it was their jurisdiction and I think they were hoping to bribe huge amounts of money for our release. He only had room for six of us in his vehicle so two of the team plus Dean and I offered to wait behind for one more night while the others were evacuated. After the vehicle departed and it was just the four of us I felt lonely. Ten of us crammed into that small space had offered comfort and a security of sorts and I now felt nervous and vulnerable. The soldiers checked on us sporadically and when they did Dean would jump to his feet and meet them at the door or window to distract them from discovering that half of us were gone. None of us slept and as the hours ticked on towards dawn I grew even more nervous. A vehicle approached the container at 3 am and we didn't know if it was a returning soldier or Alec until we heard, 'It's me guys, let's go.'

We exploded to our feet cramming our few possessions into our backpacks and throwing them into the back of his vehicle. He gave us fluorescent mining jackets and hard hats to wear with the plan to get us through all the checkpoints dressed as western workers coming off shift. It had worked for the others, now it was our turn. He told us, 'Just pretend to be asleep and don't talk.' We drove off down the winding road and into the mine. We were stopped and questioned several times by security, who shone their torches over all of us pretending to be asleep. My heart was pounding out of my chest during these moments as I fought the urge to open my eyes and stare at the light. It was the longest three-hour journey of my life before we finally arrived at a group of small, cinder block homes that made up the mining village, where Alec lived alone in a small house. He ushered us inside and as we opened the door and entered his living room there was the rest of our team, freshly showered and smiling. Their weathered faces showing their stress but also relief at our safe arrival.

Alec's home sat opposite the airfield with the helicopters' rotors being easily heard as the sun crept over the horizon. Alec told us we were scheduled to fly out via helicopter after the first few loads of miners were flown out to Timika. He didn't want to have too many eyes seeing us as we departed. We had time for a shower and a fresh meal while listening to the choppers ferry workers from the mine then it was time for us to head to the helipad. We loaded up into two vehicles and drove two minutes down the road into the makeshift airport. We all gave Alec big hugs and thanked him for the risk he took to help a group of strangers before we were ushered through security by Alec's people, who were waiting for us. We were loaded onto the helicopter and I was expecting to see the security forces roll up at any minute to demand we get off, and crush our hopes of escape. It wasn't until I felt lift-off that I dropped my head and thought to myself, 'Thank you.' We were airborne and finally being carried to safety.

We flew up out of the mine and down towards the small town of Timika. I could see the burnt vehicles pouring with smoke around the airport as we descended and landed on the tarmac fifteen minutes later. We transferred to a domestic airline and within six hours we had gone from being trapped and scared in a shipping container to having an air hostess offer us ice water and peanuts. The reality took a few moments to sink in and as I looked around at the rest of the team I gave a nod and a smile to those who made eye contact. I let the tension in my body fall away as I placed my glass of ice water against my skin and relaxed for the first time in almost two weeks. I took a long drink of the cold fluid and swallowed the taste of freedom before turning to look out of the window and noticing my dishevelled appearance reflecting back at me in the morning light. I gave a nod to the guy in the window, who nodded in return and smiled back happily.

CHAPTER 10
MOUNT ELBRUS, RUSSIA

...

The nausea and fever hit me like a Mike Tyson body shot as I was hunched over in my cramped domestic airline seat bound for Russia. I must have picked up a bug in Sydney during my short time home or it could have been something I had acquired in the jungles of Papua that had laid dormant until now. I rushed to the toilet shutting the awkward door with haste and only just managed to pull down my pants before the gates of hell swung open. I stayed in there for what seemed like hours sweating and rubbing my belly to soothe the pain. Normally I'd be paranoid about the other passengers and what they were going to experience when I opened the door but I was in such agony it never entered my mind. I would return to that toilet many times during my long-haul flight to Moscow, until my face was gaunt with dehydration and my skin took on a yellowish hue.

This was the start of my expedition to climb Mount Elbrus, a dormant volcano 5642 metres tall, which forms part of the Caucasus mountain range in southern Russia. Elbrus is one of the seven summits and is the tallest peak in Europe, and though it is considered a non-technical peak it still claims on average thirty lives per year. These death toll statistics seem to be a recurring theme on mountains that are considered 'easy' and able to be climbed by anyone with trekking poles. I have witnessed first-hand the power of Mother Nature and good climbers with well-planned expeditions always prepare for worst-case scenarios. In my eyes, no mountain is worth dying for, especially one considered easy.

My flight connected in Hong Kong where I had a six-hour layover, and as I was shuffling through the terminal, feeling like I had been beaten with a cricket bat, two airport staff pulled me aside and sat me down. I had unknowingly walked through their body temperature scanner and had lit it up like a Christmas tree. They told me I was 39 degrees, 2 above normal, and asked if I was feeling okay. Afraid I could be detained I lied and said, 'I'm fine, just a little head cold.' They told me, 'You must see the nurse, we cannot let you go,' before checking my boarding pass and seeing that I was just transferring through and not staying in China. Upon realising this they told me 'Oh you can go, you not stay in China, thank you sir.' I guess if the plague I was carrying was destined for Russia they didn't care, so off I shuffled to find the nearest toilet and then lay shaking on the terminal floor until my next flight.

I arrived in Moscow totally exhausted and still suffering from cramps and vomiting. I barely scraped through immigration without being quarantined for carrying an infectious disease. It was tough getting approval to travel through Russia and I was only given a short-term visa for my expedition. I had organised all the logistics, permits and visa myself because I was trying to save costs on this trip to put towards Antarctica and Everest, which were going to cost a small fortune. I picked up my bags at the carousel before spending some time in the airport toilet. I was hoping to see the Red Square and other tourist attractions in Moscow while I was in town and had booked a small hotel in the city centre. To get there it was going to take a bus and two trains, which in my condition at the time was not going to happen without a serious incident. I crawled into a beat-up taxi at the front of the airport, an ancient vehicle out of the Cold War era, and gave my driver the address.

My stomach began to cramp shortly after departing the terminal and as the beads of sweat started to form on my face I hoped we were not travelling too far. One hour forty-five minutes and $120 later I crashed through my hotel door scrambling for the toilet and then collapsed on the floor in exhaustion. I guzzled water from the bathroom sink and then crept into bed mid-morning and pulled the blankets over my head as my body began to shake with fever. I woke up at 2 am the next day dehydrated, exhausted but feeling like the fever had broken. I had no more cramps but my body was stiff and sore from the vomiting and the lack of food. I picked up the hotel phone and ordered a large pizza, 4 litres of purified water, one Coca Cola, one chocolate cake and two cups of tea. I knew I had to get my strength back quick to be ready for the mountain so I ate, drank and slept as much as I could until I had to make my way back to the airport in the afternoon. I didn't see anything outside of my hotel room. I would have to return another time to see the famous sites.

I was feeling a lot better as I boarded a domestic flight to Mineralnye Vody, a small town close to the mountains and my starting point for the expedition. I had arranged logistical support through a local company who had a driver waiting for me as I exited the airport. He spoke no English and I had no Russian so we played a game of charades trying to communicate as we weaved through the small town, which has a population of 70,000 people and was occupied by Nazi Germany for six months during World War II. I was dropped off at a hotel built during a time when concrete and squares were all the rage and I'd spend one night here with a truck scheduled to drive me into the mountains the following morning. I spent the afternoon and evening eating everything in sight and doing my best to rehydrate. I checked over my expedition gear back in my hotel room, making sure I wasn't missing anything, before getting to bed early for some much-needed sleep.

I was up early after a solid sleep, feeling almost fully recovered, starving for food and needing water. The hotel breakfast was great and after I had consumed my body weight in eggs, toast, coffee and water I was standing at the front of the hotel waiting for my ride. A battered truck covered in rust and missing large sections of paint rolled up and came to a stop in front of me. I had doubts about its safety and reliability but in comparison to the other vehicles on the road it was a Rolls Royce. The Russian driver jumped down with a smoke between his lips, grabbed my bag while giving me a nod and threw it into the storage lockers underneath. He gestured towards the back saying 'Elbrus', which I guessed was my cue to climb aboard. As I pulled myself into the back there was already a group of climbers inside, all wearing multicoloured layers of Gore-Tex ready for the mountains. It was an Adventure Consultants expedition starting their trip on the same day as me and they were all in great spirits.

We journeyed together through the back streets of Mineralnye Vody and into the lower hills outside of the town, slowly ascending into the Caucasus mountains. We had been winding and bouncing along the mountain roads for six hours before I saw the shiny summit of Mount Elbrus appear, snow and ice covered its peak with the bottom remaining free of snow in the summer months, showing fields of grass and rocky outcrops. I love the first approach of an expedition whether it's in the back of a beat-up truck or walking in with donkeys, the first glimpse of the peaks always takes my breath away and I felt grateful every time for the opportunity to climb. The truck pulled up at the end of the dirt road where it had been washed out by rain and was now a mud field blocking our way. The guide from the Adventure Consultants team told me we had to hike from there but that base camp was only ninety minutes away over a small outcrop in the distance. The driver was vigorously unloading our packs as I hopped down from the back and he was already climbing back into his cab as I pulled my pack on and stood to the side of the road. I gave him a wave as he turned the prehistoric lorry around and with a nod and a point in the direction we had to walk he was gone.

I hiked along the muddy trail taking in my surroundings, breathing in the fresh mountain air and chatting to the other climbers. While I told stories and got lost in conversation time flew by and it wasn't until I saw the group of tents gathered together in the small grassy valley up ahead that I realised we had arrived. Base camp was a halfway home set up by local Russian adventure operators for anyone who was climbing Elbrus to use. I walked over to the biggest tent, assuming this would be the cook/

camp operators' hangout, and it was. Victor was a Russian mountaineer and had been a guide his entire life after discharging from the military in his youth. He now provided logistical support to western companies or solo warriors like myself, who came to climb Mount Elbrus. He was a tall, well-built man who was in his late fifties, had a handshake of steel and looked fighting fit.

Victor invited me in for tea, biscuits and a local food that was some sort of cracker with slices of pig fat on top. After only recently recovering from sickness I wasn't excited about the pig fat but I didn't want to be rude so I shoved a few large slices in my mouth. The greasy salted texture and the crunch of the cracker actually wasn't all that bad but a few extra spoons of sugar in my tea made it all the more bearable. Victor and I chatted about the military and mountains for the rest of the afternoon until a young Russian, fresh from Elbrus, poked his head into the tent. Valentine sat down beaming a smile while shaking my hand and showing respect to Victor. He was twenty-six years old and worked for Victor as a guide. Valentine was going to be my guide and climbing partner for our summit attempt. He was excited, looked mountain fit and I felt instantly comfortable in his company. We all sat and chatted for another hour as the sun set but when Victor pulled out the vodka I knew it was time for me to retire to my tent. Valentine said, 'We will leave tomorrow after breakfast for camp one.' Victor gave me an assortment of biscuits, chocolates and slices of various animal parts before he would let me go to bed.

I slept for ten hours straight through that night as my body was in recovery mode, and when I was woken up by Valentine just before dawn I felt like a new man. I still had a slight chesty cough but I felt energised and ready to get moving. Over a breakfast of coffee, more biscuits and some toast Valentine told me we would do one push to camp one without the typical load-carry. I was fine with his strategy – I had spent plenty of time at altitude that year so could handle less acclimatisation and I was feeling strong. Before we departed I quickly went through my gear and cut out any superfluous stuff I wasn't going to need. I didn't want to be carrying anything that wasn't vital, especially when we were not breaking up our loads. After culling some random items my pack weighed in at a comfortable 25 kilograms. I shouldered my pack, shook hands with Victor who gave us a big weather beaten smile and said, 'Good luck.'

Valentine set a cracking pace and within the first few minutes I was breaking a sweat and stripping down layers. He was young and excited to be climbing with me and asked a thousand questions about Australia, the Army and the outside world. Between panting breaths I'd reply in depth and we didn't stop for our first water break until two hours into it. After a short rest we were off again. I was definitely feeling the weight of my pack but I was happy with my fitness. I had to keep reminding myself to stop and look around because the mountains were absolutely incredible. The trail wound its way along rocky outcrops, through grassy valleys and small waterfalls created by the melting snow. As we crested a ridge my eyes fell onto Mount Elbrus with its snow-covered slopes reflecting the sun in the distance. It was a beautiful contrast of green valleys, rock formations and white snowfields that I hadn't seen on an expedition before. Elbrus didn't seem as intimidating as the other peaks but I knew not to underestimate it, it was still a mountain and needed to be respected at all times or you could pay the ultimate price.

Three hours and fifty minutes later, while carrying a full load and ascending 1200 metres, Valentine and I walked into camp one at 3800 metres. Throwing my pack down in front of a large hut I was very tired. Valentine turned to me with a big smile saying, 'Good climb, time for lunch,' and disappeared into the shelter. Camp one was a year-round military outpost and was utilised by climbing and skiing companies during the alternate sporting seasons. The camp contained four timber shelters that could each hold a team of climbers or a platoon of soldiers. Outhouse toilet facilities were built close by and there was an assortment of communications towers scattered among the rocks.

From the comfort and security of camp one I could look up at Mount Elbrus and see the east and west summits standing proud against the horizon, both fully covered in a blanket of snow with clusters of black rocks protruding through the veneer. It was a beautiful view but all I could appreciate at that point in time was a drink of water and a place to sit down. I followed Valentine into the shelter, which upon entering I could easily recognise as the kitchen and dinner hut. Inside was a small group of soldiers all holding onto AK-47s, who didn't return my smile as I came through the door to join Valentine, who was chatting with two other climbers and drinking lemon tea. He had prepared an extra one and slid it in front me as I sat down beside him. He patted me on the back and then began to tell his two friends in Russian all about me. They nodded acknowledgement and smiled as I heard him mention the Australian Army and I took a quick glance at the Russian soldiers who were now staring at me but had smiles on their faces and were nodding as well. The mutual respect shared between soldiers was something I continued to come across during my travels. I was also happy that Australia was an ally of Russia's at the time.

We all sat chatting together for the remainder of the afternoon, drinking tea, eating chocolate, biscuits, toast and a variety of spreads that I wasn't totally sure what they were made of, and didn't really want to ask. Valentine was my patient interpreter the entire time and as the sun set he told me that the next day we would go through our skills training to make sure we were safe to attempt the summit in a couple of days' time. I exited the dinner hut on stiff legs, grabbed my pack and hobbled into the adjacent structure made of timber and tin. I was given permission to sleep in the soldiers' shelter, which was empty apart from two sleeping soldiers in the corner. I quietly unrolled my sleeping pad onto one of the wooden bunks and lay down with a bottle of water beside me. I was grateful for the accommodation and to not have to set up my tent and sleep on the ground.

Even the soldiers changing over for their night shifts couldn't wake me as I slept for ten hours, busting at the seams for the outhouse as I staggered into the morning light. I had stiffness in my legs and back from the hike but I was feeling energised and healthy again. Valentine called me over from the kitchen and we sat down for some coffee and planned out our day's training. A short walk from the safety of the camp lay snowfields, crevasses and ice cliffs, a perfect location to practise all of the skills I'd need to get to the summit and back down safely. We first went through the basics of walking with crampons on flat snow and steep ice, followed by self-arrest procedure if one or both of us ended up sliding out of control down the mountain. The only way to really train for this was to go for a slide down the slope on my belly and practise flipping over and burying my ice axe into the snow to bring myself to a complete stop.

I had done plenty of this type of stuff before but it was always great to go over everything and it was more for Valentine's confidence in me to go through it all again. When climbing with a new partner we must know each other's abilities, strengths and weaknesses if a worst-case scenario presents itself. Over the following four hours we went through travelling together on a rope, crevasse rescue procedures, traversing and jumping over open crevasses, climbing ice walls and rappelling from ice screws down steep sections. If all went to plan I wouldn't need to utilise any of these skills but it was great to know we could do it when we need to and it gave me a confidence boost in our strength as a team. We retired to the kitchen for drinks and chats for the remainder of the afternoon, in preparation for an acclimatisation climb up to an outcrop called Lenz Rocks at 4700 metres the following day.

The morning skies were clear and the weather was perfect. After an early breakfast Valentine and I pulled on our packs, which only contained a big jacket, food and water, and started up the mountain. Following the well-trodden trail towards the glacier and the snow line, it was such a huge contrast to what I had climbed in the past – one minute I was walking on dirt and gravel and the next I was kicking steps into the snow and looking across at crevasses. We had continued an hour into the snow line before I told Valentine, 'Hold on mate, I'm putting my crampons on.' He seemed to be in his element but I wanted the added traction of the crampons for safety. He placed his on as well and after a mouthful of water and a piece of chocolate we were off again. We held a cracking pace, only stopping for short water breaks every ninety minutes until we reached Lenz Rocks, three and a half hours after departure, and gaining 900 metres in altitude.

Lenz Rocks is also the location of camp two for large expeditions who needed to break up their summit day into smaller sections. Our acclimatisation climb was going to be our test day to see if we wanted to try for the summit from camp one instead of setting up an extra camp at the rocks. Judging by how well we moved together I knew we would be attempting the summit from the bottom. We climbed an extra thirty minutes and passed camp two before turning around and making a very fast descent all the way back down. It was a great day; Valentine had pushed me hard but my fitness was up to it and we had climbed together confidently. As we took off our crampons and trekked back along the dirt trail he turned to me and said, 'We will go to summit from camp one.' I smiled, nodded at him and said, 'Absolutely.'

Another solid sleep and a rest day followed our acclimatisation climb. I was feeling great and spent the day making video blogs, eating and getting photos of my surroundings. One of the young Russian soldiers assumed he was the intention of my camera instead of the glorious mountains behind him and he raised his AK-47 and pointed it at me, yelling something in Russian. I lowered my camera and put up my hands in surrender as he became louder and more aggressive. Valentine came bounding out of the kitchen to see what was happening and after some hostile words back at the startled soldier he lowered his rifle and walked away. It was an intense moment and afterwards Valentine told me I had to be careful, the soldiers were suspect of all foreigners and incidents like that have escalated into violence in the past. That brought an end to my photography for the day and I spent the rest of the afternoon preparing my equipment and checking everything for our summit attempt, starting at midnight.

I managed a few hours of sleep before my watch told me it was time to get up and get ready. I was dressed, fed, watered and ready to step off by 12.45 am; not having to get ready inside a tent in a freezing environment made it so much easier. Valentine and I attacked the mountain from camp one at 3800 metres at the same cracking pace we had set on our acclimatisation climb. The conditions on departure were great but as we stopped to put on our crampons two hours later the wind had risen and was blowing strong and unrelenting, straight into our faces. We pushed on regardless and by the time we reached Lenz Rocks at 4700 metres the orange glow on the horizon was hinting at dawn and the wind was still increasing. We stopped for a drink and a chat about how to proceed. Conditions were not ideal but we were feeling great and the weather was manageable. We decided to push on.

The wind was roaring down the northern face of Elbrus and showed no signs of easing off, but we had pushed on past the rocks and past our turnaround point from two days before. The sun was up when we stopped to rest and we could clearly see the snow whipping off the summit and the clouds forming in the south heading our way. We were almost six hours into our summit attempt and approaching the saddle ridge that connected the east and west summits of Elbrus. We were heading to the west summit, the higher of the two by 20 metres, and at our estimated height of around 5300 metres we were only 340 metres below our goal, but in worsening conditions that could take us many hours to reach.

We sheltered together behind a small rocky outcrop to get some respite from the wind and looked at each other knowingly. I stared at Valentine for what felt like minutes before saying, 'What do you think, mate?' The weather was worsening by the second and I knew what he was going to say but he put it far more eloquently in that moment than I ever could. 'It's better to come to the mountains ten times and go home, than to come once and never go home.' I lowered my head in defeat knowing he was right and as a tear formed in my eye I turned my head back up to him and said, 'Let's get down brother.'

I took a long look up towards the summit before turning around and taking my first step in retreat. I hadn't turned around on a mountain before and the emotions inside me were a roller-coaster. At one point I was about to say let's try and go up again, but a well-timed gust of wind ripped the words away before they could materialise. Snow was getting whipped up around us in the gale-force winds and visibility was deteriorating rapidly. Valentine yelled out 'Follow me', as we detoured off our trail towards a small rocky outcrop. It was close to white-out conditions and I thought I was seeing things as a helicopter appeared in front of me. As we moved forward, on closer inspection I could see it was actually a badly damaged helicopter, lying slightly on its side, the blades bent and broken and its body crumpled. Valentine moved in beside it and grabbed the handle of the door, and I understood what he was doing, getting us some shelter.

The door cracked open and we fell inside pulling the door shut behind us and cutting off the roar of the wind. I saw the muzzle of the rifle in my face before I heard the Russian soldier yelling in my ears. The AK-47 was pointed at my head as Valentine yelled at the soldier who was yelling at us. It was my second time that week having a gun shoved in my face and I thought this time my luck had run out.

It was impossible for him to miss the shot, and as I looked at his trigger finger already moving into firing position I had that moment that others have written about, the flashback to times gone past, to family, friends and crazy adventures. The last thing I heard was Valentine yell something in Russian. I could have easily shut my eyes and turned my head away but I chose to stand tall with my eyes wide open, to meet what was coming as I have with everything in life. I thought, please don't let this be it. I noticed the howling wind outside, before the silence.

The seconds ticked by in slow motion before the rifle was hesitantly lowered and reality returned, Valentine once again using his charisma to calm the situation down before mistakes could be made. We were inside a crashed Russian military helicopter at 4820 metres on Elbrus. The soldier whose duty it was to protect the sensitive material on board lived inside twenty-four hours a day, so no wonder he was agitated. He accused me of being a spy, which Valentine laughed off, but also told us we were not welcome to stay and had to leave immediately.

We pleaded with the soldier as the storm raged outside, telling him we could die if he made us leave. Our concerns fell on deaf ears and as he got more and more aggressive Valentine said to me, 'We have to leave now.' We cracked the door, forced it open against the wind and stepped out into the chaos. We short-roped together for safety and continued our descent down the mountain. The wind slammed into our backs forcing us down the slope as fast as we could walk and chased us down towards Lenz Rocks. We noticed a few yellow tents camped among the rocks and ventured over to see if they could help us. When we were close enough we called out to the tent, which opened up and we heard the reply 'Hey lads, what are you guys doing out there?' I smiled at the familiar language and we both crawled into the vestibule to say hi.

The small area at the door of the tent was just big enough for Valentine and I to stick our upper bodies into, so we lay on our sides with our legs hanging out in the storm and our heads in safety and chatted to the climbers. We realised immediately that we wouldn't be bunking in with these guys; they already had three climbers jammed into a two-man tent and with all of their equipment it didn't leave much wiggle room. They made us a hot brew as we lay at their feet and told us they were hoping to summit that day as well but had to change plans and return to their camp at the rocks to wait out the storm. We sipped our brews and for those few minutes it took me to drink it I forgot about the storm outside and our turnaround from the summit. Reality came rushing back as Valentine gave me a nod and said, 'We must go down.' We said a big thankyou to the climbers for their hospitality and crawled back out into the storm, continuing our retreat.

We moved as fast as we could without compromising our safety – we still had to be on the lookout for crevasses and a slip by one of us at this stage of our descent could mean disaster. An hour after leaving the rocks the white-out conditions had lifted slightly and we could make out the bottom of the snow line in the distance. I could finally relax a little and I thought to myself that we were going to get out of this unscathed. The wind was still blasting onto our backs almost as if the mountain was forcing us off its slopes – the unworthy climbers who didn't have what it took to stand on top. Once the adrenaline had begun to wear off from the danger of descending I started to feel defeated; it was my first turnaround on an expedition and I wasn't sure how to react. I knew we had made the right decision but there was always the question burning in the back of my mind, what if?

The dirt and gravel at the end of the snow slope was visible up ahead and as I looked up to the summit, shielding my face against the wind, I noticed beautiful snow crystals being whipped down the mountain around us, reflecting the sunlight in an amazing display of nature. Valentine said to me, 'Look, Luke. Diamonds,' as he pointed to the crystals. I replied, 'We are rich, Valentine,' and he replied, 'We are rich because we are alive.' His words stuck with me as we trudged back into camp and I threw my pack and axe onto the floor of my hut and sat down to remove my boots. It had been almost eleven hours since we departed early that morning and it had been an emotional roller-coaster of a day, one that ultimately ended with us not summiting but being alive to tell the tale.

When I arrived in Russia my visa was granted for the expedition but on strict guidelines – I had to report and write down my name and passport details at every hotel I stayed in and I had limited days to attempt the climb. With the confidence of the naive I thought the number of days I was given were ample to get the job done, but as I sat in my hut defeated that night, adding up the days I had been in Russia and how many I had left before leaving, a gut-wrenching reality dawned on me. I could only give myself one more day to attempt the summit before I had to make a run for the airport.

I was caught with a tough decision. If I didn't summit the following day did I stay and violate my visa to finish the climb, which would guarantee me never being allowed into Russia again, or should I leave the country and come back another day? I didn't know what to do so I decided to let the weather dictate. If it was good when I got up I would attempt the summit again and let fate take its course; if it was no good, I'd decide then what to do. My alarm woke me from sleep and my ears immediately heard the sound of the wind on the hut's tin roof. The sinking feeling in my stomach was confirmed by the look Valentine gave me as he entered my hut. 'Sorry, Luke, weather is no good,' and Valentine dropped his head in a show of failure. I said, 'That's okay buddy,' and I gave him a big pat on the back, 'It wasn't meant to be this time.'

I walked out of the kitchen hut later that morning with a coffee in my hand, found myself a rock to sit on and stared up at the summit. It was obscured by cloud and snow and I knew that no-one would be summiting that day. I pulled out my small camera and recorded a short video blog in which I announced my defeat and withdrawal from Elbrus to the invisible crowd. They were tough words to say even to myself and as I watched it over and over again while sipping my coffee, I stared at the man in the video and told him, 'It's better to come to the mountains ten times and go home, than to come once and never go home. You will be back.'

CHAPTER 11

VINSON MASSIF, ANTARCTICA

...

Antarctica has been home to some of the greatest adventures of all time; many stories have told of feats of courage and endurance on the continent by some of the most stoic men in history. The early polar explorers would spend years in her frozen embrace, out of touch with the rest of the world, focused purely on survival and achieving their missions. I had read books growing up on Robert Falcon Scott and his South Pole Terra Nova expedition of 1910, where he spent almost three years striving to reach his goal. Upon finally making it to the Pole on 17 January 1912 he was struck by the reality that a Norwegian team under the charge of Roald Amundsen had beaten him there by four weeks. Scott's team perished on the return journey, paying the ultimate price for pushing the human body to its absolute limit in one of the harshest environments on earth.

These stories of human courage ending in tragedy might deter some people from venturing into these myth-making places but for me they always conjured up one question: do I have what it takes to do what these guys did? I was drawn to these wild places and when an attempt on Vinson Massif – the tallest mountain in Antarctica at 4892 metres

– became a reality in January 2012, I was jumping out of my skin to get down there. I was about to go where the pioneers of polar exploration had gone before me, men who forged a lifestyle as professional adventurers that allowed guys like me to follow in their footsteps over 100 years later.

I flew to the small town of Punta Arenas on the southern tip of the Patagonian region in Chile. The town's population was 100,000 varying greatly between summer and winter, with the warmer seasons inviting tourists and adventurers from all over the globe. Its location was used as a staging point for all kinds of tours, ocean voyages and Antarctic expeditions. I had signed on with Adventure Consultants, who were leading the expedition and had employed logistical support from ALE (Antarctic Logistics and Expeditions), a company that had the only large-scale operation capable of flying climbers, scientists and tourists down to the Antarctic. In the days of Scott and Amundsen it took years to reach the South Pole, but now a tourist could pay a small fortune, around $50,000, to a company like ALE, who could fly them to the Pole on a daytrip for a photo and a 'cup of tea'. Times have indeed changed and I wonder what the great men of polar exploration would think of it all.

I stepped off the plane with Vitidnan, my old Thai comrade from Carstensz, who was joining me on this climb. I had stayed in touch with him and we had become great friends since our saga in the jungle. We were met at the airport by Mark from Adventure Consultants, who was the lead guide and a local to Wanaka in the South Island of New Zealand. He had been to Antarctica on multiple expeditions and was a professional mountain guide who had grown up with snow and ice in his blood. Mark was a really friendly guy and we all got along great from the beginning, with the Australian and New Zealander banter breaking the ice for all of us. The rest of the team arrived shortly after with George and Stephen landing from Canada and Robert from the USA. We were a small international team all beaming big smiles and shaking hands. We loaded into a van, piling all of our duffle bags into the trailer, and made our way over to the hotel.

That night Mark took the team out for our first dinner together and our first briefing of the upcoming adventure. The wind was blowing steady and the temperature was cold as we walked through the historic little town that was founded in 1848, originally as a penal colony. We followed the cobbled streets down to the waterfront and made our way to a small restaurant that looked out over the ocean. Inside it was warm, friendly and bursting with conversation from the locals and travellers who were all enjoying the food and drink. We sat down and I immediately started to devour the fresh bread and butter that lined the table while the others ordered wine and beer. I wasn't interested in drinking plus I was starving and fresh bread was one of my favourite foods on the planet. Growing up in the centre of Australia we lived thousands of kilometres from the closest bakery so Mum made bread herself and that fresh bread smell always took me back to my childhood.

Over dinner Mark gave us a rundown on current events, weather conditions down on the ice and our plans over the next few days. We had to prep all of our gear and be ready to fly down to Antarctica at a moment's notice. ALE would find a weather window when the conditions were good for take-off from Punta Arenas, and good for when we landed on the ice runway in Antarctica. It all had to be coordinated precisely so we had to be flexible and ready to run to the plane at a moment's notice, day or night; night not being much of an issue as the sun stays up for twenty-four hours a day during the summer season, which was when we would be climbing. During winter however, the Antarctic is plunged into darkness for up to three straight months. I was buzzing after our first team dinner and couldn't wait to get on that plane and see the ice with my own eyes.

I didn't have to wait long. After two days of sorting gear and buying the bits and pieces I needed in Punta Arenas the call came through from ALE at 6.40 pm telling us to be at the airport ready for our flight by 7 pm. We had an open weather window but it was closing fast and if we missed it bad conditions were forecast for the following three days. It was panic stations as we crammed gear into duffel bags and piled into the waiting van. We made it to the plane right on time and we all climbed aboard the intimidating looking craft. The Ilyushin was a Russian-made cargo plane designed specifically for extreme weather conditions, and was the lifeline to the ALE base in Antarctica. It was a monster of a craft that flew in people, vehicles, fuel and food, and ferried out all human waste on the return journeys, urine included. My first thought upon seeing it was 'how the hell does that thing land on ice?' The inside of the plane was fitted with old passenger airline seats and as we were ticked off the passenger list by the waiting crew we all found a seat and settled in for take-off.

The temperature in Antarctica when we landed was going to be minus 20 degrees Celsius so we had to wear all of the protective clothing on the plane, ready for when the door cracked open. Hearing protection was handed out by the crew, and as the Ilyushin fired up her big engines, I quickly put them in my ears; the noise and vibration was deafening as we taxied to the end of the runway. This definitely wasn't a commercial airliner, and to be honest, I was happy about the discomforts, as it gave me the feeling that the adventure had finally begun. We roared forward and as the wheels separated from the ground, the safety, and the known, a big smile crept across my face. We were headed to the unknown and I couldn't be happier, my dream was becoming a reality.

Four and a half hours later we were descending towards the ice, the lack of windows on the Ilyushin only allowing views of the cargo plane's interior, and as the engines wound back and the wheels touched down we could have been landing anywhere. We came to a stop and the doors cracked open, letting the midnight sun beam through the opening. The freezing air forced its way inside, which quickly made us all zip up tight and pull our gloves on. I stepped into the doorway and stopped, allowing the glare to slowly fade and let my eyes adjust. The scene in front of me was an image that can never be described accurately with words, it's something that can only be witnessed and felt in real time.

Ice and snow were everywhere, deep blue under our feet forming the concrete-like runway the mighty Ilyushin had touched down on. In the distance, pyramids of black stone rose sharply out of the whitest snow I had ever seen, the bold formations in absolute contrast to the pristine whiteness of their surroundings. The air was crisp, clean and cold, and harsh on my throat as I breathed it in, my lungs never having sampled unpolluted, minus-20-degree air before. I stepped down onto the snow, which made a crunch under my boots, and as I took in the 360-degree view of Union Glacier and the surrounding Heritage Range it felt like I was on another planet entirely.

There was a gentle breeze blowing and it was more than enough to make me pull my puffy jacket tight around my face. I tentatively walked across the sections of blue ice and onto the thick snow piled at the edge of the runway. The landing strip itself is a true feat of human engineering that is maintained throughout the summer season by graders, trucks and personnel. Specific care is taken to safeguard the environment against oil and fuel leaks, and every winter the entire base is shut down and all human waste is flown out to South America. We were loaded into vehicles that were a mix between a normal four-wheel drive and a tank. The wheels had been replaced by belts similar to that on a tank, which gave the vehicle much more traction and manoeuvrability on the snow and ice.

It was a short drive to the dome tents, small structures and antennas we could see in the distance. At 3 am in the morning we pulled up at the ALE base. It was quiet while everyone slept but a staff member tasked with settling us in was up and greeted us as we stepped down from the truck. We were shown where the kitchen was, the designated camping areas and the toilet blocks. All faeces were collected in airtight barrels and flown out on return journeys inside the Ilyushin. Next to the toilets there were large white barrels full of orange liquid, these were the urine depositories. At night while camping in freezing conditions we would use 1-litre bottles to collect our pee and in the morning the urine barrel was where it would be emptied. All urine was then flown out to Punta Arenas for processing. The regulations around waste management were repeated to us multiple times; not even toothpaste was to be spat on the ground, it was to go into the barrels as well. It was great to see everyone doing their best to look after the environment down on the unspoiled frozen continent.

We erected our tents and crawled inside. My sleeping bag that was once overkill and made me sweat now proved essential in the harsh snowy expanse. The storms that were forecast and initiated our panicked departure from Punta arrived shortly after we bedded down. The wind picked up and the snow fell in large fluffy flakes covering the top of my tent. The adrenaline and excitement of the day had dissipated and I drifted off to sleep listening to the snow slide down the side of the tent like a mini avalanche coming to rest in a pile a few feet from my face. I awoke hours later to the same sunlight that was present during the night – the sun not going down was going to take some getting used to. It was 10 am, I was still fairly tired but my hunger forced me to my feet to go searching for the kitchen. The kitchen tent was for everybody at the base and ALE employed full-time cooks for the summer season, and what they had prepared that morning blew me away.

I walked into the kitchen after removing my big puffy jacket at the double-door entry, and inside the second set of doors was a warm oasis smothered in the smell of coffee and bacon. It was a free-for-all and as I loaded my tray and devoured bacon, eggs, toast, coffee and juice it was easily the best breakfast I had enjoyed in months. Nobody looked like they were holding back on the portion sizes; for many of us it would be our last hot meal before we ventured out into the wild white wilderness and battled against the cold. When it comes to surviving extremely cold environments extra calories are your friend so as I loaded my plate with helping number two there was not a hint of guilt present.

The rest of that day was spent reorganising gear into sled-loads and practising our rope-tying skills while wearing gloves and with big down mitts on. That last thing we wanted to get was frostbitten fingers while up on Vinson, so being able to do intricate tasks with big mitts was an essential skill. From the ALE base a number of small bush planes flew climbers, scientists, photographers and tourists out to destinations within flight range of Union Glacier. These flights had to be well coordinated and planned to current weather forecasting. No flights were heading out our first day at the base; weather conditions were average and everyone was held in limbo waiting for the weather to clear. After dinner I found myself standing at the edge of the base, staring out at the vast white desert. Facing away from the mountain range the ice stretched as far as the eye could see and then much further. The sheer scale of Antarctica was mind-blowing and to think about the early explorers hauling all their supplies for many months out there in the wild was extremely humbling. I hoped I could live up to their courageous example of what humans were capable of.

I slept for eleven hours that night and woke up to a cold morning feeling refreshed and ready for anything. The weather was slightly better with minimal snow falling and the winds had calmed. After another delicious breakfast we ventured out onto the glacier to practise moving together as a team dragging sleds, wearing crampons and using snow shoes. We then spent time practising crevasse rescue procedures in preparation for anything that might happen during our ascent of Vinson. The Antarctic ice in places can be 4 kilometres thick and the mountains that we can see, including Vinson Massif, are actually the top of the mountains protruding out of the ice shelf. The constant movement of the ice causes fractures and huge crevasses, especially in the glaciers sloping down from the mountains. The harsh environment made our ability to deal with crevasse rescue all the more important and we spent many hours going over the drills until Mark was satisfied everyone had a good understanding of what to do.

Halfway through dinner that night an ALE staff member came over to our table and said, 'Get your gear guys, your flight to Vinson base camp is on.' We exploded into action, and I yelled 'Game on lads!' simultaneously devouring what was left on my plate and dismantling my tent with lightning speed. I heard the Twin Otter's propellers start to wind up and we loaded our gear into the back of the small craft and climbed aboard. The little Otter roared to life and all of us were wearing big smiles as we became airborne and watched the small clusters of tents fall away below us. The white horizon expanded in our view, the higher we climbed the more ice and snow we could see in all directions. The black tips of mountains exposed to the wind could be seen clearly along with the gaping black cracks of the crevasses. The mouths of large crevasses lay open, gaping wide, ready to receive their next meal; smaller ones were covered with a thin veneer of snow, like a hidden predator behind a light blue veil, still big enough to swallow a climber whole.

The fifty-minute flight flew 151 kilometres over some of the most incredible scenery a human being could ever witness. It was an unspoilt spectacle of Mother Nature and its intimidating beauty made me feel very vulnerable yet privileged at the same time. We descended towards the Sentinel Range with the highest peak, Vinson Massif, standing proud in the distance. The skis attached to the Twin Otter touched down gently at a flat point on a large glacier; the pilot's skill on landing reminded me of the bush pilots in Alaska. These guys were a rare breed and I was very grateful for their expertise. We unloaded our gear while the pilot stayed in his seat and kept the propellers spinning. Once we were clear he spun the aircraft around, pointed the nose downhill and roared away. We all sat huddled around our pile of packs and sleds watching the tiny plane disappear on the horizon, the roar of the engines was replaced with the deafening silence of the Antarctic.

We organised our gear and dug some flat areas of snow to erect our tents – it was close to 9 pm and I was ready for bed. I kept my tent open so I could stare out at the ice in the distance until the drop in temperature forced me to close it and zip up my sleeping bag tight around my face. It was minus 25 degrees Celsius which meant having my water bottle and pee bottle in my bag with me so they wouldn't freeze solid overnight. I also needed to have all of my batteries in with me as well, the cold would empty a battery of power in a single night, so I kept them all in my pockets close to my body. I drifted off to sleep in a cocoon of comfort, surrounded by a deep-freeze wilderness.

It was cold but I managed to get a great sleep and trying to use my pee bottle halfway through the night without spilling it into my bag was my biggest challenge. Our first day at Vinson base camp was a rest and acclimatisation day. We were camping at 2100 metres and the following day we would move up to our low camp at around 2800 metres. We busied ourselves preparing our sleds for the climb, and for lunch Mark whipped us up some toasted ham and cheese sandwiches. We had a practice sled haul, moving together as a team up the glacier to the start of the open crevasses and back down again. Everyone was moving well, we had gelled together as a team and we were all keen to get climbing the following day.

Getting up early didn't have the same meaning in Antarctica, as the sun was always shining when it wasn't hidden behind the mountains, and if it was 6 am or 6 pm it all felt the same to me. Sleds were packed, team gear was split among us evenly and everything was tied down ready to haul. After some oatmeal and coffee we roped in together and began our climb up to low camp. It was freezing when we were stationary, but once we started moving and hauling a sled, I warmed up quickly and had to take off a couple of layers. The sun was shining bright, it was a beautiful day and as we worked hard making slow progress up towards Vinson I was having the time of my life. We stopped every ninety minutes for water and a rest and I made sure I grabbed a few pictures every time we did. Mount Tyree, the second highest mountain in Antarctica at 4852 metres, and Mount Shinn, at 4661 metres, were looking incredible as we trudged into our low camp position, seven hours after leaving base camp. It was a tough day carrying packs and hauling sled but we had all done really well, moving together at a steady pace without any injury or incidents.

By the time we had set up tents and enjoyed a meal together it was 11.30 pm and the sun was about to disappear behind the mountains. It was a comfortable minus 15 degrees but when the shadow of Vinson descended on us we were in a deep freeze again. I crawled into bed stiff, sore and happy with my fitness. If I wasn't fit and able to do this stuff comfortably I would miss out on so much of the beauty around me. I could see at times when other climbers were head down, panting and struggling to move with efficiency, that it became a totally different expedition for them. It becomes one of physical struggle and mental endurance, an internal battle instead of wonder and enjoyment in the beautiful Antarctic. In all likelihood none of us would ever get to see this place again and we needed to be so grateful we even had the chance to be there in the first place. I was proud of the hard training I had put in back in Thailand and in Sydney and I made a conscious decision while lying there in my bag to always be at the top of my physical game so I could enjoy every little bit of this incredible world.

The sun returned and hit my tent at 11 am. I had enjoyed another perfect sleep and the altitude wasn't affecting me to any great extent. I had a small headache when I woke up but that was due to dehydration rather than altitude and a few big gulps from my water bottle would remedy it. The frost on the inside of my tent began to melt and drip on top of me so it was time to get myself dressed and crawl outside. The temp at night was minus 25 degrees but as the sun warmed the tent it was a comfortable zero, which made getting ready much easier. Today we planned to do an acclimatisation load-carry halfway up a section of the climb called the Headwall. It was a steep ice incline that our high camp would be nestled on top of. The ice slope was fitted with fixed lines earlier in the season, similar to the fixed lines on the steep sections of Denali and Carstensz. This would give us an added degree of safety if we happened to fall while climbing the wall. We enjoyed a brunch together and everyone was all smiles and feeling strong. Vitidnan was making his documentary again and he asked me, 'Can you film me climbing the Headwall brother?' I said, 'Absolutely mate, happy to help out.' We came up with a game plan to capture the best angles and as we began our climb that morning I was carrying a few extra kilograms of camera equipment, and it dawned on me that I had become a mule.

We were carrying packs only, which meant that the gear from our sleds that was comfortable to haul was now crushing down on our shoulders. It made it much tougher going and by the time we had made it to the bottom of the fixed lines I was panting and sweating. I was trying not to sweat too much due to the possible hypothermia when I cooled down, so I took off another layer of clothing before clipping into the fixed line and starting up the Headwall. It was slow progress upwards taking three steps up then taking three deep breaths to recover. The higher I climbed I remembered to take the time to look around, as the new elevation had opened up a staggering view below me. I kicked myself a small ledge in the snow, pulled out the camera equipment and took some footage of Vitidnan ascending the wall, with an epic view of the glacier and surrounding mountains below him. My voice came out clear on the video as I whispered to myself 'Bloody amazing'. I thought I was a real Steven Spielberg until my fingers began to go numb and I started to shiver. I placed the cameras away, put my gloves back on and started up again, moving a little faster to try and get warm.

When we were 300 metres higher than our low camp and almost to the top of the Headwall, we stopped at a big, naturally forming rock ledge for a drink and some lunch. We cached our equipment in a small snow ditch and buried it. We would retrieve it again when we made the final push to high camp in the coming days. Once everyone was rested we clipped back into the fixed lines, except this time we were facing downhill and rappelled down feeling lighter and moving a lot faster. The trick to fast rappelling was to always watch your feet and never get out of control. I was almost running down the face making sure my crampons were clear of my pants and being placed down correctly. Growing up in North Queensland and spending weekends running down dry mountain river beds, hopping from rock to rock with ever increasing speed, had prepared me for climbing like this. I was in my element and was back at the bottom within thirty minutes, a section that had taken hours to climb safely was super fun to come barrelling down. My heart was pounding as I unclipped and sat down in the snow to wait for the others.

The weather was forecast to be windy the following day but as we crawled out of our tents with the warming sun the next morning it was looking fine. Mark made the call for us to push up to high camp that day if we were feeling up to it. He was trying to avoid getting caught at low camp in bad conditions and wanted to secure our camp up high, to be ready for an attempt on the summit. We all agreed to push on so after brunch we were loaded up again to make our way back up the Headwall. We moved quietly and confidently together to the base of the wall and up to our rest ledge from the day before. My legs were fatigued but moving well and we loaded the extra kilograms of supplies from the cache into our packs and moved off again into new territory. The climbing was incredible and every time I glanced around I had to pinch myself to believe that I was actually in Antarctica and not simply dreaming. The bad weather that was forecast had not eventuated and we had clear skies and perfect conditions as we made it to the top.

We rested for a short time before shouldering our loads again and pushing across an easy traverse to our location for high camp at 3750 metres. We had gained almost 1000 vertical metres in six hours of climbing, a great performance from the team. We were all very tired by the time we had erected tents, built snow wall protection around them and enjoyed a meal together. I crawled into my sleeping bag at 1 am with the sun still smiling at me outside. We would no longer be thrown into the shadow of Vinson, we were now sitting high on her shoulder and if all went to plan would be sitting high atop her head very soon. The temperature dropped to minus 25 degrees Celsius throughout the night but I slept like a baby, wrapped up tight in my down sleeping-bag cocoon. I poked my head out of my tent the next day to see the summit of Vinson covered in mist and what Mark described over breakfast as 'lenticular clouds'.

The conditions were not ideal for a summit attempt but Mark was confident in our ability and strength as a team to get the job done. After a quick breakfast we prepared our gear and were formed up ready to go for the summit. We had to climb over 1100 vertical metres to the summit from high camp and I was feeling confident and ready to attack. My pack was almost empty apart from some water and snacks, which gave me a big confidence boost considering we had full loads the day before and ascended 1000 metres in half a day. We moved off as a team across a steadily sloping snowfield, slowly getting into the mountaineering rhythm. A summit day is not a sprint, it's a slow walk that would get much slower the closer we get to our goal. Ninety minutes after leaving high camp the clouds and mist had lifted and the top of Vinson could be seen.

'She is going to let us climb today,' I thought to myself as I stared upwards at her beauty. But that confidence was crushed only an hour later as an unseen blizzard descended on us and within ten minutes I went from picturing myself on top to being caught in white-out conditions and an ever increasing wind. Mark made the tough call to turn us around and descend back to the safety of camp. It was the right call to make but it didn't make it any less devastating to my morale. As the storm chased us down the mountain I was reliving my Mount Elbrus expedition all over again and I quietly hoped that history would not repeat itself. I crashed through my tent door and quickly zipped it up to escape the wind, snow and chilling cold. We had been defeated, but unlike Elbrus, we had a few days to wait out the weather and try again. I lay down and anxiously waited for the drop in the weather. Mark yelled out from his tent across the howling wind, 'If it's clear tomorrow we will go again team so rest up.' I drank some water, ate my snacks and fought off the negativity that was trying to burrow into my mental state. It was a tough fight.

I woke up the next morning to no wind and clearing conditions. I had actually enjoyed a great sleep after I finally drifted off and felt fully recharged from the previous day's retreat. The team came together for a hot brew and a meal where Mark put it out there: 'The weather looks decent guys, who's keen to go again?' I prompted the team with an 'absolutely' and it was a unanimous verdict from everyone that we should get going. Geared up and roped together we stepped off again towards the summit at 11 am. The weather continued to clear for the first hour before it changed its mind and started to snow, enveloping us in white-out conditions again. There was no wind so Mark decided we should carry on, much to my relief, and for three hours we climbed in white-out conditions. Climbing with nothing but pure white in all directions including underfoot was an intense scenario. It is so easy to get disorientated and a few times while we continued on I actually thought we were heading down instead of up.

The conditions didn't change much for the following four hours, the team only stopping twice for water but continuing on after only short periods to avoid getting too cold. It was a fine line between sweating and fogging my goggles to getting hypothermia as we rested. The team receded into their own minds and we all climbed onwards towards the summit ridge. I wanted the conditions to remain the same and deteriorate no further – if we had to turn around again this far into our second attempt, a third shot at the top was going to be a big ask. We made it to the summit ridge six and a half hours after setting off. Just as we made it to the ridge the white-out began to lift but in its place came a wind of 25–30 knots. This dropped the temp dramatically and extra care had to be taken to have no skin exposed to the elements. A lost glove or exposed cheek while ascending the summit ridge would almost certainly guarantee frostbite.

I had climbed well all day and I must have been looking in decent shape because Mark nominated me to lead the team along the ridge to the top. I looked up and across to the exposed rock standing high on the summit. The wind was gusting, causing the snow that had accumulated on my face to get blown away down the mountain. Mark asked me, 'Luke, are you good to lead?' Without hesitation I said, 'Of course mate. Let's do it!' He pulled me to the side and said, 'Don't muck around on the summit, we need to get down soon.' I knew what he was saying; we still had a long way to go to get back to camp, the winds were increasing and the team was tired. We wouldn't be wasting time up top – it was only halfway.

I tied into the front of the rope and once everyone was tied in behind me we moved off. Mark stayed at the back to help out one of the team who was moving steadily and I kept my eyes on my feet and the rope. There was no fixed protection on the ridge so as we shuffled along I made sure to throw the rope over rocky outcrops that could arrest a fall if one of us made a mistake. We were traversing a 45-degree slope in strong winds and freezing temperatures so we were literally on the edge. It was minus 40 degrees Celsius before the wind chill, and my camera had stopped working hours earlier due to the cold so there was no need to stop and pose for pictures. The ridge came to an end and I shuffled the last few steps onto a small build-up of exposed snow at its zenith where I stopped and lifted my ice axe in the air. I was standing on top of Vinson Massif, the highest point in Antarctica at 4892 metres, my fist clenched tight around the axe held high above my head in celebration and salute. The icy landscape stretched to the far horizon in all directions, the wind was howling and the temperature was plummeting. I had never felt more exposed or more alive. Before the tears could form in my eyes a gust of wind almost knocked me off my feet and brought me menacingly back to reality.

I turned after mere seconds on the summit and started to make my way back along the ridge as the next in line shuffled up to the top. We all had our special moment standing proud on the summit before we made our way back down safely to the start of the ridge and the sloping snowfield leading us home. We dropped below the wind as we headed down over the ridge, getting some relief from the bone-chilling cold. We stopped for rest and gave each other big hugs in celebration, all knowing that the hard work and suffering so far was worth those few seconds at the top. I gave Vitidnan a big hug saying, 'Well done my brother.' He hugged me back, not letting go for a few seconds, before breaking away and saying, 'Now let's get down safely bro.'

Over the following hours, slowly but surely, we descended back the way we had climbed. My body was tired and exhaustion had started to kick in after the adrenaline of the summit had worn off. I had consumed all of my water and my tongue was screaming for moisture, I'd throw a handful of snow into my mouth to soothe the dryness and take my mind off the aching pain in my feet and legs. Twelve hours after departing for the top the team staggered back into high camp and I sat down onto the snow next to my tent. I was totally spent. I could feel the blisters on my toes and heel throbbing inside my boots but I had a mission-accomplished smile on my face. I crawled into my sleeping bag that night after copious amounts of fluid and a hot meal, free of doubt and without a care in the world. I had achieved another goal and another summit on my journey for the seven and I slept like the dead.

Enjoying a long sleep-in the next day we departed high camp at 1 pm to go back down the fixed lines and across the snowfield to what was our low camp. My legs were stiff and sore and everyone was hurting in some way but the entire team was in a festive mood and moved confidently together down the mountain. At low camp we broke out the cooking stove and had a fry-up of eggs, mushrooms, onion and cheese that Mark had been saving for the return journey. It tasted incredible, and after we had all enjoyed our fill, we loaded our sleds, tied into the rope and began the haul down to base camp. As base camp came into view I made out the Twin Otter plane parked in the snow and ready for our arrival. The weather was perfect and the flight had been arranged by Mark before we departed low camp. As we marched along Mark turned to me and said, 'The weather conditions are great. With any luck we will be back in Punta Arenas tomorrow night.'

The Twin Otter's skis lifted from the snow effortlessly and below us the ice, crevasses and hardships fell away. It had taken years of training, months of organising and weeks of climbing to make it to Antarctica and summit Vinson Massif and now we were on our way home. I kept my face glued to the window of the Otter the entire flight. What I was seeing was a rare privilege only a tiny percentage of the population got to see and I was truly grateful. I was staring out at the ice that was dotted with jagged unclimbed peaks when Vitidnan, after sensing my remoteness, patted me on the shoulder and said, 'Well done mate, you did it.' I gave him a nod before returning my face to the view and whispering back, 'Thanks mate.'

I looked down at an enormous gaping crevasse and remembered the early polar pioneers. Some of them had been taken whole into these ice tombs and even today they could still be held firm in her frozen embrace. I hadn't been tested like those men had been and I envied them. It was in that moment that I made the decision to return one day. I had unfinished business, and looking down I noticed another crack in the ice in the shape of a smile. I took this as a sign that Antarctica was not done with me yet either; I would be back.

CHAPTER 12

MOUNT KILIMANJARO, TANZANIA

...

I arrived in Tanzania to the famous Swahili song 'Jambo Bwana' by Them Mushrooms playing on the radio with the taxi driver singing along jovially at the top of his lungs. Translated it means, 'Hi, hi sir. How are you? Very fine.' Accompanied by an African rhythm and a bouncy beat, these simple words were hard to ignore. The entire nation had adopted this melody as their own and before long I would be humming along with them. I had flown into Moshi, a district of Tanzania, ready to climb the tallest peak in Africa, Mount Kilimanjaro. On this expedition two friends had joined me, John's brother George and Rob the owner of Rev X, as well as my very own dad, Clive. I was so excited to have Dad with me as it was our first adventure together since I was a boy. He had shown me how to fish and hunt, now I was proud to show him the way of the mountains.

I was just a boy when my grandfather gave me one of my first books, *When the Lion Feeds*, by Wilbur Smith, a story of hunting safaris and adventures into the untamed bush of Africa before World War I. This one story followed by many more ignited a yearning to see it all for myself. In my early twenties I was fortunate enough to travel from Nairobi in

Kenya all the way to Cape Town in South Africa. Although that journey had taken almost three months to complete, it only gave me a taste of the continent and I was left wanting more. So here I was, returning to the blood-red landscape of East Africa to attempt the summit of its highest mountain, a mountain which has a unique silhouette known around the world, and one of the most summited peaks on the planet. Kilimanjaro or 'Kili' as it is known in the climbing community is a dormant volcano rising 5895 metres above sea level and is visited by an estimated 25,000 people every single year.

Even with the easy accessibility of Kili and its well-versed climbing guides and porters, summit success is only 66 per cent. Many inexperienced climbers, believing Kili to be an easy trek, succumb to the extreme cold or altitude sickness on summit day and are forced to retreat. No mountain should ever be underestimated and time should always be taken to acclimatise correctly and have spare days in case you need multiple attempts to summit – I learnt this fact the hard way on Elbrus. We were lucky on the flight into Moshi as we had a close-up view of the summit with clear skies. We flew directly over the top of the snow-capped peak, with shimmering glaciers looking out of place in the surrounding black lava rocks. The glaciers have been melting exponentially each year and rough estimates forecast the extinction of the northern glaciers by 2030.

The extra risk factors on this trip were my dad and George, who were both in their fifties and had never climbed a mountain before. Rob was a full-time fitness coach and in fantastic shape so I wasn't too concerned about him, but I needed to watch the other two. The unknown element was the altitude and no-one knows why some people suffer greatly while others simply shrug it off. While Dad and George were in good shape physically and had put in the time training before the trip, I planned to keep a sharp eye on them, especially on our summit day, when we would need to ascend over 1100 metres in one day. Actually, Dad was lucky to be alive after rolling his car returning from work only six weeks before we were due to leave. In true cowboy fashion he shrugged it off and resumed his training regime of 20-kilometre walks with three milk bottles full of water in his backpack.

If you have never been to Africa it's hard to describe with words the sensory overload we experienced as we stepped out of the airport doors. The first thing that hit me was the heat and the sticky humidity. Sweat started to pour from my face and within seconds my shirt was soaked through. Looking around I noticed that all of the local men were wearing trousers and long sleeve shirts and it baffled me how acclimatised to the heat they were. Then the smells began to break through the fog of heat and enter my nose. It's a scent of dust, unwashed humanity and an ancient land all blended into one. Every developing nation has its own particular smell but the scents of Africa are my favourites because they remind me of my desert home directly before a monsoon rain. The smell of dust in the air hours before the yearly rains fell was an incredible scent and it brought with it a sense of comfort and relief that the drought was broken and that the green grasslands were soon to grow. In Tanzania, as we loaded into our taxi, the similar smell didn't bring with it the knowledge of breaking drought however, it carried with it the hopes and dreams of the millions of Africans living on a dollar a day and working hard for a better life.

Moshi brought that better life to many thousands of locals due to the booming climbing and trekking industry. Tourists like us brought our money into the country to climb a mountain hiring locals as guides and porters, stimulating the local economy. We drove through the townships towards the centre of Moshi with the Jumbo song playing loud enough for the people on the street to sing along. We were all glued to our windows taking in our surroundings before pulling up at the large entrance of the Zara campgrounds, where we would be spending our first few days. Zara was a local logistics company that arranged Kilimanjaro expeditions as well as safaris and excursions into other parts of Africa. They also acted as the local operator for many western companies that offered Kili trips. What can sometimes happen is that a person will book a trip online with a company from their own country at an inflated price, and upon arrival get given the very same trip I had organised locally at a much cheaper rate.

We would only be there a few days to prep our gear, meet our local guide and porters then get going. The camp was bustling with activity; climbers and trekkers from all over the world were either getting ready to depart or had just arrived back from the mountain. The place had a great energy about it and I couldn't wait to get going. We were settled into some basic accommodation containing a mattress covered in a mosquito net and a small fan to combat the stifling heat. Malaria was a real concern in Tanzania and the other guys, including Dad, had arranged prescriptions of Doxycycline before leaving Australia and would now take their dosage of one tablet per day while they were here to fend off the infection. I had spent six months on Doxy while in East Timor and I knew all of the drug's side effects and decided I'd go without it this time around. Doxy makes you very prone to the sun and can cause nausea and also vomiting in some cases, so I preferred to just take extra precautions against mosquitos for this trip. I would keep my arms and legs covered, sleep under a net and use spray when they were at their worst.

Zara camp supplied meals for everyone each day and we all sat down in our small team, enjoying our first dinner together in Africa. Dad and George were from two different worlds but they were getting along like old friends. Dad grew up on the land, working with his hands his entire life, and George was big in business in Sydney, owning restaurants and managing real estate. It did not matter what they did for a living, here they were in Africa, eating the same food and about to climb the same mountain; they were equals. I was listening in to their conversation as I devoured my dinner and George was explaining to Dad how affectionate his wife got when he went away and Dad replied, 'Who with, mate?' George stared at Dad for a few seconds, not sure how to react before they both burst out laughing and I joined in. George said, 'You are different Clive, but I like you.' The team was bonding together well.

The following two days were slightly chaotic, searching for George's bags that didn't turn up, and finally tracking them down at the airport ourselves. We also met our local porter team and lead guide who would show us the way, carry our cooking equipment, extra gear, and of course the toilet. We opted for our own toilet to save us using the often crowded communal camp toilets on Kili and to give another local a job. Having a toilet for our convenience was roughly $150, and although being allocated the job of toilet porter is by no means glamorous, it's still work, and it was great to have another smiling face along on the climb. After some research, we had decided on the Rongai route for our ascent, a trail that begins in the north-east, and seemed to have retained its sense of unspoilt wilderness. It's a less crowded route that joins a popular route called Marangu after about five days. Once all preparations were complete we loaded into a four-wheel drive and departed Moshi, bound for Kili.

Pole pole was a saying we would all know well by the end of the trip – as we stepped off on the trail the porters, all noticing my eagerness, yelled out together 'pole pole', meaning slowly slowly. This was actually the key to every mountaineering or endurance expedition; go slow and steady, conserve energy and you will get there safely. It also aids with acclimatising correctly, especially on a climb like this one with minimal trekking days and high altitude, it's critical we acclimatise as best we can. It was fantastic to have Dad next to me as we trekked along and we finally had a chance to catch up on years of stories that we never shared. He was in good shape, easily keeping pace with me and not losing his breath at all during our conversations as we made our way towards the mountain.

The scenery along the Rongai route was amazing, starting off in cypress plantations and in fairly open country, it soon transformed as we moved through montane forests. The colobus monkeys kept us entertained along the way and Dad, who had only seen kangaroos most of his life, was loving it. The first day was a short one, five hours of easy trekking before we arrived at our first camp called Simba camp at 2626 metres. The trip really was a luxury one for me after battling through conditions on Denali and Vinson Massif. As we arrived at camp our tents were already erected, some warm water was ready for us to wash our faces in and there was fresh popcorn. I couldn't believe the trouble the local guide and porters had gone to to give us some lovely comforts.

After a nice dinner prepared by our cook we all settled into our tents to rest. Dad and I were sharing a tent together and as we chatted into the night, we would regularly erupt into bouts of laughter. The guide must have thought we were losing our minds but we were simply best mates catching up and sharing funny stories. The following day the scenery changed into moorland as the altitude climbed higher and we left the forests behind. Kilimanjaro is made up of three volcanic cones, Kibo, Mawenzi and Shira. As the trail narrowed it veered towards the jagged peaks of Mawenzi before we arrived at Kikelewa camp at 3679 metres, after a six and half hour day.

Dad was in a great mood after another solid trekking day, George and Rob were also smiling and everyone was adapting to the trail and the altitude well. Dad was stirring George up as I sat down for dinner saying, 'Mate, I swear I saw the guy who carries the toilet making our soup.' George looked worried before Dad burst out laughing, just in time for the hot soup to arrive from the cook. George was very tentative with his first spoonful of the potato soup, that actually looked almost identical to the carrot soup of the night before.

Day three was a steep ascent of four hours, leaving the forest and moorlands behind and emerging into the alpine desert. We arrived shortly after lunch to camp three at Mawenzi Tarn at 4300 metres and situated in the shadow of the magnificent Mawenzi Peak. We took the afternoon to explore, rest and acclimatise. Soup for the night was onion soup, and as the cook left us with a smile on his face, we all burst out laughing – it was most definitely the same soup every night but we played along and enjoyed its nourishing warmth none the less.

The first three days of the climb readied the legs for day four, which was a ten-hour ascent from Mawenzi Tarn to Kibo Hut at 4700 metres. The route was desert-like, dry and inhospitable, gradually climbing higher and over the saddle formed between Mawenzi and Kibo peaks. The consolation for the effort was the spectacular views of Kibo and the valley stretching out below us. We arrived at Kibo Hut tired but excited for what lay ahead. From the hut the only way to the summit was literally up: over

1100 metres of ascent between camp four and the highest point in Africa. We were planning to leave for the top at midnight so after a quick wash, a hot meal and plenty of water we crawled into our sleeping bags to grab a few hours of sleep before show time.

$$\bullet\ \bullet\ \bullet$$

It was bitterly cold that night and sleep was restless for me. I felt like I had only just shut my eyes before the alarm in my watch told me it was time to get ready. I turned on my headlamp, waking up Dad beside me, and together we pulled on our gear, packed some water and snacks into our packs and stood up outside. Looking up at Kili we couldn't see much through the darkness but then I noticed the line of headlamps creeping their way up the side of the mountain. There looked to be twenty climbers up on the trail already, and as George and Rob came over to where we were standing staring up I said, 'Game on lads, let's go join them.'

It was a slow, steep ascent right from the beginning and it was very cold. I had to keep burying my hands into my pants to warm them up as we went along and I could see that Dad was having issues with his hands as well. This unexpected cold was one of the biggest problems for people with limited experience in the mountains. Only a couple of hours into the climb we were passed by climbers going down, being escorted by their guides, some with obvious hand issues and some stumbling and incoherent from the altitude. I felt the effects of the altitude as we made our way higher in the darkness and as a small headache crept in behind my eyes I made a mental note to keep an eye on George and Dad – this was the danger zone for them.

I was staring at the few metres of illuminated ground from my headlamp for five hours of switchbacks across scree fields and rocky terrain. We made it to the top of the crater rim at Gilman's Point at 5681 metres and had a good rest and devoured some biscuits before setting off again across friendlier ground towards the summit. The team were doing well, everyone was still focused and feeling strong, even as the light-headedness of the altitude began to affect us all. The glow on the horizon hinted at dawn, and as it slowly lit up the landscape, the balance of power between my lamp and the sun shifted towards the latter. I turned off the artificial torch and was mesmerised by Mother Nature.

Climbers were passing us on their way down in numbers, telling me that the summit was surely within our reach. As we made our steady walk up the final slope it felt like I was in slow motion and I was incapable of moving my legs any faster. Almost as if I was drunk, the altitude had slowed my mind down and I felt like I was drifting along in a dream. I had been at altitude many times before, but even I hadn't climbed to almost 6000 metres in a four-and-a-half-day push; we were all under the influence. We crested the rise together and in front of us, nestled among a group of climbers, was the summit and the infamous sign reading:

> CONGRATULATIONS YOU ARE NOW AT UHURU PEAK TANZANIA
> 5895 METRES
> AFRICA'S HIGHEST POINT, WORLD'S HIGHEST
> FREESTANDING MOUNTAIN
> ONE OF THE WORLD'S LARGEST VOLCANOES
> WELCOME

...

We had made it. The view from the top was breathtaking, stretching as far as the eyes could see, and bathed in the early hours of sunrise was Africa. Together we hugged and shuffled our way into the group to get our very own picture under the sign to prove we had done it. I pulled Dad in beside me and I told him something I had never openly told him before, 'I love you, Dad.' He turned to me and said something in return that he had never openly told me either, 'I love you too mate.' We crushed each other in a hug as tears swelled in my eyes and once we had taken plenty of photos it was time to start thinking about the return journey.

The summit was only the halfway point so after we had refuelled with snacks and rehydrated with water, we turned from the top and joined in the line of climbers making their way to the bottom. The descent was tough on the legs but the consolation was that the rising sun was warming us up. Special care needed to be taken over the scree fields, especially when fatigued; this was an unroped descent and a slip or fall down the rocky face could end in tragedy. Nine hours after first staring up at the line of head torches at midnight we walked back to our tents at Kibo Hut. We had stood on the summit of Kilimanjaro and the highest point on the African continent. I was so proud of my dad; he struggled in places and was obviously working hard but never once looked like giving up.

We ate a nice hot meal prepared for us by the cook before packing up and starting a further descent down to Horombo Hut. It took us four hours of steady downhill trekking on tired legs before we could finally call an end to our thirteen-hour summit day. We all sat together enjoying our onion/carrot/potato soup of the day and giggled to ourselves before crawling into our sleeping bags for a well-earned sleep. The following day, on stiff legs, we made the trek down the Marangu route almost 20 kilometres to the gate at its entrance and the end of our expedition. We were issued with a summit certificate from the park headquarters then loaded into our vehicle and made our way back to Moshi.

• • •

I walked through the dirt streets of Moshi the following day taking a few hours for myself away from the team. I loved the feeling of being alone and vulnerable in a place like Africa, it gave me a heightened sense of things. I'd notice the kids playing with plastic bags, the street dogs lying under the shade of a verandah and I'd notice the toothless smiles on the faces of the locals as I walked by. Africa is humbling to say the least. In my opinion, everyone should spend some time walking the streets of a developing country, it will give you an appreciation for the simple things we take for granted like running water, air conditioning or an unlimited food supply. It will also put a human face to the commercials we typically flick through that ask for donations for another poverty-stricken community in a faraway place. Those places are very real and they have very real people living in them doing their best to survive.

I turned a corner and was enveloped by a gust of wind carrying red dust and the scent of the desert. I closed my eyes, breathed in deep and thought of home. I opened them again, smiled and started walking back towards my dad, my friends and my flight home. Along the way a tune entered my mind and I began to sing that old Swahili song, 'Jambo Bwana'.

CHAPTER 13

BUSINESS OR ADVENTURE

...

I had completed five out of the six summits I had attempted and I was planning to attempt Elbrus again on my way to Nepal to climb Mount Everest. During the fundraising event, one of the highlights of the night was a pledge of $50,000 for Everest, with me completing 100 push-ups shirtless to lock it in. The reality of the pledge and how events unfolded were slightly more depressing.

When the time came to pay for the Mount Everest expedition, I travelled to the building of the CEO who had made the pledge, ready to tell my stories and pick up the cheque that he told me would be waiting. Once I was called into his office though, something had changed. He was no longer the friendly and cheerful guy full of champagne and bravado, he was now all business.

He told me fairly directly that he would no longer be able to give me the sponsorship, and without even saying sorry, simply acted like it was no big deal. I was in total shock and didn't know what to say. I tried to protest by saying, 'You promised in front of 400 people, how can you go back on you word?' But it didn't make a shred of difference to him. I would learn repeatedly in the coming years that money is never guaranteed until it is cleared and in the bank, it doesn't matter what comes out of someone's mouth. John was as upset as I was but it didn't seem to come as a big surprise to him. I guess he has been in business long enough to know that people just talk it up sometimes and never deliver.

After realising I had no money in my bank and none due to arrive anytime soon I had a big decision to make. I was contemplating my return to the mines while still training and working at the gym when John and Chris the Greek made a decision for me. They wanted to open a gym of their own in Sydney and would like me to be involved. Once again I was in for a roller-coaster experience, with John leading the way. Of course I agreed to become a partner thinking that at the very least I'd learn a bit about business and be in a position to save money for Everest. Anything was better than going back into the underground hell of a coal mine.

The boys hit the ground running, securing a builder named John as a partner and another guy, Stewart, as an investor and manager. That made up our team of amigos, five guys all keen on health and fitness looking to open our own place. After a thousand meetings ranging from comfortable chats to screaming matches, one trip to China to source gym equipment, three months of pre-sales in shopping centres, long endless nights of building on the site and seven months of waiting, BOX HQ opened in Five Dock in Sydney's Inner West to a great reception.

I was in charge of running all CrossFit classes, ten per day when we first opened, and we had employed a good mate of mine named Patchy to run the outdoor bootcamp. Stewart was in charge of managing and paying all the bills, John the builder was all over the maintenance, while John and Chris worked their networks and sales skills to bring in the members. It was a great team, great opening and we were off and racing in our first six months of business. My stake in the business was as a minority shareholder as I didn't have a single dollar to put towards its opening, but I knew if we were successful I could make some good money as well.

By the end of our first year the gym was doing really well, so well that Chris and Stewart wanted to expand and offered to buy out the rest of us and go it alone. It was a big proposal and after talking to John about it we decided to accept the offer. It had been an eighteen-month fast-track business degree for me and I had never worked so hard in my life. I ran classes all day seven days per week and cleaned the gym floors on my Sunday afternoon off. I made good money and had managed to save a decent amount as well, but with the high cost of living in Sydney I still had nowhere near enough to climb the mighty Everest.

Shortly after selling Box HQ I stumbled upon a building site that was vacant and sitting in a perfect location for another gym. It was located in a suburb called Drummoyne and sat at the water's edge of the 'bay run', which is a hub for walkers and runners who journey around the 7 kilometres of the bay. I decided to do it all again but this time with me making all of the tough decisions and with Patchy as my partner. I wanted to change the business model and simply open a CrossFit/bootcamp space and not have all of the standard gym equipment. So once again it was six months of planning, building and marketing but before we knew it OLOC Fitness was born and it was the most incredible place to go to work every day.

I would teach classes with a view out over the beautiful bay and I had pictures from all of my adventures next to a massive OLOC logo graffitied on the wall. We had opened really well again – access to all the people walking by our front door made it an easy place to market, and with John's constant advice it was a total success. I moved into an apartment two minutes' walk from the gym, which had water views as well. I was trying to live the dream everyone wanted but there was something missing that I couldn't quite put my finger on.

A new app had exploded onto the market that took the awkward bar room conversations out of the equation and changed the dating scene forever. Tinder was something totally new to me, an app that essentially involved swiping through pictures of people in close vicinity and choosing whether you liked or disliked them purely on looks alone. It may seem like a very superficial way to meet someone, which it is, but if we are really honest with ourselves isn't that what we are all like anyway? I would always need to be attracted physically to someone before I made an approach and tried to start a conversation that often ended in utter humiliation. It would take a few stiff drinks to remedy my embarrassment but ultimately I would be out there trying again. Tinder however took away the humiliation, and while I was working fifteen hours a day, it was the perfect fit for me.

That is how I met Elise. She was a personal trainer in the city not too far from where I lived, and like me didn't have the time to get among the nightlife to meet people. Her photos were incredible and she must have thought the same about mine because after both swiping yes we exchanged messages and caught up for a coffee. We were inseparable from that moment on: she was beautiful, smart, loved training, worked in the same industry and had a desire for travel. Within three months we would be living together in my apartment and she would be working full-time at my gym, running classes and doing her personal training.

At face value I was living the dream, but the reality was that I was yearning for adventure. Every time I would stare at my photos on the wall or explain to new members what OLOC was all about I would get a little depressed. It had been almost four years since my last mountain, and in that time I had been successful in business, made money, built a great network and met an amazing girl, but I was hungry for something else. The normal life was eating at me a little bit more every day. Everyone around me was talking about buying houses and having kids but I just couldn't accept that as my reality and slowly I was getting more and more unhappy.

OLOC had been open for a year when I turned to Elise one afternoon and asked her, 'How would you feel about selling up everything and going travelling?' She said, 'That would be awesome, let's do it!' At that moment I knew that if Elise was willing to give up the money, the apartment on the water, the business, the nice car and fine dining to go travelling, she was the one for me. I also knew that I was making the right decision because it felt like a weight had been lifted off my shoulders as soon as the decision was made. The business was above break-even but not generating staggering amounts of profit, so I handed over the reins to a friend of mine named Sara, who already owned one gym and was excited to get a second. She would go on to stamp her own mark on Inner West Sydney and the fitness industry.

Elise and I hit the road with our backpacks, travelling all around New Zealand and taking in the incredible mountains of the South Island. It wasn't long before I suggested that we go to one of my favourite places to train for a while and think about our next move. We landed in Phuket and once again I found myself back on the street that had helped saved my life more than five years earlier. The street had evolved over the years and now there were multiple fitness camps to choose from, plenty of options for accommodation and an endless selection of healthy food. One of the big camps on the street was called Unit 27 Total Conditioning, offering top-shelf fitness classes based around high intensity and functional movement. We loved the place and when the offer came from the manager asking if we would like to be coaches, we accepted immediately.

We were training every day, eating healthy and working twenty hours per week instead of ninety. Going to the beach was a daily occurrence, so was getting massages and drinking coconuts. We lived in a tiny bungalow, did no cooking or cleaning and our laundry was done twice per week for $5. Now we were really living the dream and the best part was, since the cost of living was so cheap compared to Sydney, we could save money for adventures. I had my mind fixed on Everest again but little did I know that a random chain of events and a phone call out of the blue would set me on a course for the greatest adventure of my life.

This adventure would push me to the edge of human endurance, where I would learn and respect the raw humbling power of Mother Nature. I wouldn't climb one foot in elevation but the heights of my euphoria would be unprecedented. Where I was going would not contain a single grain of dirt, and when I finally smelt the scent of civilisation again I would be a world record holder. What had I gotten myself into?

CHAPTER 14

ROW2RIO

· · ·

I used the term 'ready for anything' many times while coaching classes in fitness at Unit 27: if the world economy collapsed tomorrow or if an environmental disaster struck, would you be capable of physically and mentally surviving? I had always prided myself on being ready, and above all else, ready for adventure. On 3 February I took a Skype call from friends of a friend who were planning to row across the Atlantic Ocean from Portugal to Brazil, 6000 kilometres, all under human power. Appendicitis had claimed a crew member two weeks from departure and they were asking if I was able to join their crew. I said yes immediately, without any hesitation. Nothing could really prepare me for a task of such monumental undertaking, but I knew I had a skill set that could give it one hell of a go.

I had never rowed more than five kilometres before, and that was on an indoor rower, so the morning after I had agreed to join the team I jumped on an indoor rower at the gym and plugged away for ninety minutes. My bum was numb and my hands were aching but all in all it felt fairly comfortable so I called it a day. I was very naive thinking I was anywhere near ready for what this trip would throw at me.

Three days later I had resigned from my job with the blessing of the boss and I was on a plane to London, anxious to join Jake, Mel and Susannah on their Row2Rio 2016 campaign, all in the spirit of adventure and to raise money for Macmillan Cancer Support. Leaving Elise behind in Phuket was hard; this was our first time apart since we had met eighteen months earlier and the separation would add a new dimension to the mental battle I'd have to endure. I touched down in London, a city I had not returned to since fleeing the drug scene years before. The weather was cold, damp and grey, just as I had left it, and the memories of my time spent there all came flooding back as the sites, smells and sounds of London overwhelmed me. I caught the Piccadilly line into Central station and caught the Northern line down to Tooting Bec. From there it was a short taxi ride to Jake's apartment on the other side of the common. It was close to 9 pm as I carried my bags in the freezing wind to his front door and pushed the buzzer. I had never met Jake before and I was about to spend a couple of months at sea with him.

Jake answered the door with a smile and it was obvious he had just been sleeping. 'Welcome mate, come on in,' he gestured for me to enter out of the cold and we hugged like long-lost family. He was a solid-set guy but not fat, and at 6-feet tall he carried himself well. He was twenty-nine years old and his British accent came across posh but he was simply well-spoken and wasn't lazy like we Australians with our slang and rounding of words. He made me feel right at home and we immediately started to chew into the details of the expedition. He brought me up to date with what had been done up until then and what still needed to be done before we left for Lagos, Portugal in a few days time. I was starting to get very excited as we went over the details of the row. Part of me felt like it was all an April Fool's joke and not really happening but as we discussed food, water and safety support it was quickly becoming reality.

We chatted late into the night until jet lag was pulling my eyelids south and Jake decided to let me sleep and he went to his girlfriend's place not far away. We were planning on meeting up the next day and getting stuck into the last few jobs that needed doing. It was freezing cold in the apartment but after a hot shower and curling myself up under a huge duvet I was asleep within seconds.

The following few days were busy and stressful for the team who were all trying their best to pull the trip together with limited funds and support. Susannah, who I wouldn't meet until Portugal, was finishing her PhD as well as organising oars, safety gear, navigation equipment, sponsor graphics for the hull and much more. Mel was going to be towing the boat from the shipyard south of London to Lagos with her dad and needed to leave very soon in order to get down there in time for our scheduled departure. Jake and I were doing the leg work delivering oars, buying supplies and constantly hunting for more sponsors. I was lucky, looking back, to only have had to deal with the stress of a big expedition like that for two weeks and not two years like the rest of the team.

Jake and I drove down to the shipyard to deliver the much-needed oars that were donated to us by Water Rower UK. They were lightweight, top-of-the-range oars built for river rowing. Their durability for crossing the Atlantic was a question mark so we asked for spares as well, which were readily given. After a ninety-minute drive through the English countryside we arrived in the small town of Christchurch, Dorset and the waterside shipyard of Rossiter Yachts, who were doing the last-minute building of the boat. As soon as I saw our boat a smile spread across my face and I was jumping out of my skin with excitement.

It was 8 metres long and not quite 2 metres wide, two small cabs were located at either end for sleeping, but in reality could only hold one person in them at a time, who would be semi-comfortable. When in the water she would only have 30 centimetres of clearance from the deck to the surface of the ocean, making her very vulnerable to splashing waves and rolling in big seas when hit side-on. There were no engines, no propellers and no sails, just the three spaces for rowing seats and the locking lugs to put the oars into. I was like a kid at Christmas poking my head into every little nook and crevice and I couldn't wait to get out there on the ocean. We loaded the boat with absolutely everything we were going to need to survive at sea for a few months and anything we couldn't carry on board the plane to Portugal.

Mel arrived with her dad in a big four-wheel drive vehicle loaded with even more supplies, ready to tow the boat to Lagos over the following two days. Mel was quiet and very polite, her shyness concealed a sharp mind and a steadfast British determination. She had done plenty of rowing before and was a member of the local rowing club. Her dad's name was Roger and he and I got along straight away. He was a farmer and reminded me of the tough, no-bullshit country folk I grew up with back home. We hooked up the boat, making sure everything was firmly secured in place and bid them farewell on their journey. Jake and I drove back to London, mentally checking off our to-do lists, having only one more day to gather any last-minute items before we flew out to join them in Lagos.

...

Less than twenty-four hours later Jake and I were running to catch the train with our bags loaded onto our backs. We had misread our flight departure time and were making a sprint for the train to hopefully get us to the plane in time. All was well, as we checked in with seconds to spare boarding our flight to Portugal. We touched down at the airport and caught a taxi into Lagos, a city of 35,000 people and a port town for Atlantic crossings by trade ships during the age of discovery. It was also a central hub for the European slave trade for almost 400 years and its shoreline has beautiful sand beaches spliced with amazing rock formations, some containing fortified towers used for the city's defence as early as the sixth century.

Lagos was our departure point for an attempt at a new ocean rowing route to Brazil, 3500 nautical miles away. We checked into a hotel on the harbour and waited for Mel and Roger, who were on schedule to arrive before dark with the boat. Jake and Mel had been to Lagos already as part of the greater mission of Row2Rio. The team's intention for Row2Rio was a bike ride from London to Lagos, rowing the Atlantic to the east coast of Brazil and finishing with another bike ride to Rio in time for the Olympic ceremony of 2016. They successfully completed their first ride, finishing in Lagos two weeks earlier, and it was at that point I received the invite to join them on the second leg of the journey. It was an ambitious project and I was going to give my absolute all in helping get the team across the Atlantic safely.

Mel and Roger arrived in the late afternoon that day and Susannah arrived the following morning. Susannah was our team leader and nominated captain for the voyage. She had successfully completed a row across the Pacific two years earlier and had been a competitive rower all her life. At 6 feet tall, powerfully built, with long limbs, I could see why she had been so successful in the sport of rowing. She came across as slightly dorky, very intelligent and had great attention to detail, which is exactly what we needed to pull off this mission. Once we were all finally together we sat down and shared a beer to discuss all the remaining preparations to be done and a possible departure window.

We hired Chris Martin, a very accomplished solo ocean rower himself who holds the Pacific Ocean Rowing race annually, to be our full-time weather router. He would send us up to date weather forecasts every twenty-four hours containing wind direction, wind speed, wave height/direction, ocean current direction/speed and suggested rowing bearings, all to help us maximise our distance covered per day. We had a team Skype call with him to get to know each other and he gave us our departure window for seven days' time. I wanted to get out there immediately, however he told us there was a weather system due to move through the area in a couple of days and it was best to wait it out and let it pass.

We needed to have a window of good weather for at least three days so that we could get ourselves away from the coastline as far as possible. If we didn't get far enough away and bad weather hit us we could be pushed back onto the coast and be in big trouble. Once clear of the coast we could ride out bad weather without fear of being pushed ashore. The boat was designed to be self-righting, meaning in big seas when it was too dangerous to row we could cram ourselves into the cabins and seal the hatches. The boat could be flipped, rolled and even forced underwater and it would come back to the surface and turn itself upright.

The following seven days flew by in a blur of preparation. We had so many small jobs to finish off in order to be shipshape and ready for departure, it seemed like the list in the captain's notebook just got longer and longer. We made our first sea trial off the coast of Lagos, testing the water maker, trialling different rowing positions and deciding on where to cook, when to sleep and where to go to the toilet. Our rowing schedule would be two hours rowing and two hours of rest repeated twenty-four hours a day continuously for as long as the crossing took, which could be up to seventy days. I quickly realised during our sea trial that rowing on an indoor rower in a gym is absolutely nothing like rowing in an ocean rowing boat. I had all the fitness but seriously lacked the technical side of rowing, the two girls made me look like an amateur.

Finally the morning arrived for our departure. I was so anxious after two weeks of waiting that I had no idea how the rest of the team handled waiting through two years of preparation. Jake and Mel had family and friends there to see us off and the local sailors turned out as well. At 10.05 am on 16 March 2016 we made our first stroke towards Brazil. Kicking off from the dock and waving to everyone on the shore we navigated our way through the harbour and pointed our tiny boat towards the mouth of the inlet and the open ocean. A flotilla of local boats followed us out and a drone hovered above us, shooting the departure scene for the media at home and abroad. It was only when the last boat had departed back towards the safety of the harbour and the first wave splashed over the side that I stared out at the shimmering horizon and thought to myself, this is it, there is no going back now.

I completed my first two-hour rowing shift that first morning, which at the time was the longest row I had ever done. Afterwards the muscles in my back were sore, my hands were chafed and the biggest discomfort was my backside. In two hours my bum got very painful and in the two hours rest it barely had time to recover before I was back on shift again. As the sun was setting on that first day a pod of dolphins dropped by to say hello, no doubt thinking to themselves what the hell are you idiots doing out here?! They are such beautiful and graceful creatures; it was great to see them so early in our voyage and I took it as a good sign of things to come. As we pulled further away from the coast the waves were beginning to get bigger, nothing dangerous just rough enough to get the boat rocking and my stomach starting to rumble.

Our food for the entire crossing was dehydrated meals due to their light weight and each member brought their own snacks of what they enjoyed. The team had acquired some leftover meals for a cheaper price off another expedition team so variety was in short supply, the main meals consisting of chicken korma, spaghetti bolognaise and chilli con carne. Even though Jake was the nominated cook and offered to make me meals using hot water each day, I decided early on that I'd make my own meals with cold water. I did this for two reasons: it was more convenient to make my own food at any time instead of waiting for water to boil at meal times; I also realised that a nice hot meal is fantastic, however, if the gas burner was to break and I had to go from hot meals to cold meals the drop in morale would be monumental. So I decided to eat cold meals from the beginning and learn to love them, avoiding any possible scenario for morale loss on the high seas.

I chewed down a fairly average meal of chilli con carne just after sunset and settled into our tiny cabin for my first sleep at sea. Lying flat on my back the walls of the cabin were one foot either side of me, my feet touched the end and my head was at the entry, it was a tight fit. I had just dozed off when I woke up about to be sick, spinning over as quick as I could, reaching outside for the toilet bucket and grabbing it just in time to power spew inside it. Chilli really is a miserable meal on the way back up. Seasickness had kicked in and it was only minutes after I started to vomit that I heard Mel and Susannah doing the same. Mel was rowing with Jake as I continued to be sick for a few more minutes and then realised it was time for me to relieve Jake and start my next two hours of rowing.

The first night was a really tough time for me; apart from the discomfort of rowing itself, the seas had picked up causing small waves to break against the side of the boat, soaking us every few minutes. On top of that I'd be stopping to grab the bucket for a spew every twenty minutes. My body was tiring as I got more and more dehydrated from the seasickness and as soon as I finished my shift I'd drink as much water as I could and chew down a snack, knowing full well I'd be seeing it all again shortly. It was also bitterly cold. The others, coming from the UK, seemed to be used to the temperature but my last splash in the water was at 35 degrees Celsius in Thailand. I was wearing a big waterproof jacket and pants, beanie and gloves to keep myself from shivering. If there was ever a baptism of fire into ocean rowing, that first night was it. In the middle of the night at my lowest point, while staring at the bottom of the bucket, I thought to myself, 'I don't know if I can do this.'

The toughest rowing shift was from 12 to 2 am when all my body wanted to do was sleep but it was forced to row for another two hours. I caught myself falling asleep while rowing a few times. I would doze off and my rowing rhythm would fall out of sync with Mel's or Susannah's causing our oars to clash together startling me awake again. We staggered the rowing shifts between all of us so that an hour after I started my shift the girls would change and an hour after that Jake and I would be changing. This made sure that every hour there would be a fresh set of eyes on deck. On my 4 to 6 am shift the sun was starting to show itself on the horizon and as the light of a new day forced the darkness back into the depths of the ocean, morale was lifted.

We had some teething issues in those first two days and the auto tiller that was supposed to help keep us on a straight bearing decided to throw us into donuts every few hours. This would turn us side-on to the waves and give us a good soaking. Susannah battled through the user manual for a couple of hours and eventually remedied the problem. I was feeling better by midday on the second day and I could eat, drink and finally keep it all down. I had to do both in abundance to make up for the previous twenty-four hours of dehydration. Chris Martin sent us through our first transmission of weather updates and according to him we had done very well and covered 60 nautical miles our first day.

We each had jobs to do on board during the hours of rest. Mel and Susannah were in charge of navigation and communication, Jake was the boat's cook and prepared hot drinks when we were in need of a morale boost and I was in charge of the water. During one of my rest periods I fired up the water maker to refill all of our bottles. It was a remarkable piece of technology, pumping in the sea water, forcing out the salt and leaving us with beautiful fresh water at the end. It was a temperamental machine but when given a little love it produced 32 litres of water for us in ninety minutes. With the amount of energy we were all expending and with the number of calories we needed to consume of the dehydrated food, fresh water was the number one crucial element we had to have every single day and I was more than happy to take on my job.

While resting in the tiny cabin, getting ready for my second night at sea, I could feel the boat moving underneath me in all directions as we were shoved and pushed by the waves. I could feel the team rowing and the pull forward through the waves when their oars were working together and a strong stroke connected with the sea. The echo and noise of waves crashing against the fibreglass sounded much more ferocious than they actually were. When I crawled out to begin my shift and gazed out at the endless water as far as the eye could see, it took my breath away. We truly live on an amazing planet and it was in that moment, while exposed and vulnerable in the middle of the ocean, I started to really appreciate its power and majesty.

• • •

My first rogue wave experience occurred on the fourth night. Mel and I were on shift and we had turned off the navigation lights to enjoy the stars and save our battery power. We relied on pure solar power out there to run all the electronics and the water maker so conservation was key to avoiding flat batteries on cloudy days. We were leaving the lights on when we could see other ships on our radar, enormous cargo ships were passing by at night and the last thing we wanted was to have a collision with one of those. I doubt the cargo ship's captain's coffee would even ripple as they ploughed over the top of us in the middle of the night, so we had to be on guard at all times.

I had settled into two hours of misery when I heard the rumble of a big breaking wave, a split second before it slammed us side-on and swept the deck with its power. I managed to grab the safety line just in time but Mel was swept out of her seat and was just able to hang on to the side of the boat, stopping her from being taken overboard. We were told before departure that this scenario was going to be a common occurrence, so while on deck we were wearing our life jackets with personal locator beacons for possible rescue. We also had an ankle leash to attach to our foot plate when it was really rough and another safety line attached to the boat. The rogue wave definitely rattled both of us, and for the rest of our shift any rumble from the ocean had us grabbing the safety lines with lightning speed.

We were averaging over 60 nautical miles per day, which was a great number to be hitting so early on in the row, granted we had the wind and waves assisting us over the previous five days and I was quietly hoping for the wind to keep nudging us along for as long as possible. Our bodies were slowly adapting to the twelve hours a day of rowing and I knew that as we adapted to the task and started to get strong we could influence the miles a lot more with our effort. The marine life was everywhere and in abundance, we were sighting turtles, dolphins, fish and birds almost daily. It was always a nice break from the monotony of rowing.

• • •

Our voyage was going to cover almost 3500 nautical miles (6000 kilometres) by the time we hoped to reach the Brazilian coastline. That figure was simply too huge to comprehend so we broke our voyage into stages. Stage one was to make it from Lagos to the Canary Islands, situated off the coast of the Western Sahara, 650 nautical miles (1200 kilometres) away, and at the speed we were travelling it was going to take around ten days. I made a calendar on the roof of our cabin with masking tape and a felt pen. Every morning after my last night shift of rowing I'd cross off the day before and write up the miles we had travelled in the last twenty-four hours. Apart from keeping my mind occupied, this also gave me targets to hit and it made me push harder on the rowing to beat the previous day's total.

Next to the calendar I stuck a picture of Elise and underneath wrote three phrases that have come to give me great comfort and strength: 'Be grateful', 'You deserve this' and 'Thank you for allowing me to suffer'. These words were told to me by my good friend and mentor Ken Ware. I first met Ken out in Emerald, central Queensland, while I was working in the mines. He owned and operated a health and fitness centre in town and I was training there twice a day. He is the founder of NeuroPhysics Therapy, which is a program designed to trigger the human system to resolve many of its issues without the use of drugs, surgery or manipulation. He is a former Mr Universe and current Australian powerlifting record holder who has gone on to lecture at some of the biggest non-linear science conferences in the world, where his results and findings still stun the scientific community. His programs have helped literally thousands of people remedy a wide variety of disorders. From easing pain and restoring movement to getting spinal patients out of wheelchairs and walking again. He has been a pillar of guidance and a supporter of mine for over a decade. Out in the middle of the ocean when my hands went numb from rowing, I'd use his NeuroPhysics tremor therapy to dissipate the pain and adapt to the environment. It is truly amazing stuff.

• • •

It was the morning of day six when personal catastrophe struck. To go to the toilet on our floating paradise we had no option but to use a plastic bucket within arm's reach of each other. Due to the constant instability of the boat the bucket had to be placed in the centre back section of the rowing deck so as not to cause the boat to tilt to one side during use. I scooped up some salt water into the bottom of the bucket to act as ballast and help keep it from sliding around during the rougher than average morning swell. I was due on my first shift of the day fifteen minutes later and was in the middle of my morning ritual of eating, drinking and using the toilet before I started. I had completed my use of the bucket and was pulling up my pants and preparing to empty its contents overboard when a wave hit us side-on sending the bucket and myself skidding onto the deck. I swore out loud as the bucket's contents emptied onto the deck and the gravity of the clean-up job sunk in. As I was picking up my waste with my hands, I first thought about the last time I was covered in my own filth all those years ago in London, then I thought about the people at home drinking their flat whites and starting their normal days. I envied them for a brief moment as I looked at what was in my hands, but as I lifted my head to the amazing sunrise I didn't want to be anywhere else. Jake, after being woken up by my swearing, and who was always the gentleman, offered to give me a hand. I declined, chuckled to myself and wondered, if I had said yes, would he have actually helped me?

...

Our first close encounter with another vessel occurred late into our seventh night. We had been making good progress when the auto tiller decided to throw a fit and send us into donuts again. This usually wouldn't have caused great concern except that at the same time, our AIS (automatic identification system) alarm, which warned us if we were in close proximity to other boats, started going off. Scanning the horizon we immediately noticed a mass of lights in the darkness, and not knowing what was out there, we read the description on the AIS. A 180-metre-long cargo ship was coming directly at us and was within half a mile of our location. The ship's crew, who would have been alerted by their own AIS, switched on a huge spotlight and started to scan the water, searching for us – on their system we would register as an 8-metre sailing vessel, not an ocean rowing boat. We switched on all of our lights and tried to raise the ship on a VHF radio and, on making contact with the ship, told them that we are unable to alter our course as we were a row boat. Moments later the ship altered its course to pass us on our right side and the collision was averted.

The following morning brought with it 4- to 6-metre seas and our first taste of the awesome power of the sea. The waves were big and could toss our little boat in any direction they chose so we were lucky that the waves were coming from behind us and not from the side. If a 6-metre swell caught us side-on we would be capsized for sure. A wave swept through and picked up the back of the boat, which forced us to surf down the face of the wave before it spat us out over the top. We were gaining twice to three times our average speed, reaching up to 11 knots in the ten seconds of surfing as each swell rolled through. It was a tense, scary yet exciting day and once again, the power of Mother Nature was helping us tally up some easy miles. We covered 85 nautical miles that day, our biggest total so far.

The night of day nine was a surreal experience for me as we battled rough seas throughout the entire night. I sat in my rowing position and everything was pitch-black, with not a star in the sky due to the cloud cover and the drizzling rain. The wind was howling, the surf was crashing around me and I was getting launched left, right, up and down with the ferocity of the waves. It was like being blindfolded on a roller-coaster, not knowing what turn is coming up next. The toll on the body and mind was immense and I fought to stay alert and not be thrown overboard by a rogue wave when it swept the deck. On top of that, every few minutes an oar jumped out of my hand and slammed into my shins, knee or hip, as if to jolt me back to reality saying 'stay awake this isn't over yet'. Welcome to the Atlantic rowing roller-coaster, and it was in those dark moments that I'd ask myself the hardest questions and in answering them dictate my future.

• • •

Stage one was complete, we had made it to the Canary Islands and covered 650 nautical miles (1200 kilometres). It had been a baptism under ocean fire and I was beginning to feel as if my body was adapting to the two hours on two hours off roster. Passing through the islands at the end of day ten the seas began to grow again and within an hour had grown to a massive dumping swell, making it too dangerous to be rowing. We threw out our drogue anchor, which is a small parachute on a long rope that's pulled into the current and acts like an anchor. This little device kept us in line with the waves and prevented us getting flipped end over end. Once the drogue was tied off the girls both crawled into their cabin and Jake and I squeezed into ours.

With Jake and I both inside the cabin and the hatch shut the space becomes water- and air-tight and it gets hot and uncomfortable very quickly. Every so often we had to risk opening the hatch to let some fresh air circulate with a 50/50 chance of a blast of sea water rocketing through the small opening, soaking everything. My body was begging for sleep and even though it felt like we were inside a washing machine I dozed off. It was amazing how easily we could fall asleep when we really needed it; crammed up inside a tiny space with another human, hot and sweating, being battered in the enormous swell with no comforts at all, I slept like a baby.

The following morning as the sun broke over the horizon the waves had calmed down only marginally. I poked my head out of the hatch and noticed our position was in between two of the islands and fairly close to both. We decided as a team to try and get rowing again and get ourselves into deeper water away from the land, where the waves should be calmer. I heaved in our drogue anchor and on inspection noticed it had been shredded by the ferocity of the ocean overnight. We reset the tiller, Jake and Mel climbed into the rowing seats and we turned south with the wind and waves. The acceleration was immediate and we were hurtling along at an average speed of 6–10 knots, triple our normal rowing speed. Huge breaking waves came up behind us and when we weren't lucky enough to surf away from them they broke onto deck with incredible power. At one stage we were forced side-on to the swell as a wave broke on top of us. I watched through the cabin door as Jake's oar snapped and the bracket that held it in place was shattered to pieces.

We were now in a very dangerous position sitting side-on to huge swell, as I scrambled over the deck fixing the bracket and unlashing a new oar for Jake. I thought that at any moment we were going to be capsized and going for a swim. It was the most scared I had been on board so far and I could see in the faces of the others they were feeling the same. While being battered by the waves I finished replacing the bracket and we were rowing again, narrowly escaping disaster. Ten minutes later it was my turn to go out on deck and row and I thought to myself that we were going to capsize for sure at some stage of my shift. So I pulled on my jacket, placed the emergency beacon around my neck and then proceeded to eat an entire tub of Nutella. If I was going to be hurled into the freezing Atlantic I was going in satisfied.

The seas were huge and at one time Mel and I were chest deep in white water after a breaking wave swallowed the boat, but we didn't capsize. It was an adrenaline-fuelled ordeal not knowing what the next wave was going to bring and believing that at any second we were going to be broken to pieces in the ocean. I turned into a man possessed, rowing with such ferocity while trying to surf the waves that I was testing my physical limits to their extreme. We fought on for another hour but the speeds that the boat reached were literally out of control. Susannah had the idea to throw out the tattered drogue again in order to slow our speed and increase our stability. As soon as it came to full length in the ocean we were slowed down by half and the violence of the waves seemed to dissipate to a more manageable level. It was a great call from the captain, and for the first time in fifteen hours I could relax a little and we all laughed about how close we had come to disaster. In calming down I let my eyes wander over the horizon and the islands, it was then I noticed the white-capped volcano rising huge above the ocean as part of Tenerife island. The skies had cleared and this ancient, 3718-metre giant called El Teide stood watch over our progress. The summit was the highest point in Spain and it was one of the most incredible sites I had ever seen.

...

Stage two was upon us, we had safely navigated through the Canary Islands and our next checkpoint was Cape Verde, 780 nautical miles (1444 kilometres) away. The Cape Verde islands were another small group of volcanic outcrops situated directly west of Dakar and 500 kilometres off the coast of Senegal and the West African shoreline. This would be a slightly bigger stage and if the weather stayed behind us and lent a friendly nudge along we should cover the distance in just under two weeks. We had a visitor drop by that morning in the form of a 7-foot-long blue marlin. He followed behind the boat for a while, every few seconds giving us a flash of his bright blue side as his fins stuck clear above the surface. It was a beautiful sight and a nice change from staring out at the endless rolling waves.

After our ordeal through the Canaries I was completely exhausted and was falling asleep within seconds of closing my eyes. My body had adapted to the sleeping schedule and I was now managing to get three blocks of ninety minutes sleep during the night in between shifts. I'd also try to squeeze in a power nap whenever I could, usually after making water and eating during my day shifts. Even though ninety minutes is not a long time, whenever I woke up after sleeping my body would be stiff, I'd be slightly dehydrated yet I'd feel alert and energised. In the initial moments after waking it felt as though I had slept for eight hours, but after two hours of rowing I would be craving the sleep again – it was the never-ending cycle of work and rest.

Day twelve was a long day. The sea had become choppy and the night turned into what I called the 'oblique abs workout'. The small swell was coming at us from all directions and even though the conditions weren't dangerous, the constant left and right erratic rocking was seriously tough on the body. Our backs were getting very sore and stretching breaks were needed to relieve the tension. Day twelve also started with my second toilet disaster. In our cabin I used a two-litre plastic pee bottle so that I didn't have to venture out on deck to use the bucket at night. I was pouring it out over the side and a gust of wind caught the yellow nectar, swirled in around before my eyes and sprayed it all back into my face. If that wasn't bad enough I found out shortly afterwards that Jake had used my pee bottle for emergency release during the night. Getting sprayed in the face with your own pee isn't so bad, but someone else's is just mean.

The journey south to Cape Verde came with its own set of challenges and a strong undercurrent had been pulling us west towards the traditional trade routes across the Atlantic. We were trying to pioneer a new southern route to Brazil and needed to get across those currents, which had dramatically slowed our pace. It was tough rowing throughout the day. The westerly pull finally eased off as sunset was approaching and we managed to get ourselves into a southerly current, picking up speed slightly and allowing us to settle into a comfortable night of rowing. The weather had calmed and the clouds cleared for the first time since we departed Lagos. With all the deck lights off it was pitch-black apart from the luminescent plankton in the ocean, which glowed when disturbed by our oars, and the shine of the stars.

The next day was perfect, sunny and calm, and boat maintenance was desperately needed. We had taken a battering getting through the Canary Islands and with calm seas it was time to do a thorough inspection of our floating home. Our boat had a dagger board which is a small fibreglass fin that slides down through the centre front deck and protrudes one metre into the water below. This board helps to keep us on a straight bearing while in rough seas. If the dagger board isn't in position when we are hit side-on by a wave it would swing our nose around into dangerous positions. It had done its job well when we were being battered by big waves but in the process had broken off close to its end. It now caused a problem slowing us down and with a little effort we removed it to be repaired. Noticing our rudder was not responding as well as it should be, we believed there could be some rope from our drogue anchor wrapped around it. I volunteered to go swimming and inspect it, putting on goggles and attaching an ankle leash so I wouldn't be swept away from the boat, I lowered myself over the side and took my first swim in the Atlantic. The water was cool and refreshing and on a closer look the rudder did have tattered rope restricting its movement. I had no problem clearing it and before climbing back on board I dove under and stared out at the endless blue water all around me. The bottomless expanse of deep ocean made me feel like a spectator to one of the greatest shows on earth.

I really enjoyed the weather south of the Canary Islands. I didn't want to jinx our situation by thinking it but we were having perfect conditions, with half a metre to one-metre swell and cloudless skies. The temperature had risen a comfortable 10 degrees and we were down to shorts and shirts for rowing shifts instead of the triple layer waterproofs we were wearing five days earlier. The current was giving us a nice bump along and we were making steady miles. The route we were on must be a common cruise-ship route because we saw four in a day and a half. At night they light up like Christmas trees and I was imagining the hot showers and cold beers on board. One was so close and looked so inviting we joked about faking a rescue for a few days rest on board. When I took my shirt off I could see my body shrinking even after only two weeks at sea. The rowing schedule was gruelling and I was using up so much energy my body began consuming any muscle that was not getting used. Loose skin started appearing above my knees where my quads use to be and my bum was disappearing at a rapid rate.

I had come to learn the hard way that body maintenance is so important while ocean rowing. I started to get small sores on my bum from sitting in the rowing seat for such long periods. I was too tired and shell-shocked in the first week to worry about them, but they had since turned into large salt sores and were extremely painful. I had to adhere to a strict regime to keep them under control because the last thing I needed out there was an infection, especially in an area so sensitive and crucial to the task at hand. Before every rowing shift I'd coat my backside in Sudocrem and apply Vaseline to any sensitive areas to cut down on friction. Immediately after my two-hour shift I used baby wipes to clean my entire bum and reapply Sudocrem or one of the antiseptic creams before bed. This was the only way to keep the sores stable and slowly decreased their size; one of the many joys of rowing an ocean.

I had brought along some fishing gear in the hope of catching a fresh meal for the crew and had thrown a line in using a plastic lure as bait on a few occasions with no success. It was day fifteen and I had the lure in swimming most of the day but it wasn't receiving any attention. In the endless hours of rowing I started to calculate the amount of drag the act of fishing was accumulating. Our rowing speed dropped 0.1 knots when the line was in the water and over a twenty-four hour period of fishing this equated to 2.4 nautical miles of lost distance. In the long run, over our possible sixty-plus-day voyage the simple act of fishing could cost us two extra days at sea. After coming to this conclusion I wound the line in, making a deal with myself to only throw it in again if I could see the fish swimming in the water beside me. I would buy everyone a seafood buffet when we arrived in Recife two days ahead of schedule!

• • •

It was the middle of the third week and my normal day at the oars looked something like this. First rowing shift 8 to 10 am, followed by breakfast of a dehydrated meal, brushing my teeth and completing morning toilet rituals. Back on for another shift from 12 to 2 pm, followed by collecting empty bottles and making water for the team. If the machine was functioning well I could have the water finished in an hour, leaving me time to eat again and have a short rest. My last day shift was from 4 to 6 pm and my favourite as the temperatures would typically be the most comfortable and it was close to sunset. We would crank some music through the boat's speakers and enjoy all being out on deck. I'd eat again, drink plenty of water, grab a quick nap if I could before my 8 to 10 pm shift. Between 10 pm and midnight was when I'd get my first solid block of sleep, at least ninety minutes. A quick wipe down after rowing, Sudocrem to sensitive areas and it was straight to bed. From 12 to 2 am I was back at the oars and fighting the desire to sleep for two hours; this was always the hardest shift for me. Between 2 and 4 am was my second glorious block of sleep followed by my last shift from 4 to 6 am. I would awaken from my third sleep just before 8 am ready to start the day over again. It became the ultimate groundhog day experience and I wondered just how long I could keep it up.

Twenty days at sea and we were all adapting to life on the ocean. My body had already changed to suit the environment, dropping fat and any muscle that was just for show. My mind also began adapting to the monotonous hours at the oars, Noam Chomsky's and Sam Harris's podcasts were a great aid in getting me through the long nights. When I'd hear Noam speak about the never-ending conflict in today's world, spending time with friends paddling a boat seemed like a luxury.

In the three weeks at sea we had had a few close calls with container ships and were visited by fishing boats who came out of nowhere to give us a round of applause before speeding off. Who knows what they made of these strange foreigners in their tiny boat in the middle of the Atlantic. We had all forms of marine life join us on deck, from flying fish and squid to sea birds and insects. It's so surprising to see the abundance of life out there hundreds of miles from the coast of Africa. The weather had been on our side for a week and the sun warmed our bodies and morale. Our distance covered each day was remarkable, averaging 60–70 nautical miles every twenty-four hours. At that rate we would be at the beginning of stage three in no time, although I had an inkling that Mother Nature had only just begun to show us what she was capable of.

I missed Elise constantly, with endless hours of rowing giving me time to ponder how she was feeling while I was out on this crazy adventure. Before I departed Thailand bound for London she handed me a large envelope that contained a series of smaller notes. Each note had an 'open day' written on the front. Day three, day ten, day sixteen and so on for the duration of the sixty days. I opened the first one on day three.

MY PRINCE, THIS IS YOUR DREAM RIGHT HERE RIGHT NOW. AN INTRODUCTION TO THE NEXT SEVENTY YEARS. ONE FULL OF CHALLENGES AND BREATHTAKING ADVENTURES. ONE PUSHING BOUNDARIES AND TACKLING FEARS. SO BEGIN ALL OF YOUR SUNRISES WITH GRATITUDE. TAKE EACH FIRST STROKE WITH PRIDE. AND EVERY DAY WHEN THE SUN COLLIDES WITH THE MOON I AM CERTAIN YOU WILL BE GLOWING INSIDE. ON YOUR JOURNEY WHEN YOU LOOK UP AND SEE THOUSANDS OF STARS. A SIGHT SO FEW HAVE THE CHANCE TO BEHOLD. THINK OF ME, BECAUSE I'LL BE THINKING OF YOU. WAITING, EXCITED TO HEAR YOUR BRAND NEW STORY RETOLD. I LOVE YOU BEYOND WORDS

• • •

These notes were a huge part of my morale and determination, I would use each one as a goal to reach and when some nights got really tough I would focus on how long it was until my next note and that would give me strength.

Day fifteen.

> I'M THINKING BY NOW YOU WILL HAVE FOUND YOUR GROOVE. A RHYTHM TO YOUR STROKES AND A FEW BUM SORES TO MATCH. JUST THE MERE FACT THAT YOU PUT YOUR HAND UP WITHOUT QUESTION MAKES YOU EXTRAORDINARY. THIS ADVENTURE, ALTHOUGH I KNOW YOU WILL GET IT DONE, WITHOUT QUESTION IS ABOUT SO MUCH MORE THAN THE FINISH LINE. SIMPLY LOOK AROUND YOU. YOU ARE SEEING A PART OF OUR WORLD THAT MOST HUMANS HAVE NEVER AND WILL NEVER SEE. EVERY STROKE OF THIS JOURNEY FIND THE JOY. THE JOY OF THE ACTIVITY, THE SURROUNDINGS, THE NOISES, THE GIFT YOU HAVE BEEN GIVEN. I LOVE YOU WITH EVERYTHING I AM.

...

In reply to her beautifully written words and the fact I was unable to write well with the constant rocking of the boat, I was filming a series of videos that I titled 'Reasons why I love you'. I was shooting the videos inside the cabin, out on the deck and whenever I was able. It was something I could do to show her that the notes she had written me were reciprocated ten-fold in my feelings towards her.

...

What is valuable on land has literally no value at sea and as our voyage progressed the crew and I had developed a new form of currency in snack food. There were certain commodities we each brought on board that could be easily traded in an equal value swap. Some of my chocolate for Mel's biscuits and nuts for example. However there was a product valued by all that required greater amounts of less desirable items to initiate the trade. Top Herd jerky was the most desired item at sea at this stage and once acquired it was near impossible to part with. This jerky with its many varieties and flavours was a little treat I looked forward to daily and its long-lasting comfort was cherished.

Stage two had been completed and on day twenty-two we had arrived at the point in between Dakar on the West Coast of Africa and Cape Verde, located 500 kilometres to its west. Unable to see either of those landmarks, we received our confirmation through our navigation system. Covering 780 nautical miles (1440 kilometres) in twelve days, we maintained a fantastic pace and we were well on target. The next stage was the biggest stage of the crossing, the 950-nautical-mile (1760-kilometre) push from Cape Verde to the equator. This stage would determine whether our new route across the Atlantic was even possible.

With 86 nautical miles in a twenty-four hour period on day twenty-four, we had completed our biggest daily total so far. The wind, waves, current and rowing effort all came together to achieve such a massive distance. The seas were rough and I felt like I'd played back-to-back games of rugby but it's the trade-off to getting nudged along by the swell. The girls decided to change to three hours rowing, three hours rest instead of the two and two that we were doing because they were having trouble sleeping in the two-hour rest blocks so wanted to try a longer row to get longer rest. Jake and I stayed on our same schedule. We were sleeping well and I didn't think my bum or body could take a third straight hour of rowing on night shift – by the time my two hours were up I was begging for sleep. Jake also let me in on his secret to combat bum sores and chafing. He filled a baby wipe with petroleum jelly and would insert it in between his bum cheeks. He called it his bum tampon and swore that it helped him escape the worst of the soreness in the first few weeks. We all had a great laugh at his new patent and applauded him for his initiative.

•••

The halfway point of over 1800 nautical miles was reached at the end of day twenty-six; we allowed an extra 200 miles for route deviation to be certain. We could finally say we were in the second half of the voyage and team morale took a nice little boost in passing this milestone. We continued to endure rough weather and big waves as we departed Cape

Verde however during the night it calmed and I woke on day twenty-seven to calm seas. It's amazing the difference a day can make. To me this was real rowing – no assistance from waves, just our own power in the oars driving us onwards. It was starting to get really hot during the days and hydration and heat exhaustion were our biggest concerns. We received snippets of news from home and we had just heard about the latest terrorist attack and the thirty-two civilians killed in Brussels. It was another tragedy that was a weekly occurrence in our world, and if I had been at home I'd probably have been writing an in-depth blog about it. Out on the ocean however, life was very simple and all I had time to do was row, eat, sleep and then keep rowing.

I made a trade of chocolates for fruit cake with Mel and it brought back memories of my time in the Army and the fruit cakes my nanna would send me overseas. The one I was now holding wasn't made with that kind of love and attention but the effect was similar. A shark also visited us that day, 2 metres in length but not overly huge, he swam by to say hello and disappeared into the beautiful blue water below us. With clear skies and calm seas the nights were amazing. Stars covered the sky from horizon to horizon and I'd find myself gazing up at them for hours while at the oars. It is truly an amazing world and universe we live in, between the expanse of the sea and the blanket of stars I felt very insignificant in the grand scheme.

The heat had become inescapable, beating down with ferocious intensity between 11 am and 4 pm. In between those hours rowing was literally grilling me alive and resting while lying in the tiny cabin was like being roasted in an oven. I had come to enjoy the night shifts with my shirt off and the slight breeze keeping me cool. We took an hour off the rowing schedule for maintenance on day twenty-nine as we had acquired a slow accumulation of barnacles and little organisms growing on the hull of the boat. As a team, with Mel staying on board for safety, we dove into the Atlantic to scrape the hull. There was actually lots of scraping to do and it took the best part of thirty minutes to have everything in shipshape condition again. Before climbing back on board and letting

Mel have a swim I drifted away from the boat holding onto a rope to shoot a video and take the greatest selfie of all time. While treading water with the boat behind me in the distance and endless water all around, I managed to shoot a short video for Elise, trying not to drown in the process. As we set off rowing again the increase in speed due to the lack of hitchhiking barnacles was noticeable immediately; we may have saved ourselves another day until arrival.

Our second big storm of the trip, although not as scary as the first one, was definitely more uncomfortable. We were pushing south towards the equator and a giant weather system hit us from the south-east. The wind, rain and waves were so intense there was no possibility of rowing. We lashed down everything on deck as quickly as we could, threw the drogue anchor into the water and crawled into our cabins, sealing them behind us. The weather outside intensified as the heat inside our tiny cabin rose by the minute. Jake and I were pouring sweat as we lay there crammed together and any time we cracked the cabin door for a breath of air we were battered with wind and salt water. It took six hours for the storm to ease off enough that we could crawl on deck, unleash the oars and start to get back on track. The storm had pushed us north-west and we had lost valuable miles but we didn't capsize and nobody was hurt. The wind was still howling as we struggled the rest of the night towards the imaginary line around the centre of the world.

...

We marked the end of stage three when we crossed the equator, thirty-seven days after leaving Lagos. Stage three had felt like it was never going to end, especially when the heat was really beating down, and I was positive someone was moving that invisible line just to spite us. We gathered around the navigation screen to watch our northern position count down to zero, meaning we were directly on top of the equator. We had covered 1000 nautical miles (1852 kilometres) in fifteen days and we were over the moon. Susannah had been saving some pita bread and Mel had been saving Nutella, peanut butter and jam for a celebratory picnic. The food was delicious and Jake pulled out a bottle of Captain Morgan rum to wash it all down. I decided not to partake in the rum since my track history with alcohol wasn't good and I didn't want to tempt the demons. To conclude our equator crossing ceremony Susannah produced a tin of sliced peaches that were the single greatest thing I had ever tasted in my life.

Stage four was now upon us and our goal was to reach a point in the ocean 5 degrees south and 25 degrees west, roughly 420 nautical miles (780 kilometres) from our current position. We would be travelling through uncharted waters for ocean rowing and in an area of the ocean called the Doldrums. The Doldrums were famous in maritime history as areas of the ocean void of wind, current or waves and renowned for sending sailors crazy who got caught in her gentle embrace for weeks at a time. This meant no help from Mother Nature to push us along, just more human power under the baking equatorial sun.

The night shifts had been relatively cool and we had encountered short, bursting monsoonal rains. The humid patch of ocean seemed to be an emerging point for weather systems that continue travelling north, gaining in size and intensity before crashing into the Caribbean, sometimes as devastating hurricanes. To avoid getting our cabin soaking wet during shift change, standard procedure became stripping down nude on deck and leaving all wet clothes outside. The person leaving the cabin would lay out a towel for the one entering to dry off straight away. The big downside of this system was that after having a glorious ninety-minute sleep I had to leave my cosy habitat, put on wet, cold clothes, and start rowing in the drizzling rain. Fifteen minutes after I started rowing however, my back and bum would hurt sufficiently to enable me to forget about how cold and miserable I was.

One of the biggest things I'd come to realise about ocean rowing, and this is something we can relate back to everyday life, is that things can always be worse. Often we would be going along steady then the boat would be battered by side waves, causing my back and bum to burn from trying to stay on the rowing seat. Instead of getting frustrated I would tell myself 'it can always be worse'. The next minute a headwind would build up slowing progress to a crawl and intensifying the effect of the side waves, 'it can always be worse'. The auto tiller decided to throw a fit spinning us in circles with a headwind and side waves, 'things can always be worse'. Then it was a rogue side wave towering up unseen in the dark and breaking directly on top of the boat rendering us sopping wet. With this new mantra I could control my frustration and just get on with the job knowing full well at any moment 'things can always be worse'.

Mid-morning on day forty-one Mother Nature was giving us another taste of her power. An increasing headwind had halted our progress south and instead forced us directly west at 3 knots. We had to do everything we could to keep heading south; if we didn't get far enough south by the time we were near the coast of Brazil the trade winds and currents would sweep us north and we would not be able to make it to Recife or even Brazil. The wind was unrelenting and as the waves built up around us we were doing everything in our power to get some southerly movement. The sun was setting and the waves were breaking onto the deck, we pulled on our life jackets, personal locator beacons and clipped into the safety lines. It was going to be another rough night at the oars. The brutal conditions were holding strong and by the third night I was starting to take micro sleeps while rowing since we were all totally exhausted and begging for a break in the weather.

That break came on the morning of day forty-four when conditions had calmed, giving us a chance to claw back the ground we had lost. The wind, waves and current were all trying to nudge us north-west but we were forging ahead south-west. I was trying to enjoy every moment of this adventure, knowing I would never be in this exact spot ever again, and I wanted to remember every little detail. After my rowing shifts at night I'd strip off my wet clothes and stand up at the front of the boat and stare at the stars. In calm conditions, the quiet sound of oars breaking the water and the Milky Way shining bright above me were the most beautiful moments.

I opened another note from Elise that read:

• • •

Seven days after leaving the picnic at the equator we finished stage four and had notched up another 420 nautical miles (780 kilometres). Our aim was 5 degrees south and 25 west, however with the hammering we had taken from the weather we drifted to 26 degrees south 30 west. We reset our bearing in a straight shot towards Recife and with a more westerly bearing we were hoping for some assistance from the current to get us to land within a week. We set ourselves back into our routine after this little milestone and change of direction and focused on the final 600 nautical miles (1100 kilometres) to the beach and our waiting families. Elise would be waiting for me on arrival along with my parents, who were travelling all the way from Charters Towers, a tiny town in central Queensland, to the remote coast of Brazil. I couldn't wait to see them and I spent many hours focused on our reunion to give me the strength to finish the job.

With 400 nautical miles to go the conversations between the team began turning to food and everything we were going to eat when we got to land. I believe this conversation is timeless and would have been held by sailors in the 1800s. I'm sure the food of choice would have changed over the ages – I doubt the men of the trading fleets would have enjoyed my beloved Vegemite that Elise was ordered to bring me over from Australia. Fresh fruit and vegetables were high on the list and I could feel my body slowly breaking down and in desperate need of nourishment. I had sores everywhere, 60 per cent of my body was covered in prickly heat rash, my right knee was swollen and giving me a really tough time and my hands had reformed into one solid callous. Nothing forty-eight hours of sleep, a few fresh eggs and some carrots couldn't remedy, I was sure.

We had encountered the good, the bad and the ugly on this trip so far and on day forty-seven we had a combination of all three. The good being that we made great speed and progress towards Recife, the bad being that it came with a push from some massive waves over our right side leaving us drenched. The ugly was throughout the day when not rowing, having the choice of staying on deck and getting battered by waves, or getting in the cabin with the door shut to get soaked by your own sweat. I chose the deck option – it was the less uncomfortable choice for me.

It was Sunday, day forty-eight with 320 nautical miles (600 kilometres) to go, and if the tailwind stayed strong for us I predicted a Friday morning breakfast of scrambled eggs, Vegemite on toast and fresh Brazilian coffee. We hadn't had any sightings of cargo ships for weeks but as we got closer to the coast they were showing up on the horizon again. Every time I saw one I imagined a nice air conditioned cabin and a breakfast buffet, probably with the captain and I chatting over a coffee. As they disappeared out of sight I forgot the daydream and refocused my attention on the job at hand.

We had been fighting our way south-west for over a week, a constant battering of strong winds and waves trying to push us north-west. Even though it had been brutally hard we managed to progress in the direction we were hoping for to reach Recife. We were within three to five days of finishing this monstrous journey and just when I thought the exhaustion and physical battle couldn't get much tougher, it did. Late afternoon on day forty-nine our auto tiller decided it had had enough and broke down. This device kept our bearing steady for us even when being pounded by big waves and when it wasn't working we were at the mercy of the sea and got pushed in all directions. Susannah sprang to action and changed fuses, rewired circuits and created a bypass in the system, all in an effort to keep us on track. Nothing was working so we unpacked the spare auto tiller, this one slightly smaller, and we were immediately worried about its ability to stand up to the conditions. Once it was installed it seemed as though we were full-steam ahead, until in the middle of the night when it too broke down and wouldn't start again.

This left us with only one option, manual steering with two thin ropes attached to the tiller. Pull left you go left, pull right you go right – a very simple steering method. Manual steering in good weather isn't such a hard task but when you're trying to row hard on a tight bearing through tough conditions it's a nightmare. Every time a wave hit the boat side-on we were forced off bearing and it took maximum effort of rowing on one side to bring her back on course; by that time the next wave had hit and the process repeated itself. This new development meant we were unable to stick to our bearing and had to aim off to the west. We had given ourselves a three-day goal to see if we could get to Recife on a more westerly heading, if not we were going to have to come up with a plan of action to get to the coast anyway and anywhere we could.

...

I ran out of my own food at the end of day fifty-one, successfully having eaten seventy-five days worth of snack bags, and meals. I had ten chilli con carne dehydrated dinners that were like the Alamo of starvation due to their disagreeable taste and heartburn after effects. I knew rations were going to be tight while aiming for three meals per day plus snacks but I couldn't factor in how hard the intensity would be at some stages and how much food I'd need to keep me going. I'd easily lost 10 kilograms but I'd say it could be closer to 15 by the end of the trip. Now I was relying on the team to feed me some of their meals, which being so close to the finish line, they were happy to sacrifice. There were a couple of plans getting thrown around by the team for our final approach to the coast, one was to get as close as possible to Recife and if we got pushed too far north by the currents organise for a chartered boat to give us a tow the last 30–40 nautical miles. The other option was to make landfall anywhere we could, on any beach or into any creek that would allow it. I was all for option two and so was the team. We started this voyage under human power and we wanted to finish it the same way.

Progress had been tough at best and soul destroying at worst and we decided to up the intensity of the rowing to get us on a solid bearing and to the finish line quicker. We had an extra rowing seat as a spare in our hull hatch the whole trip so we set it up with the spare oars as a third rowing position. We were doing two hours of rowing then two hours of rest, and we continued to do the same but after we finish our first two hours we moved to the third seat for some overtime, an extra thirty minutes each per shift. This left us with ninety minutes to get clean, eat and hopefully have a little sleep. It may not seem like much but with three people rowing it gave us more power and held a better bearing south, which would get us as close to Recife as possible. We were so close now I could taste the cold beer, and even though the next forty-eight hours of extra-time rowing would be hard, it would make the glory of arrival so much sweeter. I just hoped that wherever we ended up landing the locals were ready because I was going to set off every flare we had in celebration, it was going to be like a Sydney New Year's Eve special in a backwater creek of Brazil.

I stared out at the horizon on day fifty-four, searching for the first sight of land with only 60 nautical miles to go. The first day of three people rowing was a shock to the system but we were hanging in there now that we had the finish line in our sights. Studying our charts of the coastline, we had our eyes set on a few different landing options. There was a beach and two different creeks, and depending on where we ended up along the coast, we would be aiming for one of those. Our final challenge would hit us on our last night shift, where there was a 20-nautical-mile section of really strong northerly current we would have to fight hard to get across to ensure we didn't end up too far north up the coast. We were almost done, surely the body could last just one more day.

We pushed hard through our last night trying to gain as many miles as we could so our arrival could be in daylight hours. The seas stayed friendly and with three of us rowing at different stages we managed to get through the predicted northerly currents without many miles lost to the north. Our new landing spot was a small beach at the mouth of a river 30 nautical miles north from our first target of Recife, we set the new bearing into the navigation system, set the steering ropes and made good progress towards it through the first half of the day. It was a hot day again so Jake and I had a shade towel up whenever the third rowing seat wasn't being used and this gave us some respite from the heat when we ate our meals. I didn't hold back on the food – if all went well we would not be needing the dehydrated rations that night. The music was blaring through the boat's speakers and we were all in a celebratory mood as we moved closer and closer to the coast of Brazil.

We were in the rowing zone as we counted down the miles and it wasn't until I stood up after my 10 to 12 midday shift that I saw a thin blue line on the horizon. We were 13 nautical miles away from our destination and I could finally see the coast of South America. Feelings of success, happiness and ultimate safety overwhelmed me as I stared at the land in the distance. Jake was asleep under the shade towel and after a few shouts of 'wake up' his eyes were open and I told him, 'I can see land buddy, we did it!' He was up like a shot, the towel being ripped down in the process, and he locked his eyes on Brazil. Rowing came to a stop as well and we all exchanged hugs and high fives and stared off into the distance. On the breeze came the damp scent of the jungle and civilisation, and now anytime I wasn't rowing I was staring at the land mass getting bigger and bigger on the horizon.

Thirteen miles to go and we were all recharged after seeing how close we were to accomplishing our goal. Some local fisherman stopped by to see us, shouting something in Portuguese that we couldn't understand and me shouting back in English to no reaction. Instead it was thumbs up and big waves before they sped off towards the coast. We were coming up on our last 5 nautical miles and the satellite phone was making a constant racket as calls and messages were going back and forth between us and our families waiting for our arrival. They were given the location of where we were hoping to arrive and Mel was chatting to her boyfriend Shaun and father Roger to do a reconnaissance for us and hopefully guide us in through any reefs or hazards.

Shaun told us they were trying to hire a boat to come meet us and guide us the last few miles to safety but so far this was not confirmed so we continued to push hard on the oars, desperate to make it in before sundown. It was late afternoon as we saw another boat coming over for a visit, expecting more fisherman, we were blown away when we saw the faces of our families smiling and waving at us from a speedboat. I saw my dad perched up front in his OLOC Adventures T-shirt giving me the big thumbs up, bringing tears to my eyes immediately. Jake's mum and girlfriend were on board, Mel's boyfriend and the Brazilian media all crammed in together.

The speedboat was getting bucked around by the waves and it wasn't until that moment that I realised how rough the ocean was. We had grown so accustomed to the movement of the boat and had been in so many big seas that it was a great day for us with nice rowing conditions. For our family members though coming straight from land, it was brutal, and it was only a few minutes after we saw each other that people were hit by seasickness and spewing over the side of their boat. I laughed so hard when Jake's mum started to vomit overboard. We had all been through the hell of seasickness and I thought it was great that the family were having a little taste of it!

Mel asked Shaun to help guide us to the mouth of the river we were aiming for and he showed the driver of the speedboat where we were headed on a map. We followed them as they turned towards the coast, but for some reason we turned due south and off the bearing we had been following. Assuming that we had just missed the entrance slightly, we hooked into the rowing and followed. We went from having good rowing conditions and wind at our back to heading into strong wind and current as we tried to go south. It was a really tough slog, three of us going for it as hard as we could just to keep some forward momentum.

After forty-five minutes of this new bearing Mel called Shaun on the phone to confirm we were going the right way, he replied that we were and we just had to get through this tough section and make it around the point of land that was still a ways off in the distance. We hooked in again, mustering all of our strength for this final push – the ocean wasn't letting us out just yet – I was heaving with everything I had. It had been an hour and a half since we started following and we were close to breaking point. I was pouring sweat and snapping at Susannah and Mel asking, 'Why the hell are we going south?' It was at that point that the speedboat came back to us from up ahead and Shaun told us they were so sorry but they had been taking us in the wrong direction and we had to turn around.

I'm not sure what I yelled out, something along the lines of 'for fuck's sake' definitely showing my disappointment in the mistake. We turned 180 degrees, taking us back onto the original bearing. Before turning around three of us were killing ourselves to get 1.5 knots of speed but as soon as we turned, Jake and Mel alone could hit 4 knots with the wind and current in our favour again.

Back on track, only 2 nautical miles to go and I put on my last clean shirt that had the Row2Rio team logo on the front. We had no idea what the landing area was like, the speedboat hadn't checked it out for us beforehand and I doubted that the rest of our families were going to be there. Our weatherman Chris told us there should be moorings at the location and it was close to a bar, if this was a sand bar or an actual bar we had no idea; we were hoping for the latter. As we were a few hundred metres off what looked to be a small fishing village that had a small beach and moorings close by I noticed a few people running along the shore back towards the small buildings we were aiming for.

I could tell it was Elise immediately by her run and as I gave her a big wave, she jumped in the air waving back and then continued her run. I could also make out my mum walking back as well, unable to run, she was making her best speed. I thought to myself, 'It looks like we have people waiting for us after all.' I was beyond excited. The speedboat had pulled up on a small section of beach next to a concrete boat ramp. As we entered the river mouth to follow in behind them our boat was moving too fast with the wind and incoming tide behind us, we sped past the boat ramp on our right, towards some moored boats that we would smash into if we didn't do something quickly. I yelled to Susannah 'Swing her around,' as she was manning the steering ropes and I jumped into the third rowing seat as the boat came about 180 degrees and lined up to the boat ramp. The three of us heaved against the wind and tide, halting our course towards the boats and started inching back towards the boat ramp. It was an epic manoeuvre which culminated in a precision landing in between the speedboat and the concrete boat ramp. We had made it to land, and guess what? Directly in front of an actual bar!

We were absolutely exhausted and bursting with emotions. I climbed out of the boat and placed my feet into the shallow water and onto the soft sand below, stumbling immediately, and luckily my dad was there to catch me and hold me up. I crushed him with a bear hug with tears streaming down my face. All I can remember saying to him was 'Bloody hell that was hard mate.' It was then I saw Elise crouched in the sand with her head in her hands crying, she told me later that at that moment she was scared to come and hug me because she couldn't believe I was actually there. Stumbling over to her we hugged and didn't separate for a long time. We were both crying and overwhelmed by the moment. Once we broke apart she kissed me and said, 'Go and get your mum,' who was still walking towards us 50 metres away.

I let Elise go, and doing my best to walk, zigzagged and stumbled my way towards Mum, who was already crying when I pulled her in tight for a big hug. We walked together back to the boat, Mum supporting my fragile body, to the rest of the family, friends and media who were all waiting to meet us. Mel's dad Roger shoved a beer into my hand and said, 'Well done!' I said, 'Thanks mate,' as I took my first mouthful of beer in over two months and muttered, 'It was bloody tough, Roger, bloody tough.'

We had rowed 3500 nautical miles (over 6400 kilometres) in fifty-four days, ten hours and forty-five minutes from Portugal to Brazil, pioneering a new route across the Atlantic and setting two world records. It was by far the toughest adventure I had ever done and took a monumental team effort to complete. The celebrations continued on the tiny beach of a remote fishing village, surrounded by shantytown and jungle, on the coast of Brazil. Eventually, as the sun was setting, Roger and Elise set off some fireworks and we all cheered one more time. Looking around at the local villagers I wondered what they must have thought of us. Rowing from one continent to the next just to have a beer with them and set off fireworks – they must have thought we were all totally insane, and I'd have to agree.

The boat was going to be towed back to the safe harbour of Recife the following morning by the speedboat driver. Family, friends and the newly arrived rowers loaded into a bus and we all drove back along the coast to Recife together. The families had brought us fresh fruit, cold water, fresh bread, sliced meats and olives. I was devouring everything as we bounced along the back country roads heading south towards the city. It felt so strange to be in a vehicle with so many people after spending such a long time in the ocean with only the four of us. Arriving back at the hotel it was another round of hugs from everybody and Elise and I went upstairs to our room.

I was still very unstable on my legs and I was bouncing off the walls and running into tables everywhere I went. Once inside the room the first thing I wanted was a shower. Stripping off my clothes I walked into the bathroom and was stopped cold by what I saw in the mirror. Staring back at me was a broken man, a shell of his former self. I had a large red, brown and grey beard covering a gaunt face and sunken eyes. My body had wasted away, losing 14 kilograms (31 pounds) on the voyage, of mostly muscle tissue. My right leg was swollen, I had red rashes everywhere and my bum, that was now no more than two large flaps of skin, looked like it had contracted the plague. It was like a stranger was staring back at me, until I smiled. I moved in close, inches from the glass to focus on the blue in my eyes. I said to myself 'Well done.'

The warm water flowing over my fragile body was an amazing feeling. I washed myself three times with soaps and body wash to peel back the layers of salt, filth and dead skin. Getting out I looked like a drowned skinny rat and my skin glowed red from the heat of the shower. I was guzzling the cold fresh water from the fridge, not needing to worry about rationing anymore, and giving my body the much needed hydration. Elise and I curled up in bed and I wanted nothing more than to sleep for days and recover. I awoke every few hours not knowing where I was and taking a few moments to remember we had finished the row and I could go back to sleep. My body ached and my knee was pounding after I had gotten up to take a painkiller and stumbled over, crashing into the table and making a hell of a racket. Elise woke up and we both laughed at my inability to walk in a straight line.

The following morning, after a very rough sleep, I was planning to sit at the hotel breakfast buffet and graze for hours, however, before we went downstairs I wanted Elise to see the videos I had made for her on the row. I tried to downplay the videos saying to her, 'Hey why don't you watch a few of these videos I made.' She had no idea they were about her and as she lay down to watch I suggested she put in her headphones to get the best volume out of the laptop. She started to watch the series of twelve videos I made at different times of the journey. Each video was a different reason why I was in love with her and after the first one I could see the tears starting to well up in her eyes. The final video was the one I had made while treading water away from the boat at the equator. In the video I say 'I need you to do one thing for me, turn around and look at me right now.' It took a moment to register but she looked up from the laptop and turned around to face me. I stood there holding a sign that read 'Will you marry me.' Elise burst into tears, overwhelmed by the emotion of the moment. We came together and held each other tight when she answered my question with 'A thousand times yes.' At that point my heart had never been so full.

CHAPTER 15
MAGIC BACKPACKS

...

I was sitting alone in my room, watching and listening to the great Alan Watts on YouTube explaining the meaning of life. His famous quote 'What would you do if money was no object?' resonated with me as I watched clips of people climbing, riding bikes, surfing and living life to the extreme. A clip of a person BASE jumping into a cave flashed across the screen and it blew me away. It was magical footage of a jumper leaping into the Cave of Swallows in Mexico, a renowned cave big enough for this type of stunt. The sequence of flying through the air wearing nothing but a small backpack struck me as total freedom. I said to myself in that moment, I will be doing that one day.

Months had passed when I saw some videos from Dylan 'Jimmy' James, an old Army buddy, pop up on my Facebook feed. He was leaping from a cliff top in a place called Moab wearing nothing but a little backpack. He was BASE jumping, and I immediately sent him a message about how awesome I thought it was and asked how I could get myself to that level. He replied to me the following day and said that to even be thinking about getting into BASE, I had to go and get my full skydiving licence and complete at least 100 jumps. This was a substantial hurdle to overcome. I had never skydived before, the course was $4000 and to accrue 100 jumps it would be thousands more and loads of time. I placed the idea on the shelf for later and forgot about it.

It was six months later, while Elise and I were travelling around the South Island of New Zealand after selling the gym, that the road to BASE jumping entered my mind again. She had bought me a tandem skydive for my birthday and it was such an incredible experience that we bought ourselves another one the following day. The second jump was from 20,000 feet over the magnificent Franz Josef Glacier surrounded by mountains. It blew us away and from that moment we said we should definitely get our skydiving A licence so we could jump solo.

The clinching moment came when we were climbing at a famous place in Thailand called Tonsai, a beach known around the world as the limestone climbing mecca. While I was relaxing after a long day on the cliffs and enjoying a coconut, up above me some guys BASE jumped off the towering cliff and landed on the beach in front of me. It was one of the most incredible things I had ever seen and I was envious of their ability and what they must be feeling. That was the moment I decided it was time to get started and become a BASE jumper.

After plenty of research into where to complete the skydiving course, it just so happened that the cheapest place we could get it done was in Toogoolawah, Queensland, one of the states I had grown up in.

We arrived in Toogoolawah shortly after returning from Brazil and the Atlantic row, taking a few weeks to visit family, sponsors and do some much needed resting and eating. By the time we arrived for skydiving we were raring to go and checked ourselves into some very cheap accommodation right alongside the drop zone. The town itself was tiny and located in rural Queensland, where agriculture was the main economy and city folk rarely visit. The drop zone was a few kilometres out of town, a green grass landing area next to a small dirt runway. Eucalyptus trees lined the airstrip scenting the fresh air and large groups of kangaroos were feeding on the grass. It was a picturesque scene bathed in the Australian sun and made me feel like I was home, back in the outback as a boy.

We paid for the full course up-front, not knowing that most people do it stage by stage and took weeks if not months to complete it, and the next morning we were drinking coffee, waiting for the instructors to arrive. The instructors were fantastic, I could tell that they had done these courses a thousand times before yet they made it fun, energetic and made sure we knew our safety drills perfectly before they took us into the sky. Elise's instructor's name was Wado and mine was Belgy. Belgy, as the name suggests, came from Belgium and had 18,000 skydives. He was a pro. The Accelerated Free Fall course is ten stages, meaning you have ten jumps to do and you must complete all of the drills and sequences correctly to pass.

We spent the first half of the day going through theory, mainly all of the safety procedures to go with the malfunctions that can occur while skydiving. It was a lot to take in before our first jump, however, it was important and all made sense to us. Even though skydiving seems dangerous, it is one of the safest sports to get into. Deaths are rare considering how many jumps get completed each day and you always have a reserve parachute if your first one fails to open.

We threw ourselves into the course and thought about nothing else. Elise and I are both competitive, especially with each other, so it became a challenge to see who could complete the course the best and secure the bragging rights. The first jump was a tandem, which we had done before, then we were jumping solo with the instructor jumping next to us for safety. Jumping out of a plane is an amazing feeling and free fall is absolutely exhilarating.

I sat in the plane waiting for the pilot to get to the required altitude and my palms began to sweat. I was nervous to a point but not panicking. All that was going through my mind was the sequence of drills I needed to complete and what actions to take if something went wrong. My goggles fogged up and I had to continually pull them from my face to let the cool air clear them. When the door opened I was blasted by the crisp air as the other jumpers started to depart one by one. I watched as they exited the door and disappeared out of sight with amazing speed, then it was my turn. I shuffled to the door, placed my hands on the frame and moved my feet into position. I lifted my head and focused on the horizon. I looked at Belgy, who gave me the nod to go ahead, and out I went.

I pushed out and I was in free fall. The first few seconds of acceleration were exhilarating, I was holding my breath and had a sinking feeling in my stomach. I could hear the air getting louder as my speed increased to terminal velocity. I arched my body and settled into a belly-down, flat flying position. I was stable and took in the amazing view from 10,000 feet above the earth. Belgy flew in front of me and we started to go through the drills I needed to do for this jump. I completed some turns, some practice pulls and was given the thumbs up. I checked my altimeter and I was at 5000 feet and it was time for me to pull. I reached behind to my lower back, located my pilot chute and pitched it out trying not to compromise my body position. The pilot chute pulled out the parachute and in a split second I went from terminal free fall to hanging under my canopy.

It was a sense of adrenaline-fuelled relief when the canopy opened safely and I was flying over the landing zone. I loosened my chest strap to get comfortable and removed my goggles. I located the place I was going to land, checked the wind sock to see how strong the wind was, what direction it was blowing and began to make my approach. I set up my dog-leg pattern just like I was shown before the jump and lined up nicely with the grassy landing area. I came in and when I was almost about to touch down I flared my canopy to take off the speed and level me out. This time however I left it too late and landed hard, getting propelled into a front somersault and eating the dirt. I stood up and dusted myself off, pride hurt but otherwise unharmed. Elise landed perfectly close by and I had to concede this round to her. My instant reaction was to get back up there and go again.

The accelerated free-fall course literally flew by and we were completing our final stage by the end of the week. It had all gone perfectly, a few crashes and a small amount of blood spilled, however we didn't need to repeat any stages, we had passed them all first time. Once we had passed we were awarded our A licence and ordered to buy a box of beer for the instructors. Apparently this is drop zone tradition so we happily obliged. The course gave me a total of 15 jumps and I needed to have 100 before Jimmy would take me BASE jumping, so immediately after completing the course I was straight back up in the air to practise my skills and get up some jump numbers.

Skydiving is unbelievably fun but to say it is a cheap sport would be a straight-out lie. Even after the initial cost of the course a skydive rig will cost a few thousand dollars and then every jump completed will cost between twenty and forty dollars depending on where you are in the world. It definitely adds up quickly, as I was finding out trying to get as many jumps in as I could in a short space of time. At the end of the day though Elise and I are not into the traditional lifestyle and would much rather spend our money on fun and adventure than a mortgage and car repayments.

During our time at Toogoolawah I was making plans with Jimmy for a BASE jumping trip to America. I was slowly getting my skydive numbers up and I would be ready by the end of the year for BASE, or so I thought. I needed to find a BASE rig but due to my size and weight there was nothing second-hand we could find that would fit me so I went ahead and ordered a custom-made rig from Apex BASE, one of the best manufacturers on the market. If I'm going to get into a sport that has a high death rate I'm going to give myself the best chance of survival with the best equipment. After sorting out the rig we agreed on a date to arrive in Salt Lake City and from there we would drive to Idaho and the Perrine Bridge, a place where it's legal to BASE jump all year round.

Before we knew it, Elise and I were stepping off the plane in Salt Lake City, Utah ready for two months of BASE jumping, climbing, trekking and whatever other adventures we could get into. We hired a big Ram 1500 Dodge truck for the entire trip and picked up Jimmy from the airport later that same night. Jimmy had been BASE jumping for three years and had over 300 jumps, mainly from cliffs in the States, Australia and Europe. He also had a few hundred skydives before he started getting into BASE. We were best friends who grew up serving in the Army together. There was no-one I'd trust more to teach me a sport that has one of the highest death rates in the extreme sporting world.

Salt Lake City has a population of just over a million people and is surrounded by beautiful mountains on one side and the great salt lake on the other. I had a good friend living in Salt Lake, Dean, who was on the trip to West Papua with me when we were held in the container at the mine. He owns and operates World Wide Trekking and hooked us up with a ski villa up at Snowbird resort in Little Cottonwood Canyon for the duration of our stay. He also fitted us out with all the camping gear we were going to need for our two-month tour, saving us a small fortune. We spent a few days enjoying the canyon, skydiving at the local drop zone, and learning how to pack my BASE rig.

We departed Salt Lake and drove across the state border into Idaho and on to Twin Falls, a small town on the Snake River. The river winds through a steep, jagged canyon that appeared out of nowhere. One minute I was talking to Jimmy about something trivial and he said, 'Get ready.' I said, 'For what?' just as the land dropped away into a breathtaking gorge and we drove across the Perrine Bridge towering 150 metres from the water below. The next morning I'd be doing my first jump off the centre of this bridge and I was instantly nervous. Jimmy pulled over at a view point next to the bridge and we walked out to the centre, the exact spot I would be climbing over the rail and jumping from the next day. My hands were sweating again and I was scared. I've never been one to hide my fear and I said to Jimmy, 'Mate, I'm shitting myself.' He said, 'Good, that's going to keep you safe.' We walked the landing area and talked about the approach as Elise watched on in silence, not wanting to interrupt our conversation at such a crucial time, although I knew she would be as nervous as I was.

We found a room to share at the local Quality Inn, which gives discounts to BASE jumpers, and paid for two weeks up-front. The hotel was perfect for jumping, it was a five-minute walk from the bridge, served coffee all day and would let us pack our rigs in the air conditioned hallway after each jump. I didn't sleep a wink all night, lying there staring at the ceiling, going through the first jump over and over again in my head. The alarm didn't have a chance to go off, as I was lying there awake and turned it off with a few minutes to go. It was time to get up. Elise got up with us as she wanted to be there for my first BASE jump, film it and ultimately see me survive it.

I consumed a plate of glorious powdered scrambled eggs and a few cups of coffee from the breakfast room before the three of us made the slow walk down the road in the early morning chill towards the bridge. There wasn't a lot of talking taking place; I think we were all too nervous. The sun was beginning to show itself over the horizon as we arrived at a patch of grass next to the walkway leading out onto the bridge. The view was amazing in the first light of the day. Shadows were cast down from the cliff tops over the shimmering water, all bathed in a beautiful yellow glow of dawn. If I wasn't about to jump off a bridge into this euphoric scene it would have been great to sit there with a coffee and take it all in.

We laid our rigs down on the patch of grass and Jimmy started taking me through the procedure of gearing up correctly. What I quickly learnt about BASE is that you have one shot to get it right so everything has to be done meticulously the first time. My first jump was going to be a PCA – pilot chute assist – which meant Jimmy would take control of my pilot chute and pull it out as I jumped. It is the safest way to do a first jump because it will open straight away, and if I did go head low on my exit instead of keeping my chest up, which is a big problem for beginner jumpers, the parachute would fully open before I was in a dangerous position. We went through the jump and landing pattern once more and then it was time to head out onto the bridge.

When I normally walk out onto a bridge it feels no different from walking down the street, however, knowing that in a few minutes I was going to be climbing over the rail and jumping off, the walk out took on a whole new feeling. My heart rate increased and my hands began to sweat. We arrived at the centre of the bridge and I was shown how to check the wind by spitting over the side and taking note of how it dropped and moved around at different heights. Jimmy ran through the entire jump one more time and then did a final body and gear check. He then said words I'll never forget: 'Okay buddy, when you're ready, over you go.'

I don't think I could ever have been really ready for climbing over that first time. I grabbed the rail with sweaty hands and slowly brought my leg over the top. I hugged the top, keeping my body low to the rail as I swung my other leg over, ending up in a position facing back towards the bridge and at Jimmy. Slowly I repositioned my feet and hands, turning my body around and I was now staring out at the canyon with a 150-metre drop below with nothing but sweaty hands death gripping the rail behind me for support. I extended my arms so that I was leaning out, away from the bridge, with my eyes fixated on the horizon. I said to Jimmy, 'I'm ready to go.' Jimmy had moved into position behind me holding my pilot chute and told me, 'Okay mate, go ahead just like we practised.'

I took a deep breath, stared out at the horizon and told myself three things. Be grateful, you deserve this, thank you for allowing me to fly. I counted out loud, 'Three, two, one, go!', and I jumped. The sinking feeling deep in my stomach falling through dead air only lasted a split second before my big canopy exploded open above me and I was flying away from the bridge towards the landing area. The sense of relief was immediate but I didn't have time to enjoy it, as I needed to take off some altitude and begin my landing. I made two figure-eight turns to bring my height down and once I was in the right position I brought it in to land, flaring perfectly and running out my landing. It was then I let out a yell back up to Elise and Jimmy, who now looked tiny on the bridge above. I watched as Jimmy wasted no time in climbing the rail himself and launched off. He had a nice opening and came to land next to me. We high fived, hugged and yelled back up to Elise together. The sense of relief was overwhelming for all of us. The first jump was out of the way, now it was time to perfect this skill and become a real BASE jumper.

That same day we completed two more jumps, for both of them Jimmy pulled out the pilot chute as I jumped but the following day it was time to go handheld. Handheld is when I have my pilot chute coiled into my hand and when I jump it's up to me to pitch it correctly to enable the deployment of the parachute. Body position during exit is crucial, so we were doing a video debrief after each jump, and on my first jump it was easy to see me going head low, which according to Jimmy was normal for your first jump, but if I repeated that while going handheld I could get tangled in my pilot chute and it would be game over. Climbing over the rail with a hand full of pilot chute was more terrifying, but once in position looking out from the bridge, I felt in control. Three, two, one, go! I exited with a perfect body position, pitched after a one-second delay and brought it in to land nicely.

After every jump we had to repack our rigs, which for an experienced jumper normally takes between twenty and thirty minutes. For a beginner like me it was taking forty-five minutes to an hour. It's a detailed process with countless stages that all have to be done perfectly. Missing a step could cause anything from a hard opening, off heading (parachute opens in the wrong direction) or a malfunction. With BASE rigs there is no reserve like in skydiving, you've got one chance to get it right, and for that reason I was taking as much time as I needed to pack. All the responsibility was back on me, and I was starting to love that about this sport. In normal life you can pass the blame for anything onto someone else, with BASE it's your pack job, you picked the object, checked the weather and jumped it. It's all on you.

The jumps were adding up quick and the course that Jimmy had put together was running perfectly. He broke things down military style and we would practise one thing over and over until we got it right, then move on. By the end of the first week I had done eighteen jumps, averaging three per day, usually in the morning before the afternoon wind made it too dangerous for a beginner like me to jump. Whenever the wind came up Elise was ready with an adventure for us, climbing one afternoon, kayaking the next and a cheeky CrossFit session at the local box (gym) was thrown in as well.

While we were jumping, plenty of other guys and girls were jumping as well. Some were on first jump courses like I was with local guys and some were there just staying current and having a blast throwing flips off the bridge. It was guaranteed that when we were jumping there was a hoard of Chinese tourists gathered around the view point taking photos of us; they absolutely loved it. On one jump, as Jimmy and I were about to walk out we were given a standing ovation from the tourists. They called us heroes and all wanted to take photos with us – it was ego boosting and hilarious. In Australia you would get arrested and your rig confiscated for jumping, here they called you a hero and cheered you on. God bless America!

By the start of the second week I had progressed onto stowed jumps, meaning that my pilot chute was now rolled up tight in a pouch at the bottom of my rig. This added an extra dimension to my jump. My arms were now free, which was great for climbing over the rail, however when I exited I had to reach behind myself while falling, grab the end of the pilot chute and pitch it out. My body position had to stay perfect, I couldn't compromise it by starting to turn or tumble while falling, and there was always a fear that I'd fumble the pilot chute, causing a delay in my parachute opening. The first stowed jump was nerve-racking but after a few I settled down and it was amazing fun.

The worst malfunction to occur during the type of BASE jumping we were doing was an off heading. Ideally, after my parachute opens I am facing away from the bridge, cliff or whatever the object may be, and I fly away safe. The parachute, however, can open on many different angles, slightly left, slightly right or the absolute worst outcome is a 180 degree off heading, when the parachute will open facing straight back at the object. While jumping from a bridge this is no big deal as there is nothing to hit, on a cliff or building however this can be catastrophic. To handle an off heading scenario, Jimmy started to teach me object avoidance drills, which are a series of things to do in case of a 180 opening that when done fast enough will help you turn the canopy around without striking the object. These drills included turning the canopy on the risers, stalling the canopy to halt its forward movement and turning the canopy while stalled. Being proficient at these skills was crucial before we departed the bridge at Twin Falls and made our way to the cliffs in Moab.

It was our last day in Twin Falls, Jimmy was happy with my progression and we had made twenty-nine jumps together so far. There was one jump we still really wanted to do and it was called a bridge steel jump. The Perrine Bridge is constructed with massive steel arches and crisscrossing support sections with the very top of the arches accessible via a maintenance ladder from the bottom of the bridge. A jump that some of the local jumpers had done was to climb the access ladder and make their way to the very top of the arches underneath the road and jump through the steel into the canyon. This was what we wanted to do for our last jump in Twin Falls.

We all woke up early, Elise included, long before sunrise, and drove to the parking lot that was the start of the trail into the canyon. Elise was excited to come along and would take pictures and shoot some footage of us jumping. We made our way in the dark without headlamps, along the canyon trail paralleling the river to the enormous concrete foundations directly underneath the bridge. It was a short scramble from there to the start of the maintenance ladder where I repositioned my rig to the front of my body so I could climb the caged ladder effectively. The steel was freezing to touch and I had to stop every few minutes, shoving my hands into my pants to warm them up again. The ladder topped out on the huge arch beams and from there we walked the slope of the beam skyward, clinging onto the small safety rail for comfort.

The arch began to taper off as we neared the top and at its summit it was flat and stable. The beam itself was just over a foot wide and as the cars crossed the bridge above our heads the entire structure would vibrate, sending a shiver down my spine. It was time to gear up. We had been going for over an hour and the sun was just starting to show its orange glow on the horizon, illuminating the breathtaking view below us. I was ready for a handheld jump and I was going to jump first. I began to climb over the small handrail, crushing my manhood in the process, although I was too nervous to feel any pain. Once on the other side, with no more protection, I had to inch my way out onto a smaller beam to be directly in the middle of the bridge and the best area to clear all of the steel structure below me. My legs were shaking, I was terrible at slack lines and balance games and thought that at any second I was going to fall before getting the chance to jump.

After what felt like an eternity of mere seconds, I was in the middle facing a gap in the steel and ready to jump. Jimmy was completing the nut crushing rail climb as I was getting focused. Three, two, one, go! I stepped from the beam and plummeted through the steel, missing it by what felt like inches. Once clear of the structure I pitched my pilot chute and had a great on heading opening, facing towards a beautiful sunrise over the canyon. I landed safely on the grassed area and held in my burning desire to yell out with relief. I had just completed a jump that could be frowned upon by the authorities and I didn't want to attract any judging eyes. Jimmy had a great exit as well and landed safely close by. I looked up at the bridge to see Elise making her way back down the walkway underneath the bridge to safety. What an amazing way to start the day.

Our time in Twin Falls had come to a close with an epic jump through the steel structure of the bridge. The first stage of training for BASE jumping was complete and it was now time for stage two, cliff jumping. America is famous for cliff jumping and attracts jumpers from all over the world to its beautiful red towers of stone. Moab is a small town in southern Utah that is commonly described as the Mecca for adventure sports. It has a lifetime of rock climbing to throw yourself at, starting from easy routes for beginners up to hard routes that only a handful of people can climb. Downhill mountain biking, off road ATV and 4x4 driving, skydiving, water sports galore and some of the most amazing BASE jumps around.

We drove all the way from Twin Falls to Moab, stopping off for a night in Salt Lake City. I'm a firm believer in the theory that the only way to see a place is by moving through it overland and we had the chance to see the beautiful landscapes changing by the hour as we drove through Idaho and Utah. The red dirt and rock of southern Utah let us know we were getting close to Moab and we bypassed town for the first night and went camping in a local canyon called Mineral Bottoms. It was a 50-kilometre drive down a dirt road that suddenly descends into an enormous canyon with a river flowing through it. The sheer rock walls on either side of the canyon, rising up to 125 metres in places, were intimidating and as we drove along the bottom of the canyon Jimmy gave me a description of the BASE jumps that seemed to be located on every overhanging face.

We made camp down inside the canyon in a red dirt basin surrounded by boulders, with the majestic cliffs towering on either side of us. We got a roaring fire going and settled back to eat some dehydrated food packs. As I was munching through a vegan black bean and rice ensemble Jimmy said to me, 'Have a look up at that cliff mate.' I gazed up at an intimidating overhung monster being bathed in the sun's fading light and said in my most confident tone, 'Looks beautiful bro.' He replied, 'That's Sweet Spot and you're jumping her in the morning.' My heart skipped a beat, a wave of nervous energy washed over me followed by pure excitement. Staring up at Sweet Spot I thought to myself, this is what I had come to learn, this is what I had been watching in videos for years and tomorrow it's all about to become a reality.

I spent a restless night going over the malfunction procedures in my head and before I could go over them for the one thousandth time I heard Jimmy moving around getting ready and knew it must be almost dawn. I pulled my boots on and poked my head out of the tent to a picturesque canyon scene, with daylight just starting to glow on the horizon. We all drove out to the top of the canyon and walked through the desert moonscape to the very edge of the cliff. Jimmy had done this jump many times before and lead us straight to the exit point that consisted of a flat slab of rock overhanging the main wall by a few metres. This was Sweet Spot and she was beautiful, the view was amazing and the conditions were looking perfect. Down in the bottom of the canyon were our tents, which I would hopefully be landing next to in a few minutes.

I laid down on my belly and poked my head over the edge of the exit point; this was by far one of the scariest things I'd done. Without my rig on I was leaning over the edge relying on body friction to prevent me from falling, nerves kicked in, and I felt afraid. However I needed to do it so I could spit over the exact point of exit and check wind conditions all the way down the face at different altitudes. The last thing we wanted was an unseen headwind down where our parachutes would be opening – that could be disastrous. I watched my spit fall straight down without movement to the base of the rock, proving perfect conditions. Time to gear up. As I pulled on my rig Elise was filming and Jimmy was going through the jump and flight plan back down to our camp. I was going to jump first so Jimmy could watch and then critique my body position. Once he had given me a final safety check he gave me the all clear and said, 'Game on bro.'

I was standing three steps back from the edge with my pilot chute in my right hand repeating the words in my head as I stared out into the canyon. 'Be grateful, you deserve this, thank you for allowing me to fly.' I stared at the tiny spot on the edge where I'd place my last step on the run up, then made a mental note of a tiny spot on the horizon I'd focus on after leaving the cliff to help keep my body in a good position. Three, two, one, go! A three-step run-up, strong push off the cliff and I was airborne. A short delay in free fall and I threw my pilot chute and in a split second my canopy opened and I was flying away from the cliff, losing my mind with excitement. The visual of the massive red rock cliff flying by bedside me was absolutely epic and I could hear Jimmy and Elise yelling in excitement from back above me. I made my flight down to the camp ground in thirty seconds and brought it in nicely into a soft, sandy river bed 50 metres away from my tent. I let out a scream of excitement, adrenaline, nerves and pure happiness. That was one of the best things I'd ever done and I couldn't wait to get straight back up and do it again.

For the next three weeks we made Moab our home, camping in the beautiful canyons and occupying a tiny cabin at the local hostel called the Lazy Lizard as our main base. Jimmy and I would head out every morning if the weather was good and jump multiple exits with names like Tombstone, G-Spot, Parriott Mesa, Mary's Gash and Echo. If the weather was average or the winds came up Elise and I would kayak, trek or climb one of the thousands of beautiful rock walls dotted throughout the area. This place really was an adult playground. While out in an area called Castle Valley where Jimmy and I jumped a huge beast of a cliff called Parriott Mesa, Elise and I were awestruck by a tower of rock rising up from the valley floor that stood apart from the rest with its sheer walls and prominence. Its name was Castleton Tower and immediately after seeing it Elise and I wanted to climb the tower, and as I was now a BASE jumper, I thought I should at least try and jump it as well.

One problem Elise and I had was that the climb up Castleton was a traditional climbing route (trad) and we had only done sport climbing before. The difference being that in sport climbing you have fixed bolts already on the route that you can clip into for safety, with trad there are no bolts and you must place in your own protection as you climb. Lucky for us we were in a place dominated by climbing and climbing guides and after a short search we found a local guide named Marie who was free to guide us up and was happy to have me jump off the top once we got there.

We started the approach to Castleton from a small campground by the side of the road that splits the valley floor. It took us an hour and ten minutes of switchbacks and scree fields to get to the top of the talus and to the base of the rock wall where we would start our climb. We had chosen one of the most popular routes up the tower called the North Chimney, which involved climbing a crack that turns into a large chimney before topping out three pitches above us. The climb was rated a 5.9 up to a 5.10 in places, which although isn't hard climbing, it was our first crack climb and was bound to be challenging. Marie gave us a quick lesson on crack climbing techniques before we started, how to use finger and foot jams and how to squeeze your body into wider sections and use the texture of the rock to ascend.

We started up the route with Marie in the lead placing in all the protection as she climbed. Protection or gear, is made up of Camalots (cams) acting like spring-loaded anchors, perfect for cracks, that come in multiple sizes. Nuts, which can be placed into tiny, irregular shaped holes, and an assortment of other devices used for various slots and pockets are all designed to save your life if you fall. Once Marie was secure at the top of the first pitch I would climb second and retrieve most of the protection she had placed in. It took me longer to climb as I was continually fumbling around collecting the gear from the wall and trying not to fall off in the process. I secured myself at the top of the pitch and pulled my parachute and helmet up in a haul bag before Elise climbed. The bag wasn't too heavy and it hauled cleanly up the face in no time at all. Elise then started her climb, secured from the top so she was safe from falling at all times. Elise collected all of the remaining protection and once we were all at the top of the first pitch we would reorganise the ropes, equipment and gear then the process would start all over again.

The climbing was amazing, so different to anything I'd climbed before and the view of the valley below us as we moved higher and higher was absolutely breathtaking. The route was challenging in places but at no time did I feel like I was going to fall and Elise looked to be in her element. The first pitch took us one and a half hours and as we completed the third pitch and were nearing the summit we had been climbing for almost four hours. We scrambled up the last few metres of the route until there was nowhere higher to go and the breeze hit us in the face – we were on the top. The summit was the size of a basketball court, shaped more like a triangle than a square and had sheer drop offs on all sides to the talus below. The view was stunning and we were totally pumped to be up there after the challenge of the climb.

After hugs and high fives in celebration I started to look around at the possible exit points and checked the wind on all sides of the tower. The best exit point faced back towards the road 500 metres below us and had a good overhanging lip on its edge. It wasn't much of a run up, only two steps but it was the safest option for a jumping point. I checked the wind by spitting off the edge multiple times and there was a small breeze that was fluctuating from different directions but no head wind so I decided I was going to jump it.

I unloaded the haul bag and put on my parachute, helmet and shin pads. Jimmy had made his way out to the landing zone so I was able to raise him over the walkie-talkie and get a brief about what the winds were doing down below. He told me the winds were moving right to left and I made a mental note while picking out a trail in the distance that could be perfect to land along if I could glide far enough away from the tower. I checked the winds one more time and they seemed to be changing directions every few minutes, but still no head wind. I said my goodbyes to the girls and set myself up two steps back from the edge. My plan was to do a handheld jump with a 1–1.5 second delay in order to open up in the most overhung section of the cliff. I picked my last point of contact for my foot and picked my horizon focus point upon exit. Deep breath, three, two, one, go!

Two steps and I pushed off the edge into free fall before pitching my pilot chute with my right hand. I immediately started to turn and I knew something was wrong. I was flung around facing the cliff, knowing instantly I'd had a massive off heading and was going to hit. Instinctively I reached up to the top of my right rear riser and pulled as hard as I could to try and turn the canopy before I hit. Nothing happened for what seemed like an eternity, but in reality was fractions of a second, and then it turned. The canopy pulled around to the right as I drifted slightly backwards within a couple of metres of the rock and then it started to move away. While I was trying to turn the canopy I was still losing altitude and I noticed a big ledge rushing up from below. I cleared the ledge by a few metres as the canopy picked up speed and gave me some separation. I popped my brakes and the parachute did its job, surging away into open air towards the landing zone. I was safe.

My heart was jacked, the adrenaline was pumping through my body and I let out a yell in shock and celebration. I couldn't relax just yet as I still had to land, and I lined up with the trail I picked out earlier. The winds were picking up and the parachute was struggling to punch through in the direction I'd chosen, forcing me to pick out another section of the trail further down the valley to land in. I lined up with the trail and brought it in, landing safely on a soft, red dirt path. I let out a scream of relief and could hear Elise and Marie replying with yells from the top of the tower. They didn't have a clue at that stage as to how close I'd just come to having a serious accident but Jimmy did, who came rushing over to make sure I was alright. He thought I was going to hit for sure and was just as relieved as I was that I was able to turn it in time. Jimmy's training at the bridge had paid off big time and without those practice days with him at the bridge I could have been crippled or killed.

Analysing the GoPro video later that night it was clear to see I had a 200-degree off heading to the right. I was within a couple of metres of hitting the wall and my quick reactions just managed to save my own life. I was slightly shaken up by the whole thing and it did put a tiny dampener on what was an amazing climb of Castleton Tower. The crazy thing about BASE jumping is that even though I had just had a close scrape with death I wanted to go and jump again straight away. I had trouble making sense of these feelings but what I think it comes down to for me is that when I'm living life on such a knife edge like that it makes my everyday life so rewarding and you appreciate it so much more. It seems bizarre explaining that risking your life makes you appreciate it, but that's how it feels for me and maybe it's only a feeling BASE jumpers get to experience.

● ● ●

We had the most epic time running around Moab and playing on its cliffs but it was getting close to the end of our American tour and Elise and I had decided to tie the knot in Vegas so it was time to say bon voyage to this little adventure paradise and say hello to Sin City. We drove into Vegas at night, which I'd highly recommend over the day time. The allure of the glittering lights and sparkling billboards of naked women project a slightly different image than the all-exposing light of day. We stayed at a lovely hotel on the strip with all the trimmings and we had made all the arrangements for our little wedding the month before. We had decided to get married in a hot air balloon with Jimmy as our witness, and at the conclusion of the ceremony we would all jump out together. It was simple, fun, stress free and it was all about us.

Elise had purchased her wedding dress from a used clothing store for $25 and I had found a suit jacket for $8. Some alterations needed to be made to the dress so it didn't get tangled up during the jump and I wore blue board shorts to go with my jacket. She looked beautiful and I was comfortable, just the way you should be on your wedding day. The balloon guys picked us up from the strip early the following day and we drove half an hour outside Vegas into the desert. We met the celebrant who was very excited to watch us jump out of the balloon, and with a chill in the air and no wind it seemed to be perfect weather for ballooning.

We watched on as the balloon crew inflated the balloon with the roaring flame thrower and fans. The huge structure rose slowly above the basket and once it was directly overhead and fully inflated we pulled on our parachutes and climbed aboard. Within seconds we were lifting off under the roar of the gas burner. It's an amazing feeling gaining altitude without a plane and as the sun broke over the horizon and the desert stretched out below us it was truly an amazing sight. We made it to 5000 feet and the celebrant started the ceremony. It was short and sweet, filled with the dramatic quotes of love and life that we all come to expect on days like this and finished with the pronouncement of husband and wife. I was never going to get married, and had put it from my mind before I met Elise and now I cannot imagine my life without her. I love her completely and said so as we sealed the deal with a kiss. We were now Mr and Mrs Richmond and our first act as husband and wife was jumping from the balloon.

We had planned our exit before we left the ground. Jimmy was going to be jumping backwards and Elise and I would jump forwards towards Jimmy, who could capture it all on film. We climbed up onto the top of the basket and positioned ourselves as best we could. Elise had only ever done jumps from a plane and had never done an exit into dead air so I told her to keep her eyes on the horizon and keep her chest up to avoid going head low and tumbling. We all smiled at each other, picked our landing area far below on a rare patch of grass near a hotel and were ready to exit. Three, two, one, go!

We stepped off and that glorious feeling of free-fall took over. Elise went head low and performed a perfect front somersault before levelling out nicely into free fall. Jimmy and I exited well and once the air speed had increased to terminal velocity we tracked away from each other to give us good separation before we deployed our parachutes. Opening a BASE jumping rig at terminal speed can be a bit rough but mine opened perfectly and as I looked around I saw Jimmy and Elise were open and flying towards the landing area as well. Jimmy was first to land and I followed him in, performing a nice little fly-by of the small casino whose grassed front courtyard we were landing in. Elise came in last and we had all landed perfectly without incident. I let out a yell of joy that was echoed by Elise and Jimmy before quickly ripping off my parachute and running over to my wife to give her a big hug and a kiss. We were married and what a way to start a marriage! We ran over to Jimmy and had a group hug and photo to seal the day, and it was back to the strip for celebrations.

The American BASE jumping tour was one of my all-time favourite trips. The sport itself is hard to explain to non-jumpers but I'd tell anybody interested in BASE jumping to take it slow and go through all of the training correctly, don't progress too fast. Read and learn about the sport and find yourself a mentor you trust to show you the way. As Jimmy moved over to Europe to pursue the art of human flight in the form of wing suiting, it was time for Elise and I to head back to our beloved Thailand for a season of work, climbing and planning for the next adventure. We all have one life and one chance so get out there and make the most of it.

AFTERWORD

...

My life has been anything but normal and I cannot thank my parents enough for dragging me around Australia and teaching me country values when I was a boy. Adventures and sharing my story are now my full-time obsession and I cannot imagine a life without it. We don't know how long we each have left on this earth and a wise man once told me that if you get to your death bed and can tell one hell of a story about your life then it was a life well lived. All of my possessions can fit inside two duffel bags and at the drop of a hat I could be on a plane tomorrow bound for another epic adventure. As I write these concluding words my current position is N45 00.638 E96 11.195 – eighteen days into a crossing of the Gobi desert in Mongolia. Elise and I, plus a British mate named Matty, are trying to be the first to cross the entire desert while dragging carts 1800 kilometres from west to east. Every morning I crawl out of my tent and say:

BE GRATEFUL

YOU DESERVE THIS

THANK YOU FOR ALLOWING ME TO SUFFER.

ACKNOWLEDGEMENTS

...

Behind every great adventurer there is a support base that allows us the freedom to do what we love. Although I don't class myself as one of the greats just yet, my experience so far in the adventure world is no different. First and foremost I thank my parents Mandy and Clive for raising me in the outback, with country values and morals that have served me well to this day. They are still travelling in a caravan somewhere in Australia and continue to inspire me with their positive outlook on life.

I need to thank my army buddies I served with and who helped transform me from a green 17-year-old kid into a confident man during my years in the military. For those who are still serving – stay sharp, trust your gut and get yourselves home safe from wherever you are in this crazy world. To Liam Harte and Jordan McCallum, those two phone calls at a critical time changed the direction of my life from one of addiction and despair to adrenalin and adventure.

I have too many sponsors to thank across so many great expeditions but I have to make a special mention to Simon and Kerrie from Australian Sports Nutrition. You both took a chance on a young guy with no experience and have stuck with me over the years. Also thanks to the Karima Group and the Sahyoun family, you are like a second family to me and I still call on your guidance and mentorship during pivotal times.

To all of my teammates, climbing partners, and those that enjoy the suffering as much as I do, thank you for being who you are and for giving me the inspiration I needed during the tough times. To those who have died doing what they love, you will never be forgotten and I'll be seeing you all again one day, I am certain.

To Jane Curry, Zoe Hale and Eleanor Reader at Impact Press Publishing, you took a chance on an unknown author who had trouble spelling and staying in the right tense. We have come a long way, created something very special and I thank you for your guidance and support. Lauren Mitchell, my first draft editor and daily inspiration, you are a beautiful human and I thank you for all your red pen suggestions during the early days of writing.

For all of my friends whom I think of as family from around the world, you are too many to count and for that I am truly grateful. Every single one of you has impacted me in some way and have helped create the content in this book. I hope that I have given back to you in the same way you have given to me.

The final acknowledgement is for my beautiful wife Elise. Without you next to me, adventure loses its spark and the volume of life is turned down. You give me the constant support I need to pursue these challenges and never question my ability to get the job done. We have crossed a desert together, climbed the highest cliffs, and jumped out of a balloon. The next fifty years are bound to be incredible. I love you and this book would not be here without you. Onwards to the next adventure!

GET IN TOUCH WITH LUKE

Stay up to date with everything Luke gets up to or get in touch with him at:

✉ luke@olocadventures.com

🌐 www.olocadventures.com

📷 @luke_olocadventures

f Luke Richmond – Adventurer